SELF-DISCLOSURE: AN EXPERIMENTAL
ANALYSIS OF THE TRANSPARENT SELF

SELF-DISCLOSURE

An Experimental Analysis of the Transparent Self

SIDNEY M. JOURARD

University of Florida

WILEY-INTERSCIENCE

A Division of John Wiley & Sons, Inc.
New York · London · Sydney · Toronto

Preface

Man's behavior is visible, his experience is not. Yet it is man's experience that is the subject of great fascination to everyone. We want to know what a man *means* by his behavior, what he is "saying" to us and to the world by his deeds. The only way we can know what a man is experiencing is if he discloses his experience to us in language we can understand. This book reports research we have done on some of the factors involved in a person's willingness to let others know his experience. It is a book about self-disclosure.

Advances in any new field for scientific investigation are made when suitable techniques for measurement are discovered.

By 1957, I had been a working psychotherapist for about eight years, engaged in inviting suffering patients to disclose themselves to me. This they did, frequently in agonies of embarrassment and dread, sometimes with huge sighs of relief as they divested themselves of long-kept secrets.

One of the aims of any psychotherapist is to help his patient live more authentically, to stop misrepresenting himself to the people among whom he lives. An obvious factor in the background of any neurotic or psychotic sufferer is his tendency to conceal his authentic thoughts and feelings, in order to live a cosmetic life of pretense. I often found myself wondering if people became psychologically ill *because* they did not disclose themselves honestly to others.

This line of thinking led me to ask myself just what we knew, from a scientific point of view, about self-disclosure. In 1957 we knew very little. A number of happy accidents made it possible for me to invent a means of measuring self-disclosure, or at least an aspect of it. In 1958, in collaboration with a sociologist colleague, Dr. Paul Lasakow, I published our first exploratory study, using a questionnaire to measure a person's report of past disclosure to various significant people in his life.

Since 1958, I have completed and published a number of investigations employing "self-disclosure" questionnaires of varying length and content and, with the help of graduate students, made some beginnings at studying self-disclosure in the laboratory.

Interest in this work ran high, perhaps stimulated by publication of my book *The Transparent Self* (1964). Requests for reprints of my articles quickly exhausted my supplies, and I entered into lively correspondence with researchers from many parts of the United States and elsewhere. By 1970, over one hundred studies had been completed by other investigators, many triggered by our initial studies.

I think that this book will be useful not only to investigators who wish to begin self-disclosure research, but also to advanced undergraduate students of psychology who have not yet tackled a scientific study. This book offers a record of the way in which an idea for research came into being, and how one person pursued it, alone, and with help. I have mentioned throughout the text the way my work as a psychotherapist and as a teacher influenced the research, and how the research findings affected my thinking and practice as therapist and teacher. Research papers seldom reveal to the reader the groping, the fiddling, the confusion, or the excitement that the investigator goes through in order to produce the tidy, systematic report that appears in the journals. I have tried to show some of the human element that enters into pursuit of a scientific idea; since the research is about self-disclosure, it can do no harm for the researcher to reveal something of himself as he presents his findings.

The first section of the book is devoted to presentation of the findings we obtained in numerous studies of self-disclosure by means of questionnaires. Most of the studies reported in this part have been published in journals before their inclusion in this book. Hence the style of exposition is "journalese."

In Part II, I present the results of experiments that my students conducted either for their Master's theses, or as supervised projects for course credit. The experimental findings reported there are direct outgrowths of the earlier questionnaire studies; readers whose interest is primarily in experimental research may wish to omit Part I. However, I regard questionnaires and experiments as valid approaches to the study of self-disclosure.

The Appendix contains questionnaires that were employed in the studies reported here. Researchers will find these useful either in the form in which they are shown, or modified to suit their particular purposes. I hereby grant permission to investigators who wish to use our measuring devices for their research; it will not be necessary to write for permission.

I am glad to acknowledge the help of the students and colleagues who worked with me at various stages of the research reported here. I mention them in the text, but I would like to assemble their names as a way of expressing my gratitude: Dr. George Breed, Linda Devin, Lee R. Drag, Marshall Frey, Robert Friedman, Sharon Graham, Dr. Wilson Guertin, Michael Heifitz, Peggy Jaffe, Dr. Leo Kormann, Dr. Murray Landsman; my first collaborator, the late Dr. Paul Lasakow; Dr. Jim Powell, Jaquelyn Resnick, Patricia Richman, Jane Rubin, Diane Skafte, and Linwood Small.

SIDNEY M. JOURARD

Gainesville, Florida
September 1970

Acknowledgments

I want to express thanks to the following publishers and journals for permission to reprint or adapt materials first published in their pages:

Journal of Abnormal and Social Psychology
Merrill-Palmer Quarterly of Behavior and Development
Journal of Humanistic Psychology
Journal of Applied Psychology
Academic Press
Journal of Social Psychology
Psychological Reports
Perceptual and Motor Skills
Journal of Counseling Psychology
University of Florida Press
Duke University: *Law and Contemporary Problems*
Journal of Personality and Social Psychology

More direct acknowledgment of prior publication is made in the main text.

S. M. J.

Contents

PART III

Some Implications of Self-Disclosure Research

SELF-DISCLOSURE: AN EXPERIMENTAL ANALYSIS OF THE TRANSPARENT SELF

PART I

Studies with Self-Disclosure Questionnaires

It started in late 1956, when I was reading galley proofs for my textbook, *Personal Adjustment* (1958, 1963). In several chapters I spoke of the importance of "real-self being" for healthy personality. I pondered how one would do research into the process of "being one's real self in relation to others." I thought it was a question of telling others the truth, and letting one's actions reveal one's true intentions. In short, it meant letting other people know you. Then, I wondered, "Who knows *me?*" I asked members of my family, friends, and colleagues to tell what they knew of me. Their answers were so diverse, I hardly recognized the person they were describing. I wondered how they got those impressions of me, and realized I played an important part in determining how well any other person knew me. In fact, there was much about me I did not want others to know. Much of my action was aimed at misleading others, at misinforming them about the person I knew myself to be.

At this time, I was seeking another position, and almost daily, was obliged to fill out personal data sheets for prospective employers. Some of these forms asked for information I considered personal and private. Yet, to maximize my chances of getting a more suitable job, I wrote down the information. I found myself thinking, "I am telling these things about myself to strangers. Would I reveal as much to my friends and family? To whom have I already disclosed this information?"

This line of thinking led to a way of investigating the "real self." With considerable excitement, I wrote a lot of questions about a person—the kind of thing one asks another if one wishes to know him personally—and asked everyone who came across my path, "On which

1

of these questions [there were about 100 of them] have you revealed yourself truthfully to the various people in your life? How many of these questions can your wife answer? Your closest friend, Your colleagues?". I tested myself and discovered that each person with whom I was involved had answers to some, but not all, of these questions about me. On testing others by this primitive technique I learned that if people are books, then some persons have let themselves be read from cover to cover, while others have let only the title and author's name stand forth.

Such variability in a preliminary study excites an investigator. Moreover, as a psychotherapist, I was involved every day in encouraging patients to speak openly about themselves. I wondered why these patients would tell me secrets they had concealed from others for years. Obviously, it was in the hope that if they revealed the truth about themselves to me, they might help me to help them live their lives more effectively. I saw there was a connection between the customary secretiveness of people and their mental health. If this was so, then there was good reason to study secretiveness and openness, to learn something of their parameters.

I refined my list of personal questions, and produced a questionnaire listing 60 topics of a personal nature, classified into 6 categories, or "aspects of self" (see Appendix 1). I named this instrument the Real Self Questionnaire. I made an answer sheet which requested a person to check the topics he had disclosed to each of several "target-persons," such as spouse, mother, father, or closest friend. Then I was ready to begin collecting data. I enlisted the collaboration of a sociologist friend, the late Paul Lasakow, and we tested hundreds of people around Birmingham, Alabama—in such places as college classrooms, clinics, and the YMCA. We analyzed our first data, and each of us presented a paper with preliminary findings at meetings of our respective professional associations.

Someone at my meeting challenged the term "real-self communication," saying, "Isn't all communication about oneself 'real'?" I decided a more neutral descriptive term would counter the objection and, subsequently, adopted the term *self-disclosure* to describe the act of revealing personal information to others.

Now we present our first study, the result of about a year and a half of collaboration between Dr. Lasakow and myself.

1. Some Factors in Self-Disclosure*

Self-disclosure has been studied and discussed hitherto in a tangential, not a direct, way. Block (1952) and Block and Bennett (1955) demonstrated that what a person told others about himself was a function of the role he held with regard to the others. For example, a secretary revealed different aspects of herself to her boss than she did to a fellow secretary.

Lewin (1958) noted differences between typical Germans and Americans regarding their readiness to confide personal information, the Germans being more reserved than the Americans. I suggested that accurate portrayal of the self to others was an identifying criterion of healthy personality, while neurosis is related to inability to know one's "real self" and to make it known to others (Jourard, 1963). Characterological studies of Fromm (1947), Riesman (1950), and Horney (1950) called attention to a tendency, common among persons in our society, to misrepresent the self to others. This tendency is central to the "marketing personality," the "other-directed character," and the "self-alienated" individual, as these have been described by their respective authors.

It is apparent, too, that much of social science is founded on a person's willingness to reveal himself to researchers; the conditions and dimensions of authentic self-disclosure therefore bear directly upon the validity of many "facts" in the social sciences (see Part II).

From the foregoing, it may be concluded that more direct analysis of self-disclosure promises to yield information that is relevant to diverse

* This chapter was originally published in the *Journal of Abnormal and Social Psychology*, **56**, 1958, 91–98, and is reprinted here, in slightly modified form, with permission from the American Psychological Association.

areas of human existence. The following questions were proposed for this first investigation:

1. Do subjects vary in the extent to which they disclose themselves to different target-persons, for example, mother, father, male friend, and female friend? What is the effect of the subjects' marital status on self-disclosure to parents and friends? What is the effect of the subjects' feelings and attitudes toward particular target-persons upon self-disclosure to them? (This last question was investigated only with respect to the relationship between subjects' disclosure of self to parents, and their feelings and attitudes towards their parents.)

2. Are some categories of personal information more readily disclosed than others?

3. Do the sexes differ in self-disclosure? Do various racial and ethnic groups in our society differ in this activity?

METHOD

Instruments

The Self-Disclosure Questionnaire. A 60-item questionnaire was devised. As can be seen in Appendix 1, the items are classified in groups of 10 within each of 6 more general categories of information about the self (aspects). Subjects were given the following instructions for completing the questionnaire:

The answer sheet which you have been given has columns with the headings Mother, Father, Male Friend, Female Friend, and Spouse. You are to read each item on the questionnaire, and then indicate on the answer sheet the extent that you have talked about that item to each person; that is, the extent to which you have made yourself known to that person. Use the rating scale that you see on the answer sheet to describe the extent that you have talked about each item.

The self-disclosure rating scale was as follows:

0: Have told the other person nothing about this aspect of me.

1: Have talked in general terms about this. The other person has only a general idea about this aspect of me.

2: Have talked in full and complete detail about this item to the other person. He knows me fully in this respect and could describe me accurately.

X: Have lied or misrepresented myself to the other person so that he has a false picture of me.

The numerical entries were summed (X's were counted as zeros), yielding totals which constituted the self-disclosure scores.

Seventy white unmarried college students of both sexes were tested for self-disclosure to mother, father, male friend, and female friend, in a study of reliability. Since the questionnaire included 60 items, and there were 4 target-persons, a total of 240 entries were made by each subject. These 240 entries were divided into halves by the odd-even method, and the subtotal sums were correlated with each other. The resultant r, corrected, was .94 indicating that the subjects were responding consistently to the questionnaire over all target-persons, and all aspects of self.

Parent-Cathexis Questionnaires. Mother-cathexis and father-cathexis questionnaires (see Appendix 2) were employed to test subjects' feelings toward their parents. The subjects rated their feelings about 40 parental traits—for example, sense of humor, temper, ability to make decisions—in accordance with the following scale:

   1: Have strong positive feelings; like very much.
   2: Have moderate positive feelings.
   3: Have no feelings one way or the other.
   4: Have moderate negative feelings.
   5: Have strong negative feelings; dislike very much.

High scores indicated negative feelings toward the parents, while low scores signified positive feelings.

Subjects

The subjects included in the studies to be reported were taken from larger samples drawn from three Alabama college populations: two white liberal arts colleges, a Negro liberal arts college, and a school of nursing located at a medical school. For the combined sample 300 white and Negro liberal arts college sophomores and juniors were obtained, and 55 white nursing students. All subjects were tested in groups by an examiner of the same race.

For the purpose of analysis, the following randomly selected subsamples were drawn from the combined samples:

1. From the 300 liberal arts students, a subsample of 10 white males, 10 white females, 10 Negro males, and 10 Negro females was drawn for the study of differences in self-disclosure associated with race, sex, targets, and aspects of self. All subjects were unmarried, and in all cases, the parents were living. Mean ages were: white males, 21.70,

SD 1.00; white females, 20.30, SD .90; Negro males, 22.10, SD 2.02; and Negro females, 20.40, SD .45. All subjects had been tested for self-disclosure to mother, father, male friend, and female friend.

2. From all the white respondents in the combined sample, a subsample of 10 married male and 10 married female subjects was drawn for comparison with the first subsample of 10 unmarried males and 10 unmarried females to test the effects of marriage on self-disclosure patterns. These subjects had indicated self-disclosure to mother, father, same-sex friend, and spouse. Mean age for the married males was 23.40, SD 1.43, and for the married females, 20.60, SD 2.42.

3. Thirty-one unmarried nursing students comprised the third sample, used to examine the relationship between parent-cathexis and self-disclosure to the parents. Mean age for this group was 18.59, SD 3.53.

The data were analyzed according to Lindquist's (1953) Type VI model for analysis of variance with mixed "between-within" effects. Critical differences for t-ratios at the .01 level were computed between all groups, targets, and aspects of self when F-ratios proved significant. Pearsonian r's were computed between mother-cathexis scores and scores for disclosure to the mother, and between father-cathexis scores and the corresponding disclosure scores, within the group of 31 nursing students to whom these two instruments had been administered.

RESULTS

Influence of Race, Sex, Target-Differences, and Aspects of Self

Figure 1 shows the mean self-disclosure scores of the 40 white and Negro subjects classified by targets and groups. Analysis of variance and t-tests showed that:

1. The four groups differed in total self-disclosure; white subjects disclosed more than Negroes ($P < .01$), and the females disclosed more than males ($P < .01$).

2. The combined group of 40 subjects varied in amount of self-disclosure to different target-persons. Males disclosed most to mother, and in lesser amount to male friend, father, and female friend. Females likewise disclosed most to mother and less to female friend, opposite-sex friend, and father. Sex differences in disclosure to the four target-persons are shown clearly in Figure 2.

3. The combined group of 40 subjects varied in self-disclosure according to aspects of self. Two clusters of aspects appeared—a "high dis-

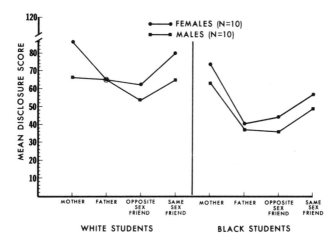

Figure 1. Mean self-disclosure scores of white and black students, classified by target-persons and by sex.

closure" cluster comprised of Tastes and Interests, Attitudes and Opinions, and Work, and a "low disclosure" cluster that included Money, Personality, and Body. These clusters are shown in Figure 3.

4. There was significant interaction between targets and aspects, groups and targets, and groups, targets, and aspects. The group-by-aspect interaction was not significant.

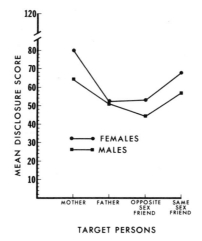

Figure 2. Mean self-disclosure scores of male and female students, classified by target-persons.

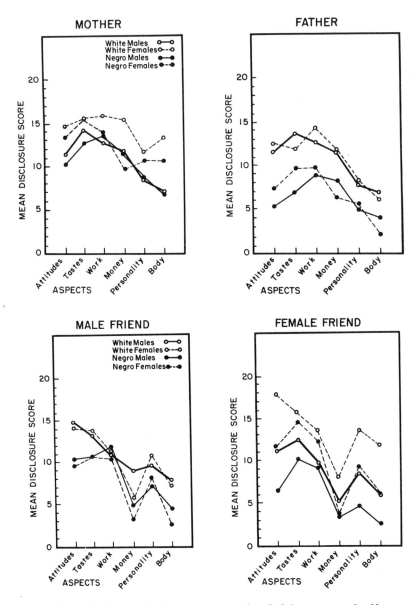

Figure 3. Mean self-disclosure scores classified by aspects of self.

Influence of Marriage

Separate analyses of variance compared married with unmarried males, and married with unmarried females. In the analyses, opposite-sex friend and spouse were treated as equivalent target-persons.

No differences were found between married and unmarried subjects in *total* amount of self-disclosure. Figures 4 and 5 show, however, that: (*a*) married subjects disclosed less to the parents and the same-sex friend than unmarried subjects, and (*b*) there was more disclosure to spouse than to any other target-person.

Marriage thus appears to have the effect, not of increasing or decreasing the total extent to which subjects disclose themselves, but of producing a redistribution of self-disclosure. The married subjects "concentrated" self-disclosure upon the spouse, and became more reticent toward other persons. In this sense, self-disclosure enters into relations similar to those of libido in psychoanalytic theory.

Parent-Cathexis and Self-Disclosure to Parents

Total mother-cathexis scores for the group of 31 nursing students correlated—.63 with scores for self-disclosure to mother; father-cathexis scores correlated—.53 with scores for self-disclosure to father. Both coefficients were significant beyond the .01 level for $df = 30$. The direction

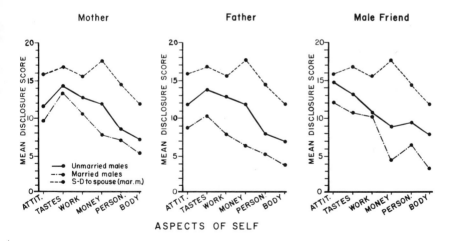

Figure 4. Comparison of married and unmarried males on self-disclosure to mother, father, and male friend. (Curve for disclosure to spouse is shown in each panel.)

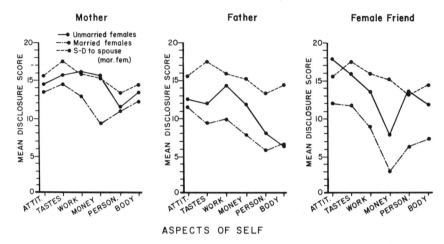

Figure 5. Comparison of married and unmarried females on self-disclosure to mother, father, and female friend. (Curve for disclosure to spouse is shown in each panel.)

of the obtained values signifies that high self-disclosure was associated with positive feelings toward the parents, while low self-disclosure was associated with attitudes of dislike toward the parents.

DISCUSSION

These preliminary findings demonstrate that self-disclosure is measurable, and that the present method for assessing it has some validity. The questions now open for exploration are virtually without limit, in view of the many possible and relevant combinations of the main factors—groups, target-persons, aspects of self, and individual differences.

Some questions suggested by the present findings may serve as guides to further exploration: Why do Negro subjects consistently disclose less about themselves than whites, and why do females disclose more than males? Why is the mother the preferred target of self-disclosure for this age group? What is the significance of the fact that some aspects of self, for instance, Tastes and Interests, Attitudes and Opinions, and Work, are disclosed more than information about Personality, Money, and Body? Is it an artifact of the questionnaire, or does it reflect cultural consensus about what is readily disclosable and what is not? What individual traits besides feelings and attitudes toward target-persons account for individual differences in self-disclosure?

SUMMARY

A reliable questionnaire for the assessment of self-disclosure was described. Groups of both sexes, white and Negro, married and unmarried, were tested with the questionnaire for extent of self-disclosure of six different aspects of self to various target-persons—mother, father, male friend, female friend, and/or spouse. The findings are summarized as follows:

1. Young unmarried subjects, both white and Negro showed the highest self-disclosure to mother, with lesser amounts to father, male friend, and female friend.

2. Subjects tended to vary the amount of self-disclosure with respect to the category of information to which an item about the self belonged. Two clusters of aspects emerged, a high disclosure cluster including Attitudes and Opinions, Tastes and Interests, and Work, and a low disclosure cluster comprised of Money, Personality, and Body.

3. White subjects disclosed more than Negroes, and females more than males.

4. There was significant interaction among groups of subjects, target-persons, and aspects of self.

5. Married subjects disclosed less to mother, father, and same-sex friend than comparable unmarried subjects. Most disclosure occurred within the dyad formed by spouses.

6. A significant correlation was found between parent-cathexis and self-disclosure to the parents. The more that the parents were liked, the more disclosures were made to them.

The Next Chapter

This first study showed we could measure an aspect of self-disclosure in a fairly reliable way, and that some patterns could be discerned in the findings. There were differences associated with sex, race, and marital status. The field was now open for comparisons between all kinds of groups in their reported level of self-disclosure. We found significant differences in the amount of disclosure which people directed toward the various "significant others" in their lives. There were differences in the degree to which various kinds of subject matter were disclosed. There were interactions among those factors. And, finally, we had shown that individual differences were involved—large standard deviations were obtained for the various scores we obtained, and we were able to show correlations between a measure of attitude toward target-persons ("parent-cathexis" scores) and the amount that had been disclosed to them.

With myriad leads to follow, I chose next to pursue the relationship between liking for a target-person and the amount of disclosure to him. The next two studies were devoted to this problem and, in the process, we chanced upon the "dyadic effect"—the reciprocal nature of self-disclosure.

2. Self-Disclosure and Liking*

The amount of personal information that one person is willing to disclose to another appears to be an index of the "closeness" of the relationship, and of the affection, love, or trust that prevails between the two people. In more general terms, self-disclosure and liking for the other person may be correlated. Evidence to support this proposition stems from both clinical observation and systematic research. Thus, psychotherapists have long noted that when a patient feels warmth, trust, and confidence in his therapist, he discloses himself more freely and fully than when he perceives the therapist as hostile or punitive, or when he dislikes the therapist. More direct evidence of the relationship between liking and self-disclosure was provided in our first study where we reported significant correlations between questionnaire measures of mother-cathexis and father-cathexis, and the amount that subjects had disclosed to their parents.

This study inquired more directly into the relationship between self-disclosure and liking. In addition, we looked at (a) the relationship between a person's liking for the other and the amount of personal information that he *knows* (from past disclosures) about the other person, and (b) the extent to which disclosure to others and knowledge about others involve reciprocal relations between people. The latter aim may be regarded as an indirect test of the hypothesis that one of the necessary conditions for promoting self-disclosure in another is to volunteer it oneself. On this assumption, a person who discloses much to another may be expected to receive much disclosure from him; and

* This chapter was originally published in the *Journal of Abnormal and Social Psychology*, **59**, 1959, 428–431, and is reprinted here, in a slightly modified form, with permission from the American Psychological Association.

a person who knows a great deal about another should be relatively well known by him. Indifference or antipathy between two persons may be expected to produce the consequences of low disclosure to one another, and little knowledge about one another as persons.

The hypotheses of the study were therefore as follows:

1. The amount of personal information that a person has disclosed to each of a group of co-workers covaries with degree of liking for each fellow group-member.

2. The amount of personal information that a person knows about each of a group of colleagues covaries with his liking for the others.

3. Disclosure-output to each colleague covaries with disclosure-intake from each colleague.

4. A subject's knowledge about each colleague covaries with the amount that each colleague knows about the given subject.

METHOD

The 8 members of a newly organized college of nursing, together with the Dean, served as subjects in the study. Mean age of the subjects was 36, with a range from 27 to 45. Several of the subjects had known one another before joining the present faculty, while others were strangers before their appointments. They had worked together for about 10 months at the time the study was undertaken.

Self-disclosure-output was measured in the following manner. Each subject was interviewed by the investigator, in order to obtain the 15 items of information that were called for in the questionnaire shown in Appendix 3. Since the questions do not presume extreme intimacy, the subjects can be assumed to have been frank in disclosing themselves to the interviewer. Each subject was then asked to indicate to which of her colleagues she had disclosed information about each item. It was thus possible to determine the total amount of disclosure-output for each subject, and the varying amounts that each subject had disclosed to each colleague. *Disclosure-intake* was computed from the same data, as the corresponding sums of information directed at a given subject by her colleagues.

Knowledge was determined by asking each subject to tell the investigator what she knew, from the questionnaire, about each of her colleagues. A score of 1 was given to each bit of knowledge claimed by a subject about a colleague which agreed with what the colleague had told the investigator about herself. Similarly, the amount that others knew about a given subject was obtained from the same data.

Liking for the other person was determined by paired comparisons in terms of the criterion, "liked best as a close friend." This procedure produced a rank-order of preference for each subject, with the best-liked colleague receiving the largest number of choices, and the least-liked colleague receiving the lowest number.

RESULTS

Significant rank-order correlations ($P \leq .05$) between the amount disclosed to each colleague and the degree of liking for the colleague were found for 7 of the 9 subjects (see Table 1, Column 3). The first hypothesis is thus confirmed.

Column 7 in Table 1 presents the data relating knowledge of others and liking. *Rho's* significant at or beyond the .05 level were found in 4 cases between amount known and liking. The data thus lend partial support to the second hypothesis.

The relationships just established between self-disclosure, liking, and knowledge about others suggest that the 9 subjects tended to develop pairs of mutual closeness and intimacy. This "dyadic effect" is more clearly demonstrated by further data in Table 1. Column 4 shows that in 6 cases, significant *rho's* ($P \leq .05$) were found between disclosure-output to colleagues, and disclosure-intake from colleagues. Correlation between the amount each subject knew about her colleagues and the amount that her colleagues knew about her is shown by the 7 significant *rho's* reported in Column 8, Table 1. The subjects tended to get disclosure back in proportion to what they gave—a lot for a lot, and a little for a little. Similar considerations applied for the relationship between "knowing" and "being known."

DISCUSSION

The present data show that liking, self-disclosure, disclosure-intake, knowing, and being known are interrelated. They show further that despite the existence of a formal role structure—specifically, a dean, various levels of academic rank, different departments, etc.—dyads had tended to develop with varying but largely mutual degrees of intimacy. The data do not show, however, whether liking precedes disclosure, disclosure precedes liking, or whether both of these factors are determined by something else altogether.

Table 1 Relationships among Liking, Disclosure, and Knowledge

	1	2	3	4	5	6	7	8
Subjects (Ranked in descending order of average liking by others)	Total No. of Items Disclosed by Subject to Colleagues	Total No. of Items Disclosed by Colleagues to Subject	Rho, No. of Items Disclosed by Subject to Colleagues vs. Subject liking of Colleagues	Rho, Disclosure Output to Colleagues vs. Intake from Colleagues	Total No. of Items Known by Subject about Colleagues	Total No. of Items Known by Colleagues about Subject	Rho, No. of Items Known by Subject about Colleagues vs. Subject's liking of Colleagues	Rho, No. of Items Known by Subject about Colleagues vs. Items Known by Colleagues about Subject
Mary	38	65	.79*	.81*	36	39	.71*	.80*
Ann	51	42	.88**	.57	27	29	.23	.34
Ruth	66	57	.72*	.65*	43	37	.49	.86**
Betty	55	58	.76*	.83**	41	27	.67*	.68*
Jean	52	40	.99**	.89**	23	26	.81*	.77*
Rose	36	34	.65*	−.14	23	22	.82*	.04
Suzy	44	46	.79*	.79*	30	44	.52	.65*
Dawn	69	51	−.14	.57	36	41	.11	.83**
Winny	23	41	.05	.80*	33	27	.34	.87**

Note: *Rho* = .64 for the .05 level (*) and .83 for the .01 level (**) with *N* = 8.

Provisionally, it may be suggested that once contact has been made between two persons, they proceed to "uncover" themselves one to the other at a mutually regulated pace. If it is generally true that intimate self-disclosure begets intimate self-disclosure, while impersonality begets impersonality, then certain implications follow for a number of areas of interpersonal endeavor. For example, it might prove to be true that therapists, in order to maximize disclosure in their patients, will be obliged to go beyond impersonal "technique" and "be themselves," that is, disclose what *they* are experiencing during the therapy hour as freely to their patients as they expect the latter to disclose to them. Rogers (1958, p. 12) already has intimated something of the sort. Possibly similar considerations apply in such fields as teaching and nursing.

Two subjects who did not show a significant *rho* between liking for others and disclosure warrant special attention. One of these subjects (Dawn) was the highest discloser, while the other (Winny) was the lowest discloser in the group. Both fell at the "least-liked" end of the average liking ranks. Direct observation showed that both subjects behaved consistently in most situations—the high discloser revealing much about herself without regard to social context, or the interest of the listeners, and the low discloser withholding her personal life even from the scrutiny of those colleagues whom she liked. If being liked by others may be viewed as a rough index of interpersonal competence (*cf.* Jourard, 1963, pp. 295–299), then perhaps failure of these subjects to vary self-disclosure with liking for others betokens contrasting forms of interpersonal (and personal) maladjustment.

It may be objected that the self-disclosure questionnaire items are so trivial that whether or not such information is revealed signifies little about an interpersonal relationship. It can be argued, however, that if a relationship between two people is close, affectionate, and personal, most of the items included in our brief questionnaire will have come up for discussion at one time or another.

An unsolved question thus far relates to the meaning of self-disclosure as behavior. Why do people vary the amount of self-disclosure in which they engage? If self-disclosure is regarded as a special case of operant behavior (*cf.* Skinner, 1957, pp. 185–226), then some answers suggest themselves. Self-disclosure produces consequences, influencing the behavior of others toward oneself for better or for worse. Possibly, then, persons disclose or fail to disclose themselves in accordance with the consequences that they expect to follow. Frequently, the expectancies may not be warranted; in such cases, one would likely find inaccurate other-concepts and either more or less self-disclosure than is appropriate to the situation.

SUMMARY

A self-disclosure questionnaire with 15 items was administered individually to the dean and 8 faculty members of a college of nursing. Subjects were asked to disclose the answers to these questions about themselves to the investigator, and then to indicate to which of their colleagues they had disclosed each item. The subjects were then asked which items of information they knew, from having been told, about each of their colleagues. Finally, the subjects ordered their colleagues in terms of liking by means of paired comparisons.

It was found that subjects tended to vary the amount of disclosure-output to colleagues with degree of liking for colleagues, and to know more about the colleagues whom they liked best than those whom they liked less well. Finally, evidence was found for structured dyadic relationships such that if a subject had disclosed much and knew much about a colleague, the other knew much about, and had disclosed much to her.

The Next Chapter

I had begun to "humanize" my way of being a psychotherapist, and I frequently shared with my patients some of my lived experience that paralleled problems with which they were struggling (Jourard, 1964, pp. 59–75). And I had taken to disclosing how I felt about my patient and myself, when this emerged in the therapeutic dialogue. These departures from my usual style of "practice" appeared to accelerate the development of a good working relationship, and considerably shortened the time of therapy. The "dyadic effect" data lent a kind of scientific support for these clinical innovations. I decided to explore the generality of this phenomenon. Using the same method I had used with the nursing faculty, I tested a group of male graduate students in psychology, with the collaboration of Dr. Murray Landsman, who at the time was a student himself.

3. Knowing, Liking, and the "Dyadic Effect" in Men's Self-Disclosure*

In the last chapter we reported significant correlations between the scores measuring nursing college faculty members' degree of liking for each of 8 colleagues and the amount disclosed to each colleague. These data provided stronger support for the hypothesis that liking was a factor in disclosure among females. It was further found that the subjects tended to establish dyads of reciprocal intimacy: they disclosed most to those colleagues who most confided in them, and vice versa.

The present study sought to determine the degree to which men varied self-disclosure to available confidants with liking for those persons, to ascertain whether knowledge of others was a closer correlate of disclosure among males than liking, and to determine whether the males, like females, would show a dyadic effect in their disclosing patterns.

HYPOTHESES

The hypotheses tested were as follows:

1. Men will vary the amount of personal information they disclose to other men according to the degree they like the others.

2. Men will vary the amount they disclose to other men according to the degree they know the others.

* The material in this chapter was published originally in the *Merrill-Palmer Quarterly of Behavior and Development*, 6, 1960, 178–186, and is reprinted here with permission from the Merrill-Palmer Institute.

3. The correlation between knowing and disclosure among men will be higher then the correlation between liking and disclosure.

4. Men will show a "dyadic effect" in their disclosure pattern, that is, they will disclose the most to men who have disclosed the most to them, and vice versa.

METHOD

Subjects

Nine male graduate students enrolled for a year or longer in the University of Florida Department of Psychology were selected as subjects from among a larger group of about 40 students. At the time the data were gathered, 5 subjects were married, and 4 were single. Mean age was 28 years, with a range from 23 to 32.

Disclosure-Output and -Intake Scores

Each subject was interviewed by Murray Landsman (a graduate student working with me) to ascertain the 15 items of information called for by the questionnaire shown in Appendix 3. Then, each subject indicated to which of his 8 fellows he had revealed each item of information. Finally, each subject was asked what information from the questionnaire he knew about each of his fellows. The number of items which each subject told his fellow students constituted his disclosure-*output* scores; the number of items disclosed to each subject by his fellows, his disclosure-*intake* scores.

The validity of the disclosure-output and -intake scores was checked by comparing what each subject knew about each fellow with the information disclosed by the latter to the examiner. The output and input scores may be deemed valid, since there was close coincidence between what each subject knew about his fellows, what he said be disclosed to his fellows, and what each subject told the examiner about himself.

Liking and Knowing Scores

Each subject was then given two questionnaires listing the names of his fellow students arranged as paired-associates. One of these was completed according to the instruction: "Like better of the two"; and the other, according to the instruction: "Know better of the two." These procedures resulted in a forced ranking of his fellow students by each subject. The ranks were called, respectively, *liking* and *knowing* scores. All 9 subjects were ranked as well from best to least liked, and best to least known, on the basis of the liking and knowing scores.

RESULTS

Liking and Disclosure-Output

Column 5 in Table 2 shows rank-order correlations between the liking rank to which each subject assigned his fellow students and the rank for the amount he disclosed to them. Significant *rho*'s were found in only 2 out of 9 cases. The males thus showed only a slight tendency to vary disclosure-output to others with liking for them.

Knowing and Disclosure-Output

Column 6 in Table 2 shows significant *rho*'s in 8 out of 9 cases between knowing and disclosure-output. Clearly, these subjects showed a strong tendency to disclose most about themselves to the fellow students whom they knew best, and least to those whom they knew less well.

Knowing versus Liking as Factors in Disclosure-Output

Comparison of the *rho*'s between liking and disclosure (Column 5) and knowing and disclosure (Column 6) shows that in 7 cases the knowing-disclosure correlation was the larger; in 1 case it was smaller; and the *rho*'s were identical in another instance. By the signs test the probability of getting 7 out of 8 larger *rho*'s is .035. It may concluded that the correlation between knowing and disclosure was stronger than that between liking and disclosure.

Disclosure-Intake as a Factor in Disclosure-Output: The Dyadic Effect

Eight of the 9 subjects showed significant correlations between the amount they disclosed to each of their fellow students and the amount that their fellows disclosed to them (see Column 9). This finding shows that disclosure was a reciprocal kind of behavior which proceeded to a level of intimacy agreeable to both parties in each possible dyad and then stopped.

Since liking and knowing were differentially correlated with disclosure, it was pertinent to determine what happened to the dyadic effect when liking and knowing were statistically controlled. Accordingly, the correla-

Table 2 Rank-Order Correlations (*Rho*) between Knowing Others, Liking Others, and Disclosure

	Rank Order		Total Items Disclosed		Items Disclosed BY Subject vs. Subjects		Items Disclosed TO Subject vs. Subjects		Disclosure-Output vs. Intake	Liking vs. Knowing	Disclosure-Output vs. -Intake	
Subjects	Liked by Colleagues†	Known by Colleagues	By Subject	To Subject	Liking of Colleagues	Knowing of Colleagues	Liking of Colleagues	Knowing of Colleagues			Liking Partialled Out	Knowing Partialled Out
	1	2	3	4	5	6	7	8	9	10	11	12
Al	1	4	33	34	.81*	.81*	.90**	.86**	.87**	.93**	.54	.57
Bert	2	6	21	34	.35	.95**	.28	.87***	.77*	.14	.74*	.38
Cal	3	9	13	22	.56	.79*	.38	.79*	.80*	.46	.77*	.47
Dan	4	7	53	38	.33	.81*	.60	.96**	.74*	.72*	.72*	.25
Ed	5	2	35	34	.49	.90**	.21	.79*	.70*	.57	.87***	.04
Fred	6	1	43	38	.49	.86**	.57	.48	.79*	.72*	.72*	.84**
Gus	7	5	31	20	.69*	.79*	.55	.59	.36	.81*	.03	.22
Hal	8	8	16	19	.61	.70*	.45	.81*	.65*	.74*	.54	.20
Irv	9	3	31	37	.62	.46	.67*	.46	.71*	.93**	.50	.63

Rho

* Significant at the .05 level.
** Significant at the .01 level.
† In order of decreasing cathexis.

22

tions between disclosure-output and disclosure-intake were recomputed, with liking (Column 11) and knowing (Column 12) partialled out. When liking was thus controlled, there were still 5 out of 9 significant correlations remaining, whereas only 1 out of 9 *rho*'s remained significant when knowing was partialled out. This comparison lends further support to the proposition that liking was not as strong a factor as knowing in self-disclosing behavior among these males.

FURTHER FINDINGS

The findings reported above supported the hypotheses proposed in an earlier section. Certain other analyses, not directly bearing on these hypotheses, were conducted and are reported below.

Liking and Disclosure-Intake

If a man likes another, does it necessarily follow that the other person will then confide in him? Column 7 shows the *rho*'s between liking and the amount of confiding which was directed *at* each subject by his fellows. Significant *rho*'s were obtained in only 2 of the 9 comparisons. It may be concluded that a subject's liking for each of his fellows was not a strong determiner of *their* disclosures to him.

Knowing and Disclosure-Intake

Significant *rho*'s between knowing and disclosure-intake were found in 6 out of 9 cases (see Column 8). This shows that the men tended to receive the most disclosures from those whom they knew best, or more probably, that a given subject's degree of knowledge about others was the outcome of being disclosed to. Stated another way, there appears to be nothing magical about coming to know another person. If he discloses himself to you, you will know that much about him, for a certainty, and no more. This finding has definite implications for psychotherapy, as well as for interpersonal relationships in general: people who wish to become known and understood must disclose themselves.

Sociometric Status and Self-Disclosure

The subjects named in Table 2 are listed in descending order of likability to their fellows—a crude type of sociometric status-ranking. The question may be raised: is there any relationship between the degree to which a person *is liked by* his fellows and his average disclosure-output? A *rho* of .05 between likability rank and disclosure-output rank, which was not significant, shows that in this group, likability and disclosure-output were not related.

A rank-order correlation of .12, which was not significant, was found between likability rank and rank for total disclosure-intake. This indicates that the persons in the group who were best liked by their fellows were not necessarily confided in more than the subjects who were the least liked.

It may be concluded that likability to one's fellows was not systematically related either to disclosure-output to, or disclosure-intake from, one's fellows.

Self-Disclosure and Degree Known

Ranks for the degree to which each subject was known by his 8 fellows are shown in Column 2 Table 2. These ranks were found to correlate .62 ($P < .05$) with rank for total disclosure-output and .54 with rank for total disclosure-intake. The latter *rho* was not significant. The fact that degree known was correlated significantly with total disclosure-output serves both as an index of the validity of the self-disclosure questionnaire and of the more obvious fact that the way one becomes known by one's fellows in a group is through self-disclosure.

Relationship of Liking to Knowing

Though 6 of the 9 subjects showed significant *rho*'s between liking and knowing, it does not mean that the subjects liked whom they knew. Common sense tells us that knowledge about someone may provide the basis for dislike. Moreover, when we correlated the likability ranks of the 9 subjects with their ranks for degree known, a low (insignificant) *rho* of —.20 was obtained. If this *rho* had reached significance, it would mean that there was a slight tendency for those subjects who were best known to be the least liked.

DISCUSSION

The present findings showed that liking for another was not as strong a determiner of men's disclosing behavior as either the degree to which a man knew each of his fellows or the extent to which each of others had confided in him. Since knowing was found to be related to disclosure-intake, it seems likely that each of the 36 possible dyads in the group commenced mutual confiding up to a point where the subjects knew as much as they wanted to know about one another and then stopped. These data did not afford any leads as to why confiding stopped at the point it did.

The relatively minor role played by liking in men's disclosure contrasts sharply with the major role it played in the disclosure patterns of the female sample studied earlier (Chapter 2). The men and women alike showed a marked dyadic effect—the men's slightly stronger than the women's—but the strong association between liking and disclosure was peculiar to the females.

There is reason to suppose that this sexually differentiated response to feelings is related to the social definition of the male and female role. Women in most societies are trained to assume "expressive" roles. The expressive role calls for especial concern with, and responsiveness to, feelings. Men, trained mainly to adopt "instrumental roles," doubtless are encouraged to suppress or distrust feelings and to base their transactions with people on cognitive factors rather than emotion. Certainly, there is some evidence to support this interpretation. Earlier study of self-disclosure (Chapter 1) showed that women were higher total disclosers than men.* This sex difference was further supported by comparison of the mean total amount of disclosure shown by the nursing faculty with that found in the present study. Although the groups were not entirely comparable (since they differed in mean age, in marital status, occupation, etc.), the testing procedures were identical; the nursing faculty members disclosed a mean total of 48.22 items (SD 4.60) compared with a mean total of 30.67 (SD 10.98) for males. The difference between means was significant at the .02 level ($t = 2.72$).

Tentatively, it may be proposed that men follow their role definitions most closely when they keep their "selves" to themselves, confiding in someone only after they have gotten to know enough about him to trust him. Obviously, the man can know the other person only after receiving some disclosures from him. The dyadic effect noted above suggests that disclosure proceeds on a *quid pro quo* basis—"you tell

---

* Rickers-Ovsiankina and Kusmin (1958) reported some data on sex differences in disclosure which conflict with our observations. They employed a "social accessibility" questionnaire which asked subjects' to indicate their willingness to confide items of personal information if they were asked by (a) a stranger they would never see again, (b) an acquaintance, and (c) their best friend. The males had a slightly higher total score for willingness to confide than the females. It is not known whether this discrepancy with our findings stems from differences between the samples tested, between questionnaire items, or differences in the set which subjects assumed in responding.

me and I'll tell you." Doubtless it is an occasion of anxiety for many men if they have revealed more about themselves to another man than he has revealed to them. Perhaps this is why the unilateral disclosure which occurs in psychotherapy is so threatening and is so often resisted by the patient: the therapist knows so much more about the patient than the latter knows about the therapist.

The fact that the men have been found to be lower disclosers than the women and that they tend to discount feelinge as a basis for disclosure seems to corroborate not only role theory, but also statements abounding in popular literature which portray men as strong and silent and distrustful of feelings; women are commonly portrayed as more emotional, talkative, overly trusting of those whom they like, and hence more vulnerable to betrayal than men.

SUMMARY

Nine male graduate students were tested with a brief self-disclosure questionnaire and questionnaires measuring degree of liking and degree to which each knew each of his fellow students. The amount of personal information which the subjects revealed to their fellows was highly correlated with the degree to which they knew the others and the amount the others had disclosed to them. Liking was only slightly correlated with disclosure within this male sample.

Additional analyses showed that there was only a slight relationship between a given subject's liking for fellow students and the latter's disclosures to him. The degree to which each subject knew his fellows was highly correlated with disclosure-intake from them. Average likability within the group (sociometric status) was not correlated either with subject's total disclosure-output or -intake. The average degree to which an subject was known by his fellows was correlated with his total disclosure-output but not significantly with his total disclosure-intake.

The males of this sample disclosed significantly less than did a sample of nursing college faculty who had undergone identical testing.

The Next Chapter

Men did not show as strong a correlation between liking and disclosure as women. I confirmed this more directly by testing a group of male college students with our 60-item disclosure questionnaire (Appendix 1) and with the patient-cathexis questionnaire (Appendix 2). I found insignificant correlations between amount disclosed to each parent, and degree of liking. The r's were .19 and .21 for the disclosure-cathexis correlations ($N = 45$) for mother and father, respectively.

The strongest finding that emerged in this study, however, was still the dyadic effect. I became fascinated with the hypothesis that "disclosure begets disclosure," and wanted to test this experimentally. Later (Chapter 15) we were able to do this. There was another test of the hypothesis possible through the use of questionnaires, and so with the assistance of Patricia Richman, we explored the question further.

4. Factors in the Self-
Disclosure Inputs
of College Students[*]

One of the purposes of the present study was to determine whether a "dyadic effect" would be found in subjects' relationships with their parents and closest friends.

A further aim was to investigate self-disclosure input as a dependent variable in its own right. Little is known about the degree to which subjects have been disclosed *to* by the significant others in their lives, and it is pertinent to ask, "Do subjects receive more disclosure than they give? Are there sex differences in the degree to which people are disclosed to by significant others? What differences in disclosure input are associated with differences in target-persons?" The present study sought answers to these questions.

METHOD

Disclosure-*output* was measured by means of the 40-item questionnaire shown in Appendix 4. Subtotals were obtained by summing the entries for each of the target-persons, and a grand total was also obtained.

Odd-even reliability coefficients for the target subtotals and the total disclosure score had previously been established with a group of 56 female college students, as follows: mother, .85; father, .89; opposite-sex friend, .90; same-sex friend, .75; and total score, .85.

[*] This chapter was published originally in the *Merrill-Palmer Quarterly of Behavior and Development,* 9, 1963, 141–148, and is reproduced here with permission from the Merrill Palmer Institute.

Test-re-test reliability coefficients were obtained from two samples of 44 and 43 medical freshmen, each group tested at 6-month intervals. The correlations were: for disclosure to mother, .67 (.77); father, .84 (.94); opposite-sex friend, .55 (.80); same-sex friend, .77 (.74); and for total, .62 (.61). These correlations are lower in some cases than those obtained by the split-half method. This should not be surprising, however, in view of the fact that over time, relationships tend to change.

The disclosure-output questionnaire, with appropriate changes in instructions and in the wording of items, was employed for the measurement of disclosure-*input*. Thus, a sample item about appearance was worded, "What he (or she) dislikes about his overall appearance." The scale for rating the amount of disclosure input was:

0: Write in a *zero* if the other person has never talked about a given topic to you.

1: Write in a *1* if the other person has talked in general terms about a topic, but not in full detail. You have only a general idea about that particular side of the other person.

2: Write in a *2* only if you believe the other person has talked fully to you about that particular topic. You will use a 2 only for those topics where you feel you have full and accurate information about the other person because you believe he has taken the trouble to confide fully to you.

As with the disclosure-output questionnaire, separate input subtotals were computed for each target-person, together with a grand total. The odd-even reliability coefficients were of comparable magnitude to those obtained on the output questionnaire.

Fifty-eight unmarried male and 51 unmarried female undergraduates served as subjects in the study. The disclosure-output questionnaire was administered first, during regular classroom sessions, followed from three to seven days later with the disclosure-input questionnaire. The subjects were told that the study was part of an ongoing series of investigations of the process of confiding, and they were assured that their scores would be kept confidential and would not affect their grades in any way.

RESULTS

The Dyadic Effect

The dyadic effect was tested by computing product-moment correlations between the input and output scores of each subject with respect

Table 3   Correlations between Reported Disclosure-Input and -Output

			Targets		
Group	Mother	Father	Opposite-Sex Friend	Same-Sex Friend	Total
Males (N = 58)	.68*	.76*	.80*	.78*	.83*
Females (N = 51)	.47*	.76*	.73*	.67*	.60*

* $p < .01$

to each target person. As shown in Table 3, all correlations for males and females, and for all target-persons, were significant beyond the .01 level.

Input versus Output in Disclosure

Both men and women reported significantly more disclosure-input than output in relation to friends and the same-sex parent. With respect to the opposite-sex parent, input did not differ significantly from output among males or females. These findings are shown in Table 4.

Sex and Target Differences in Input and Output

Inspection of Table 4 shows that the females obtained higher mean scores than males for both input and output, for each target-person, and for total scores. The significance of these apparent sex differences was tested by means of analyses of variance, conducted separately for the output and input scores. To facilitate computation, every seventh male case was eliminated, thus making the N's comparable.

Significant F-ratios were found, in the case of both the input and output scores, for the comparisons between sexes, between target-persons, and for the sex-by-target interaction. Accordingly, t-ratios were calculated for the difference between sexes in mean disclosure-output to, and input from, each of the four target-persons. The results are shown in Table 5, and graphically in Figure 6. It may be seen that the females obtained higher mean disclosure-output scores than the males in relation to the mother, the same-sex friend, and for the total output. For disclosure-input, the females obtained higher mean scores

Table 4 Differences between Reported Disclosure-Input and -Output for Various Target-Persons

Group	Targets	Input Mean	Input SD	Output Mean	Output SD	t
Males	Mother	39.14	13.24	38.79	13.38	0.25
Females		51.78	11.27	48.41	14.94	1.74
Males	Father	37.50	14.71	33.81	14.79	2.73*
Females		38.31	13.43	36.92	17.65	.93
Males	Opposite-sex friend	42.97	15.33	39.66	15.97	2.55*
Females		49.84	14.45	43.14	16.35	4.19†
Males	Same-sex friend	45.07	13.47	42.19	11.72	3.06†
Females		57.20	13.10	52.06	12.90	3.47†
Males	Total	164.68	33.31	154.45	42.08	3.31†
Females		197.13	36.71	180.53	46.14	3.37†

* $p < .05$
† $p < .01$

Table 5 Sex Differences in Reported Disclosure-Input and -Output*

	Target Persons Mother	Father	Opposite-Sex Friend	Same-Sex Friend	Total
Disclosure-output	3.32‡	.99	1.12	4.16‡	3.07‡
Disclosure-input	5.38‡	.30	2.41†	4.76‡	4.81‡

* The figures in the table are t-ratios for differences between male and female means. In all cases, the female means were higher.
† $p < .05$
‡ $p < .01$

31

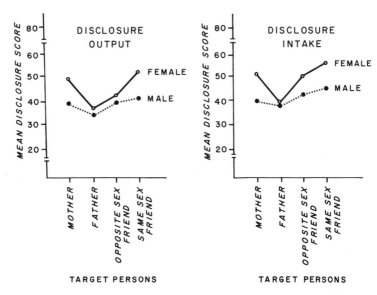

Figure 6. Mean for disclosure-output and -input of male and female college students.

than the males for mother, opposite-sex friend, same-sex friend, and for total input.

DISCUSSION

The main finding of the present study may be interpreted as follows: subjects who report they have revealed a great deal of personal information to their parents and closest friends, likewise report that those target-persons have disclosed a lot to them. In contrast, those subjects who reported they have disclosed relatively little about themselves to significant others indicate these others have not revealed much about themselves either. This finding, though obtained by a different method and employing different target-persons, supports the earlier findings obtained in occupational settings (Chapters 2 and 3). The implication is that the dyadic effect is a general phenomenon extending to many types of interpersonal relationships. Indeed, recent writings of certain psychotherapists suggest that, even in the patient-therapist dyad, patients will disclose themselves most fully when their therapist is likewise "transparent" (Hora, 1960; Jourard, 1964; Mullen and Sanguiliano, 1961) and "congruent" (Gendlin, 1959; Rogers, 1961); that is, when he discloses his experience to the patient as fully as he expects the latter to reveal his experiencing to him.

The possibility exists that the correlations obtained here reflect, not the presence of a dyadic effect in self-disclosure, but rather a "response set" on the part of the subjects. That is, subjects may tend consistently to overestimate or underestimate the extent of their own disclosure-output and the amount of disclosure-input they have received from their parents and friends. Because of the lack of independence of the input and output measures, some caution must thus be observed in drawing conclusions from these data. On the other hand, the fact that the correlations are comparable to those obtained in the earlier studies (Chapters 2 and 3), where input and output measures were obtained independently, provides some evidence that the present correlations are not spurious.

The preponderance of input over output, shown by both sexes, suggests that these subjects saw themselves as better listeners than revealers; that is, they reported being talked to by parents and friends more than they reciprocated, in spite of the correlation between intake and output. The present data do not permit us to ascertain whether this is a general phenomenon, or whether it is limited to subjects of the present age range, in relation to these target-persons.

The females were found both to disclose themselves more fully to selected others than males, and to be disclosed *to* by others more than males. The present findings thus replicate earlier results relating to output, and suggest further that women, more than men, may be viewed as the "personal interviewers of everyday life." A further implication of the sex difference in disclosure-intake is that women probably know more about the subjective side of the people around them than men do, just because they have been disclosed to the most. This implication is consistent with the fact that women are most typically socialized toward the assumption of "expressive," nurturing roles within the social system, and it may also help us better to understand why women have been found to be more empathic and intuitive than men (Dymond, 1950). If women are disclosed to more than men, then it would naturally follow that women should be more familiar with human "subjectivity" than men and, hence, better able to imagine the reality of another person's experiencing than men can.

Some final remarks may be made regarding differences between targets. The present findings are consistent with earlier findings (Chapter 1), which showed that fathers were the neglected parties in self-disclosing relationships; in the present study, the subjects disclosed less to their fathers than they did to the other three target-persons, and the fathers reportedly disclosed themselves less to their sons and daughters than did the subjects' mothers or closest friends. If fathers know less about their children than mothers do, the reverse implication holds as well—children know less about their fathers than about their mothers. The remaining three targets were disclosed to (and they disclosed to the subjects) in a rank order that has consistently been found for the age range considered in this study, specifically, for the males, in descending order: same-sex friend, opposite-sex friend, mother, and father. For the females, in descending order: same-sex friend, mother, opposite-sex friend, and father. These rankings are interesting because they show that males of this age range prefer to exchange confidences more outside the family than within—perhaps a sign of "emancipation." By contrast, the females appeared to exchange the most disclosure with other females, that is, mother and girl friend. With marriage, both males and females have been found to exchange the most disclosure with their spouses (Chapter 1), and to decrease the amount of disclosure to their parents and same-sex friends. This is perhaps less of a radical change for males than for females, since the males have already withdrawn more from family intimacy than the females.

SUMMARY

Questionnaires designed to measure self-disclosure output to parents and closest friends, and disclosure-intake from those target-persons, were administered to 58 male and 51 female college students. Substantial correlations were found between the measures of disclosure-output and disclosure-input with regard to all target-persons. Study of mean scores showed that both males and females reported more disclosure-input than -output in relation to all target-persons except the mother, where the input and output scores were similar. The women subjects were found to have disclosed more to, and to have received more disclosure from, the various target-persons than the men. The findings were viewed as further support to the hypothesis of a dyadic effect in self-disclosure.

The Next Chapter

Travellers delight in making comparisons of "national character." The small amount of travel that I had done convinced me that there were differences between nationalities, and even between regions of the same country, in the typical amount and content of self-disclosure. And so we did the two exploratory studies reported in Chapter 5, comparing American college students at the University of Florida with students in universities in England and in Puerto Rico.

Someone should check out the long-held stereotype that New Englanders in the United States are very taciturn, as compared, say, to New Yorkers or Californians. A story about a man from Maine still can elicit a chuckle: it was the fiftieth wedding anniversary for this Maine couple. At the celebration, the gray-haired husband was asked to make a speech. He stood up, put his arm on his wife's shoulder, and said to her, before the group of his children, grandchildren, and great-grandchildren, "Bessie, there's been times during this past 50 years when I felt so loving toward you, *it was all I could do to keep myself from telling you.*"

5. Self-Disclosure
in Britain, Puerto Rico,
and the United States

Britain versus United States[*]

Modal personality differences associated with different nationalities are the subject of much contemporary research in social science. Inkeles and Levinson's (1954) summary of technical literature on national character illustrates the scientific approach to the problem, but popular literature often provides valuable observations in this area. A particularly good and witty example of a literary study in "culture and personality" is Pierre Daninos' (1957) satire about Major Marmaduke Thompson, C.S.I., D.S.O., O.B.E.—a British Gentleman who enjoys comparing English manners and morals with the (to him) incomprehensible behavior of the French and Americans. In one delightful passage, Daninos describes a shipboard encounter between Major Thompson and Cyrus Lippcott, an American businessman. The narrative proceeds: ". . . *In less than four minutes, Mr. Lippcott had told us more about himself than a Frenchman does in four months, or an Englishman in several generations*" (Daninos, 1957, p. 153. My italics).

Daninos' fictional narrative contains a direct statement about national differences in *self-disclosure patterns,* and in this case, he is contrasting the stereotyped English "reserve" with the equally stereotyped American garrulousness in speaking about the self. The present study was undertaken to determine whether different nationalities would vary in their

[*] The material in this section was originally published in the *Journal of Social Psychology,* **54,** 1961, 315–320, and is reprinted here with permission from the publisher.

modal disclosure patterns. More specifically, it was predicted that British subjects would prove to be lower disclosers of self to selected target-persons than a matched sample of American subjects.

METHOD

Subjects

Twenty-five female undergraduates (mean age 19.88; range 18–25 years) enrolled at the University of Nottingham, England* and 25 co-eds (mean age 19.68; range, 18–21) from the University of Florida comprised the samples for this study. All subjects were unmarried, and all came from comparable middle-class backgrounds.

Materials and Procedure

The 25-item self-disclosure questionnaire shown in Appendix 5 was administered to the subjects with the following instruction: "If you have disclosed the information from the questionnaire to your mother, father, closest male friend at present, and closest female friend at present, then write a '1' in the appropriate space on the answer sheet. If you have not told this information to that person, or if you have only given an incomplete version of the information, then write in a 'zero'."

Split-half reliability of the questionnaire had already been demonstrated with a separate American sample; odd-even r's for each "target" subscale were all .90 or higher.

RESULTS

Analysis of variance undertaken with individual self-disclosure scores yielded significant F-ratios between nationalities and between target-persons. There was no significant interaction between nationality and target-persons. Further analysis of target-persons showed that the subjects agreed in disclosing significantly more to females than to males.

Figure 7 shows that the American girls were higher disclosers than the British girls. Though the groups did not differ significantly for amount of disclosure to any one target-person, the mean total disclosure

* The author is indebted to Joan L. Eyden, Lecturer in the Department of Social Science, University of Nottingham, for providing him with the data for the British samples.

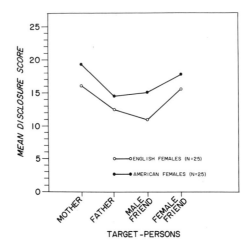

Figure 7. Mean disclosure scores of American and British female college students.

to all four target-persons combined was highest for the American subjects ($t = 5.72$, $p < .01$).

The two groups were then compared on readiness to disclose the different *items* on the questionnaire to each target-person, as follows. The number of English girls and American girls who had disclosed each item to a given target-person were employed as the *x*'s and *y*'s for Pearsonian product-moment correlations between the nationalities. The resulting *r*'s (mother: .78; father: .85; male friend: .86; female friend: .68; all significant beyond the .01 level) indicate marked agreement between English and American girls on the relative disclosability of the respective items to each target-person. We may conclude that, although the two groups differed in average disclosure-output, they agreed markedly in attitude concerning the relative disclosability of the questionnaire items to each target-person.

DISCUSSION

The present findings lend support to the common observation that British people are more "reserved" in their interpersonal transactions than Americans. Although the study was confined to comparison of female subjects, it seems likely that similar findings would emerge from a comparison of British and American males.

A pertinent objection which might be raised against the findings of the present study is that they are based on too small a sample. In defense of the present work it may be said that the subjects were well matched with regard to age, socioeconomic background, educational level, and marital status. Work on American samples has shown that these are pertinent matching variables, and so, while the samples are admittedly small, there seems little reason to doubt that they represent their respective universes.

One theoretical interpretation of these data can be made in the light of Lewin's (1936) topological conceptions of personality structure. In commenting upon phenotypic differences noticeable between German and American modal personality, he stated that the Germans had a "thick boundary" interposed between the outside world and the central regions of the personality, but this boundary was closer to the "periphery" of the person than was the case in the typical American. That is, the typical German would regard more information about himself as private than the typical American: " . . . more regions of persons are considered of public interest in the United States than in Germany . . . the American is more willing *to be open to other individuals* and to share certain situations with other individuals than the German" (Lewin, 1936, p. 18. My italics).

Lewin's observations were made regarding the comparison of British and American modal personality as well. Perhaps it might be said that the English individual, like the German, divides the "private and personal" from the "public and disclosable" closer to his "periphery" than does the modal American.

If the difference in modal disclosure patterns is a valid and general one, it is pertinent to inquire into possible correlates of self-disclosure in the two societies. There is reason to suspect (*cf.* Jourard, 1964) that self-disclosure is systematically related to mental and possibly to physical health—at least in the American culture. Self-disclosure is one means by which a person permits himself to be known by others. It is obvious that people are variably reluctant to permit others, even "significant others," to know about certain aspects of their own personality, such as, selected past experiences or embarrassing or guilt-inducing thoughts and feelings. One index of both repression and suppression is the withholding of disclosure to others; indeed, Freud chose the terms "resistance" and "repression" to describe the refusal or inability of his patients to disclose certain mental contents. Repression and suppression, in extreme degree, are factors in neurotic and psychosomatic disability. It follows from considerations of this sort that societies which produce modal personalities with differing self-disclosure habits might well produce different frequencies for certain kinds of illness, in which suppression and repression are known to be factors.

SUMMARY

Twenty-five female undergraduate students in a British university were compared with a matched sample of American female college undergraduates on amount of self-disclosure to the mother, the father, the closest male friend, and the closest female friend. It was found that:

1. The English females obtained lower mean total disclosure scores than the American subjects.
2. Both groups tended to disclose more to female target-persons than to males.
3. Both groups agreed in disclosing some items readily to a given target-person, and in disclosing other items in low degree to a given target-person.

Self-Disclosure in Puerto Rico and the United States

Spanish-speaking persons are commonly stereotyped as more open with their emotions than people raised in English-speaking societies. The question may be raised, however, whether such openness extends to the realm of confiding personal information to significant others in their life. Here, we compare the self-disclosure patterns of a sample of college students in Puerto Rico with those found in a sample of American students.

METHOD

Subjects, Materials, and Procedure

The 40-item self-disclosure questionnaire (Appendix 4) was translated into Spanish by the late Dr. Leonardo Rodriguez at the University of Puerto Rico and administered to his students in regular class sessions. I administered the English version to students in psychology classes at the University of Florida.

Thirty male and 44 female Puerto Rican students had been tested, and from these, 25 male and 25 female records were selected such that all were unmarried, between the ages of 17 and 22 years, and had both parents living. From the records of about 500 students tested at the University of Florida, 25 male and 25 female cases, all born and raised in the United States, were matched with the Puerto Rican sample on age, religious affiliation (predominantly Catholic), year in college, father's occupational level, and father's education. The matching was so close that the groups could be regarded as nearly identical in composition with respect to the variables indicated.

Scores for amount of disclosure to each target-person were obtained by summing, and the target subtotals were summed for a total self-disclosure score. The nationalities then were compared by means of analysis of variance.

The following procedure was adopted to determine whether there was a significant nationality by subject-matter interaction: for each of the 40 items of the questionnaire, the entries for that item of all subjects in each group were summed. Then, Pearsonian r's were calculated, with N corresponding to 40 items—with, for example, the sum of Puerto Rican males' entries on each item disclosed to the mother serving as x, and the sum of the American males' scores on each item disclosed to mother serving as y, for the correlation. A high r between the American and Puerto Rican males on disclosure to mother would signify that the two groups showed similar patterns of willingness and reluctance to confide the questionnaire topics to that target-person—presumably a reflection of shared norms of what subject-matter is disclosable and what is not. A low r would betoken a significant interaction between nationality and subject matter of disclosure.

RESULTS

Table 6 shows means and standard deviations of disclosure scores classified by nationality, sex, and target-person. Though the nationalities

Table 6 Mean Self-Disclosure Scores of American and Puerto Rican College Students, Classified by Target-Persons and by Sex

| | Target-Persons | | | | |
	Mother	Father	Opposite-Sex Friend	Same-Sex Friend	Total
Males					
Americans	46.28	41.16	47.20	48.36	183.00
Puerto Ricans	37.60	28.84	35.16	41.12	142.72
Females					
Americans	42.84	31.36	37.00	46.12	157.32
Puerto Ricans	46.80	27.44	29.24	42.32	145.80

appeared to differ in amount disclosed to each of the four target-persons, the analysis of variance showed a significant F-ratio only for the comparison of total scores, not for the interactions between nationality and target-person, nationality and sex, nor for the triple interaction. The combined group of Puerto Rican students obtained significantly ($P < .01$) lower total disclosure scores than did the American students. The only other significant F-ratios in the analysis of variance were for the between-target comparison, and for the sex-by-target interaction. These findings were to be expected, signifying only that the target-persons were disclosed to in varying degrees whether we combined the sexes or treated them separately.

Nationality-by-Subject-Matter Interaction

The purpose of this analysis was to determine whether the nationalities resembled one another in significant degree in their pattern of revealing or withholding different categories of personal data with respect to each of the four target persons. A high r between nationalities would signify similarity, while a low r would betoken differences in the norms governing the topics of self-disclosure. For the males, the relevant r's were .65, .69, .73, and .76 for mother, father, opposite-sex friend, and same-sex friend, respectively. For the females, the r's (in similar order for target-persons) were .73, .81, .81, and .73. These findings indicated that there was a statistically significant degree of similarity between the two nationalities in their concepts of what was disclosable and what was not.

DISCUSSION

The present data showed that, contrary to expectation, Puerto Rican college students disclosed less personal data to parents and closest friends than did comparable American college students. In the exploratory studies of cultural differences now completed by the present writer, American students have appeared more "socially accessible" than either English or Puerto Rican students. Melikian (1966) reported some self-disclosure findings obtained on 9 groups of male students coming from different parts of the Middle East, in attendance at the American University of Beirut. Although he did not report his data completely, it was possible to determine that the mean total disclosure to parents and friends on the questionnaire he employed was 205.4. In the study reported in Chapter 1, a similar questionnaire had been employed with white and Negro college students in the southeastern United States. The comparable mean total disclosure score was 248.50 for the white males, and 185.90 for the Negro males. Though we cannot subject the differences between Melikian's subjects and those in the Jourard-Lasakow study to a test of significance, the trend is clear, that the white male American college students appeared to be higher self-disclosers than the Middle Eastern group. Later, Plog (1963) reported that German college students were lower disclosers than American students. If we can extrapolate from these scanty data, it may be proposed that Americans, at least Caucasian Americans, tend to be higher disclosers of personal data to significant others in their lives than people from other societies. To use Allport's (1961, p. 500) and Foa's (1958) terms,* we might suggest that Americans, considered as a nationality, are more "transparent" (as opposed to opaque or enigmatic) than are people of other nationalities.

The similarity noted between the American subjects and the Puerto Ricans in the differential disclosure of subject-matter parallels that found in the comparison of English with American female college students. It seems that even in cultures as geographically separate as England, the United States, and Puerto Rico, similar norms govern what kinds of personal data will be more readily disclosed than others. Melikian also found results comparable to ours (Chapter 1) on the disclosability of subject matter. Thus, it appears that across at least four nationalities, such personal data as one's hobbies and interests, attitudes and opinions on political and religious matters, tastes in food and beverages, and so forth are more readily revealed to other people than one's financial and sexual affairs, and worries relating to one's health, personality, and interpersonal relationships.

SUMMARY

A 40-item self-disclosure questionnaire was administered to 25 male and 25 female college students at the University of Puerto Rico, and to a matched group of American college students. The American students differed in that they were found to have disclosed more to parents and closest friends of each sex than did the Puerto Rican students. The nationalities resembled one another on the topics of personal data they could readily disclose, and those less readily disclosed, evidently a function of similar norms.

* I think I got the idea for the title of my book *The Transparent Self* from Foa's and Allport's use of the term "transparency."

The Next Chapter

We have shown, thus far, that sex, race, target-persons, liking, knowing, disclosure from the other person, and nationality are all factors in self-disclosure to significant people in one's life. The question occurred to me, "What changes occur in self-disclosing patterns as a person grows older?" Since I could not readily follow a person from early childhood into old age, I looked at the accumulated data we had on hand and carried on a study of differences in various age groups.

6. Age Trends
in Self-Disclosure*

As young people grow from late adolescence into more mature years, their interpersonal relationships change. Parents die, and the majority of people select a mate. Since self-disclosure scores appear to be a fairly direct measure of the "closeness" between people, we might expect such scores to reflect the typical age-related changes in significant interpersonal relationships.

METHOD

Hypothesis

The specific hypothesis explored in this study was, therefore, that as late adolescents grow into later maturity, they will reduce the amount that they confide to their parents and same-sex friend, and show a concomitant increase in the extent to which they confide in the person of the opposite sex who is closest to them. Moreover, we might expect that the amount disclosed to the opposite-sex friend or spouse in the mature years will exceed the average amount disclosed to either parent or to the same-sex friend at any earlier stage. In other words, the relationship between a person and his spouse is "closer," insofar as self-revelation is concerned, than any other everyday relationship a person has entered up to that time.

---

* This chapter was originally printed in the *Merrill-Palmer Quarterly of Behavior and Development*, **7**, 1961, 191–197, and is reprinted here in slightly altered form, with permission from the Merrill-Palmer Institute.

Table 7   Characteristics of the Sample for Study of Age Trends in Self-Disclosure

Age Levels	N		Percent Married		Percent with Mother Alive		Percent with Father Alive		Mean Socioeconomic Status Score*	
	M	F	M	F	M	F	M	F	M	F
17–18	53	134	0	.7%	96.20	96.15	96.20	92.54	33.98	32.13
19–20	130	174	3.08	5.17	96.15	100.00	90.77	92.54	32.11	39.02
21–22	100	105	16.00	30.48	100.00	99.05	87.00	87.62	33.34	36.51
23–24	54	27	40.74	25.93	96.30	96.30	85.19	88.89	35.88	35.38
25–29	66	34	65.15	50.00	95.45	91.18	83.33	82.35	38.13	33.85
30–39	50	37	92.00	72.97	94.20	94.59	82.00	64.86	39.58	36.04
40–55	19	37	94.74	64.86	84.21	78.38	63.16	51.35	29.55	33.46
Total N	472	548								

* Scored by the method of Hollingshead (1959).

Subjects

One thousand and twenty students enrolled in classes at the University of Florida between 1958 and 1960 served as subjects in the present investigation. Age, marital status, percentage of parents who were deceased, N for each age group, and socioeconomic status (scored by the method of Hollingshead) are shown in Table 7.

Materials and Procedure

The 40-item self-disclosure questionnaire (Appendix 4) was administered to the subjects in group sessions.

RESULTS

The means for disclosure to each target-person at the seven age levels here considered are shown for both sexes in Figure 8.* Means for dis-

* In the first study of self-disclosure patterns, we found that female subjects were higher overall disclosers than males. The present data, based on a wider age range, provided a selective confirmation of the earlier findings, in that the females proved to be higher disclosers to mother ($CR = 8.3$, $P < .001$) and to same-sex friend ($CR = 2.40$, $P < .02 > .01$) than were the males. The differences between the sexes in mean disclosure to father and to opposite-sex friend were not significant.

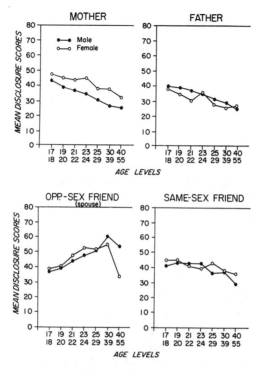

Figure 8. Age changes in self-disclosure to four target-persons.

closure to parents were calculated with *N* equal to the number of subjects with living parents. Inspection of Figure 8 shows a gradual decrease
in disclosure on the part of males and females to both parents and
to the same-sex friend. The scores for disclosure to opposite-sex friend
(or spouse) show a gradual increase with age. For the 40- to 55-year
age range, a drop-off in disclosure to opposite-sex friend was noted.
Since 18 of the 19 males in that group were married, this implies some
reduction in the amount of verbal self-disclosure exchanged between
these men and their wives. Thirty-five percent of the oldest female sample was unmarried; the score of these older spinsters for disclosure
to opposite-sex friend reduced the mean for the whole group to the
level noted. Mean scores for disclosure to mother, father, opposite-sex
friend, and same-sex friend of these unmarried older women were sub-
stantially lower than the respective means for the entire female sample.
Unless these women had close, confiding relationships with other people
besides the target-persons mentioned on the questionnaire, it may be
assumed that they were relatively lonely people.

Analysis of variance showed no significant differences between age levels for mean disclosure to any given target-person, a finding which held true for both males and females. The reason lay in the fact that the absolute differences between mean disclosure scores of any two age levels were small, and the variabilities about each mean were high. That there was correlation between age and disclosure to each of the target-persons may be seen from the slope of the curves shown in Figure 8.

Inspection of Figure 8 also shows that, beginning with the age range from 23 to 24 years, the mean disclosure to opposite-sex friend (spouse) was higher than the mean for disclosure to either parent or to the same-sex friend at any age level. The oldest female group was the sole exception to this trend.

In general, then, the data upheld the major hypothesis of this study.

DISCUSSION

The present data, beside showing age trends in self-disclosure, may also be viewed as evidence of the "concurrent" validity of the self-disclosure questionnaire, and as a partial replication of an earlier comparison between married and unmarried subjects of similar age (Chapter 1).

It would be of interest to follow the age trends into younger and older ranges. Senescence is thought to be accompanied by a process of "disengagement," and the self-disclosing patterns should reflect this. At the younger pole, suitably constructed questionnaires might permit longitudinal investigation of the constriction or openness of children's relationships with significant others.

One of the more obvious findings of the present study was the high amount of variability in disclosure to any given target-person, irrespective of the age level under consideration. This calls attention to the need for study of individual differences in self-disclosure to a given target-person and the correlates thereof. We already know that liking, knowing, and the amount of disclosure-intake from another person are all related to the amount a subject will disclose to that person, but these three factors are not independent one of the other, and leave much of the variance awaiting explanation. One wonders if anxiety level or past experiences with people who resemble a given target-person are relevant here. Certainly, whatever is pertinent to the psychology of the "transference" in psychotherapy should be pertinent in this connection.

The fact that the present data derive from a confounding of age with marital status is in some ways an advantage, because it throws unexpected light on the significance of marriage. The fullest disclosure of self seems to be reserved for a partner of the opposite sex, usually the spouse; this implies that if a person is unable to achieve a close relationship with an opposite-sex partner, he will remain with much "self" that is not expressed or realized. Possibly herein lies one reason for the avoidance of marriage—the dread or inability to "uncover" one's self before the gaze of another person, a sort of resistance against being known.

One wonders too about the significance of having much unexpressed self. We know that more self-disclosure is exchanged between spouses than occurs within any other everyday relationship. We also know that morbidity rates for most illnesses, as well as suicide rates, are the highest among unmarried people. This would suggest that there is a correlation of some kind, possibly curvilinear, between the amount of self-disclosure and variables from the fields of mental and physical health.

SUMMARY

A self-disclosure questionnaire containing 40 items of personal information was administered in group sessions to 1020 college students of both sexes, married and unmarried, and ranging in age from 17 to 55 years. A trend was noted for subjects of both sexes to decrease the amount of disclosure to their parents and to their friend of the same sex, while the amount of disclosure to the opposite-sex friend (or spouse) increased with age. No significant differences between age levels were found for mean disclosure to any given target-person, in consequence of high variabilities. The implications of the findings were discussed.

I did the above study in 1959. I was not happy with the composition of the older samples. We need to learn more about the self-disclosing patterns of people in their 50's, 60's, and older. I suspect that we would find a positive relationship between involvement in mutually disclosing relationships in that age range, and overall health and longevity. Stated otherwise, I believe we would find that people in their advanced years are sick more often, and more gravely, if they are not implicated in intimate personal relations—as betokened by mutual disclosure with significant other people.

At the other end of the age range, Rivenbark (1966) studied the disclosure patterns of school children between the ages of 10 and 16, and in 1969, Genevieve Skypek completed a master's thesis investigating children's disclosing relationships with their closest same-sex friend between the ages of 6 and 12. I will present her study briefly.

Self-Disclosure in Children Aged Six to Twelve

A sample of 98 children (94 from an elementary school in Decatur, Georgia, and 4 from a school in Gainesville, Florida) was selected for testing, as follows: 7 boys and 7 girls were chosen for each of the 7 age levels, all subjects came from white, middle-class backgrounds, and all had tested IQ's of 100 or above.

The questionnaire listing 25 topics (shown in Appendix 6) was developed, such that the content and the wording would be understandable and relevant to children in this age range. The questionaire was administered individually to each subject by experimenter (Miss Skypek). The 25 items were presented to each subject in the same order and in one continuous session. Interviews were tape-recorded and then transcribed for scoring. The subjects were asked to disclose the information to experimenter, but could decline if they wished. The subjects were then asked to tell experimenter whether or not they had disclosed this information to their closest friend of the same sex. If subject said that he had, he received a score of 1 for that item. If he had not, a zero score was given. Subjects were also asked if their friend had disclosed that information to them. Two scores were obtained by this technique—a disclosure-*output* and a disclosure-*intake* score. Since the output and intake scores were correlated .96, only the main findings for disclosure output to closest friend will be reported here.

Results

Analysis of variance of the disclosure scores, classified by age and by sex showed a significant ($P < .001$) F-ratio for age, but not for sex, or for the age-by-sex interaction. The mean disclosure output to closest friend of the same sex showed a linear increase with age (see Figure 9), the means for both sexes combined being 5.86, 7.43, 9.57, 12.00, 13.14, 14.93, and 15.86 for the ages 6 to 12, respectively. The correlation between each subject's age and his disclosure-output score was .99!

Discussion

It would have been desirable to see what happened to the scores for disclosure-output to mother, father, and closest friend of the opposite sex, in order to make comparisons possible between children of this

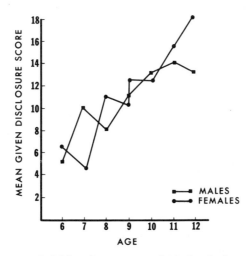

Figure 9. Mean scores of children between 6 and 12, for disclosure to closest friend.

age range, and those whom Rivenbark tested, and the subjects in my study. However, it does seem true that the closest same-sex friend is not confided in much in childhood; as a child matures, he comes to disclose much more to that target-person. Extrapolating from the data available, I will propose that children of both sexes begin life with their mother as their closest confidant. The sexes do not differ up to age 12 in overall amount of disclosure. As they enter adolescence, a difference between the sexes begins to appear, the females disclosing more than the males. As adolescence and young adulthood is reached, the typical pattern is for the amount of disclosure to parents to be reduced, with increases in disclosure to closest same-sex friend. As heterosexual relationships are commenced, culminating in marriage, the spouse becomes the closest confidant, with further decreases in confiding to parents and closest same-sex friend.

The preceding formulation is tentative because there remain gaps in the data. But existing techniques for measuring self-disclosure and other personality variables make it quite feasible to explore such questions as, "What is the connection between self-disclosure and health or illness at various age levels? Between self-disclosure and academic achievement?"

Students of human development can have a fruitful time investigating self-disclosure more thoroughly than we have done with these exploratory studies.

The Next Chapter

Another question that my accumulated data enabled me to explore was that of differences in self-disclosure attributable to religious denomination and religious involvement. Dr. Terence Cooke (1962) had done a dissertation exploring the relationship between measures of disclosure to parents, and extent of involvement in formal religious activity (Appendix 7). His subjects were 111 male Protestant college students, ranging in age from 17 to 22. He found r's of .22 and .21 between disclosure to mother and father, and religious behavior. I reanalyzed his data after classifying his subjects by age. I found r's of .47 and .49 ($P < .01$) between disclosure to mother and father, and religious activity at ages 17 to 18, with the r's decreasing to —.13 and —.20 for subjects aged 20. This suggested that as subjects matured, their religious activity became more independent of the closeness of their relationship with their parents.

I next wondered if students of different faiths would differ in their self-disclosing patterns. The next chapter describes the study we did on this problem.

7. Religious Denomination and Self-Disclosure[*]

Most religious teachings affirm the importance of love, of the ability to establish close ties with other people. Self-disclosure questionnaire scores show promise of being indices of positive regard for others and of "closeness" to others. The present study sought to explore possible differences between members of four religious denominations in degree of closeness to mother, father, closest male friend, and closest female friend, as this is measured by the self-disclosure questionnaires.

From among several thousand 40-item self-disclosure questionnaires that had been administered to students at the University of Florida, the records of 25 unmarried males and 25 females between the ages of 18 and 21 were randomly chosen from those indicating affiliation with the Methodist, Baptist, Jewish, and Catholic faiths, a total N of 200. The groups were comparable in socioeconomic status as measured by Hollingshead's (1959) index.

Analysis of variance showed that there was a significant F-ratio ($P < .01$) for the comparison of *total* disclosure scores (the sum of 4 target subscores) between religious denominations among the males but not among the females. There was no significant interaction between denomination, and disclosure to the various target-persons for either sex. A significant ($P < .01$) F-ratio was found for the between-targets comparison, and between sexes. Table 8 shows the means obtained for all groups. The Jewish male subjects obtained disclosure totals significantly higher ($P < .01$) than those found for each of the other three male groups, none of which differed significantly from each other. It may be concluded that Jewish college males are higher disclosers to the

[*] S. M. Jourard, "Religious denomination and self-disclosure," *Psychological Reports*, 8, (1961), 446. Reprinted with permission from the publisher.

Table 8 Mean Self-Disclosure Scores in Four Religious Denominations

Target-Person		Religious Denomination			
		Methodist	Baptist	Catholic	Jewish
Mother	Male	39.79	37.30	38.14	46.93
	Female	48.60	46.79	45.17	50.07
Father	Male	37.23	32.63	35.48	43.14
	Female	37.59	36.34	34.30	39.90
Opposite-sex friend	Male	33.67	36.51	39.60	43.17
	Female	38.63	40.59	42.60	42.83
Same-sex friend	Male	43.60	45.00	43.10	47.70
	Female	45.97	51.27	47.53	52.80
Total score	Male	154.29	151.44	156.32	180.94
	Female	170.79	174.99	169.60	185.60

significant people in their lives than are comparable Methodist, Baptist, or Catholic students. The present study did not control for intensity of religious participation, as was done in Cooke's study (see p. 52).

The Next Chapter

The next study to be reported was done in Birmingham, Alabama, during the year 1957. Dr. Lasakow taught a course in criminology at the University of Alabama extension, and he tested the police officers who attended his lectures. We wanted to compare the disclosure patterns of these men with a more suitable group, but we had no data available. Accordingly, we decided to compare them with married college students who differed in age, length of marriage, and social class. Not the best kind of comparison, but it produced suggestive findings.

8. Police Officers
versus College Students

Police officers, as an occupational group, are sometimes viewed as authoritarian, suspicious, paranoid, and distrustful (Moloney, 1949). It is not known whether these traits are acquired in consequence of training and experience as a police officer, or whether persons with those traits gravitate toward a police officer's career.

If it is a valid observation, that police officers are indeed distrustful and suspicious, then it might be expected that, in comparison with other males with different vocational orientations, they would engage in less self-disclosure to "close" target-persons.

METHOD

Hypothesis

Married police officers will display less self-disclosure to their wives and closest male friends than a group of young married male college students.

Subjects

The police officer sample was obtained from a university night-school class in criminology. Average age was 44.50, SD 3.30. All of the police group had rank beyond that of a patrolman, and there were sergeants, lieutenants, and chiefs of police included in the sample. Average duration of marriage was 17.48 years, SD 7.33.

The male married college group were the identical subjects employed in our first study as reported in the introduction to Part I. Average

age was 23.40, *SD* 1.43. The average duration of marriage in this group had not been ascertained at the time the data were collected, but in view of their age, it may be assumed that none of the group had been married longer than five years.

Materials and Procedure

All subjects were tested in their classrooms with the 60-item Self-Disclosure Questionnaire (Appendix 1). Responses to wife and to closest male friend were compared, as well as combined scores for both target-persons. The data were subjected to analysis of variance.

RESULTS

Significant *F*-ratios were obtained for the comparisons between groups and for the triple interaction, which are the findings of relevance to this study. The other significant *F*-ratios parallel those obtained in Chapter 1, and will not be discussed.

The mean total self-disclosure score (see Figures 10 and 11) of the police group was 92.50, *SD* 33.80 and that of the college group was

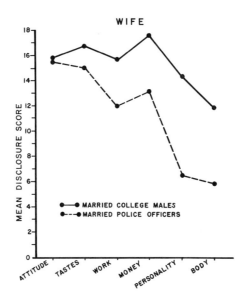

Figure 10. Comparison of married college males ($N = 10$) with married police officers ($N = 10$) on self-disclosure to wife.

MALE FRIEND

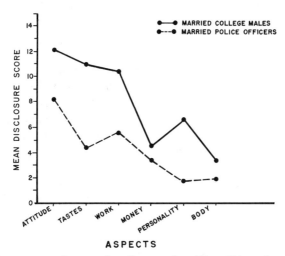

Figure 11. Comparison of married college males ($N = 10$) and married police officers ($N = 10$) on self-disclosure to male friend.

139.40, SD 30.40. The difference between these two scores is significant beyond the .001 level ($t = 10.71$, $df = 19$). Thus, the findings are in line with our prediction.

DISCUSSION

Many of the police officers thought that the questionnaires were probing too deeply, and that it would take a crazy person to reveal everything on the questionnaire to his wife or best friend. It appears that resistance to self-disclosure may be "normal" in the police group we studied and, perhaps, to policemen in general.

The Next Chapter

Someone asked me, Is there any correlation between self-disclosure and intelligence?" I had not obtained any data that sampled various intelligence levels. But I had collected enough questionnaires from students in the University and in the College of Nursing to attempt some explorations in levels of academic competence. I had been testing nursing students all along, and I ran correlations between their overall grade-point average and self-disclosure scores, and found nothing of significance. Then, I hit upon the idea of looking only at their grades and ratings for performance, in *nursing* courses alone. The reason for this lay in the fact that the nursing college had become a kind of laboratory in self-disclosure. I was working with the faculty, seeking to help them become more secure in disclosing to the students how they experienced the whole field of nursing. The students were asked to disclose their personal reactions to books they had read, patients they had worked with, and the like, in the form of "reaction papers." I reasoned that readiness to be "open" might contribute to a student's grade, both in the academic courses and in the practical work with patients. This line of reasoning led to the study reported next.

9. Academic Competence and Self-Disclosure

Self-Disclosure Scores and Grades in Nursing College*

There are educational programs in which the interpersonal as well as the intellectual aspects of student's performances are considered in the final determination of grades. Collegiate programs of nursing are a case in point; students of nursing are judged partly on the basis of their ability to learn the verbal subject matter of the curriculum, but also on the degree to which they have mastered manual and interpersonal skills. The present study was undertaken to determine whether a measure of one aspect of nursing students' interpersonal behavior—their self-disclosure to parents and peers—when obtained early in the students' careers, would predict their grade-point averages at the conclusion of their programs.

METHOD

Subjects and Procedure

The 25-item self-disclosure questionnaire was administered to 46 sophomore students of the University of Florida College of Nursing during a regular classroom session. Odd-even reliability coefficient for total scores on this questionnaire was .93. Median age of the group was 20 years.

By the time this group had become seniors, attrition had reduced

* Reprinted, with slight modifications, from an article first published in the *Journal of Applied Psychology*, **45**, 1961, 244–247, with permission from the publisher.

the N to 23. Following the completion of the senior academic year, grade-point averages of these 23 subjects were calculated for (a) all nursing courses taken during the 4 years of study, (b) nursing courses taken in the junior and senior years, (c) all nonnursing courses taken during the 4-year program, and (d) all courses combined. Product-moment correlations were calculated between these grade-point averages and the self-disclosure scores obtained 2 years earlier.

RESULTS

Table 9 shows the correlations between the various grade-point averages and the self-disclosure scores. Significant r's were found between total disclosure scores (see Column 5) and the three sets of grade-point averages in which nursing courses figured. The correlation between total self-disclosure score and grades for nonnursing courses did not reach statistical significance. Table 9 also shows correlations between each of the target subtotals and the various grade-point averages. It may be seen that the highest r's were found between scores for disclosure to mother and the three grade-point averages which included nursing courses. The r's between disclosure to female friend and nursing grades were slightly lower, and those between disclosure to father and the two sets of nursing grades were lower still, but still within the range of statistical significance. The r's between disclosure to male friend and

Table 9   Correlations between Self-Disclosure Scores and Grade-Point Averages in Nursing College Students

Grade-Point Averages	Disclosure Scores				
	Mother	Father	Male Friend	Female Friend	Total Disclosure
All nursing courses	.75†	.46*	.21	.59†	.78†
Junior and senior nursing courses	.78†	.44*	.25	.62†	.79†
All nonnursing courses	.38	.29	−.50	.39	.39
All courses combined	.70†	.38	.14	.53†	.68†

* At .05 level: $r = .41$ ($df = 21$).
† At .01 level: $r = .53$ ($df = 21$).

grades were all insignificant, as were those between the various target subtotals and grade-point average for nonnursing courses.

DISCUSSION

The self-disclosure scores may be presumed to reflect the degree to which the subjects actually have engaged in self-revealing communication to significant others in their lives. The present findings strongly suggest that this type of activity prepares a nursing student to engage in the kinds of behavior which will earn her the highest grades in nursing college. It is interesting that the highest correlations were found between scores for disclosure to mother and grades in nursing courses. This finding implies that experience at communicating openly with one's mother is good preparatory practice for communication with other female authority figures, namely, the faculty of the college of nursing. Support for this interpretation is provided by the fact that in the particular college from which the subjects were drawn, the students were required throughout the program to reveal their personal reactions to books and articles they had read, and patients they had dealt with, through the media of classroom discussion and written "reaction reports." It is likely that those students who were the most "open" in such communication impressed the faculty most favorably, and hence earned the higher grades.

Another factor which the faculty considered in assigning course grades to students was the observed facility with which the students interacted with patients. An exploratory study showed that the 10 sophomore and junior students who received the highest ratings from their clinical instructors on "ability to establish close, communicating relationships with patients" had higher total disclosure scores ($p < .05$) than the 10 matched students who received the lowest ratings on this ability (see Figure 12). The self-disclosure questionnaires had been administered a year before the time of rating. This finding too suggests that the higher-disclosing students were best able to elicit disclosure from patients, producing thereby a favorable impression upon their instructors.

That the self-disclosure scores are not indices of intelligence, or of more general academic aptitude, is attested by an insignificant correlation of .07 that was found in a sample of 52 freshmen nursing students between total score on the ACE Psychological Examination and total self-disclosure scores. Moreover, the correlation in the present study between self-disclosure scores and grades in non-nursing courses was not significant, suggesting that the attributes measured by the self-dis-

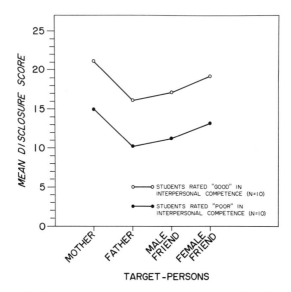

Figure 12. Mean disclosure scores of nursing students rated "good" and "poor" in interpersonal competence.

closure questionnaire played a lesser role in performance in more strictly academic courses.

The question may be raised whether the self-disclosure questionnaires employed here could have predicted which subjects would fail in the program or would leave it for other reasons. A comparison was made between the self-disclosure scores of 34 students who dropped from the nursing program before their senior year and those available from 37 juniors and seniors tested at the same time. Mean total disclosure score of the dropout group was 59.60, SD 15.79, while that for the continuing group was 62.94, SD 15.86. The difference between means was not statistically significant. Inspection of the scores of those students who failed did not show any consistent trend toward higher or lower mean disclosure scores than those found in students who left school for reasons of marriage, or who changed courses; nor did the self-disclosure scores of the failing students differ significantly from the mean total of the senior class. This observation is not intended to be conclusive, however; it is possible that study of a larger sample of failing students might point up some trends that were not apparent here.

Nursing is not the only profession in which the ability to establish close relationships with others is a desired trait; counseling, psychotherapy, teaching, military and industrial leadership all require some measure of interpersonal competence. The present findings provide further evidence for the predictive validity of self-disclosure questionnaires, and suggest that they may have promise of providing a measure of one of the important nonintellective factors which might predict success in programs of training for these vocations.

SUMMARY

A self-disclosure questionnaire was administered to a group of students of nursing during their sophomore year. At the conclusion of their senior years, grade-point averages were calculated for (*a*) all nursing courses taken during the 4 years of study, (*b*) nursing courses taken in the junior and senior years, (*c*) all nonnursing courses taken during the 4-year program, and (*d*) all courses combined. Significant correlations were found between the scores for disclosure to mother, female friend, and total disclosure, on the one hand, and all grade-point averages in which nursing courses were included. Disclosure to father was significantly correlated with grades for all nursing courses, and grades in nursing courses taken in the junior and senior years. Disclosure to male friend was not significantly correlated with any of the grade-point averages.

The Next Chapter

While I was still in Birmingham, I had lectured on self-disclosure at the University of Alabama Psychology Department. A student, Stewart Smith, became interested and wanted to do his master's research in this area. All entering freshmen at the University were required to take the Minnesota Multiphasic Personality Inventory (MMPI), and Smith had access to these records for research purposes. He went through nearly 2000 test records, and picked out 9 male and 9 female records in each of 3 categories—the "normals", who showed no clinical scales above a cutoff point of 60; "78's", who showed T-scores above 70 on the scales supposed to betoken schizoid and obsessional traits; and "94's", who showed similarly elevated scores on scales that supposedly reflect psychopathic and manic personality trends. He located these students and tested them with the 60-item self-disclosure questionnaire. There were no differences found between these groups.

But students with specified patterns of scores on the MMPI are by no means an "average" group of college students—not even those whose MMPI scores are deemed "normal." And so, several years later, I completed a little study comparing the self-disclosure scores of Smith's groups of subjects with the scores obtained in a more randomly chosen sample.

This study was the first of several in which I followed up the intention to explore personality factors in self-disclosure. In the next chapter, I report studies of the relationship between self-disclosure and MMPI scores, productivity on the Rorschach test, and scores on a test of self-concept.

10. Some Personality Factors in Self-Disclosure

Self-Disclosure and the MMPI

Sullivan's insistence (1953, pp. 13–14) that personality disturbance arises and is manifested in the context of relationships with "significant others" is commonly accepted today, and it is perhaps a reflection of his influence that much research and writing are today devoted to interpersonal psychology (cf. Heider, 1958; Leary, 1957; Schutz, 1958).

Certain forms of personality maladjustment are characterized by inability or unwillingness to establish close, confiding relationships with others. Since closeness to others and being known by others exposes one to the risk of criticism, rejection, and punishment, it is readily apparent why many persons are reluctant to permit others to know them.

Smith (1958) sought to explore the supposed relationship between self-disclosure and quality of adjustment, when the latter was measured by means of the Minnesota Multiphasic Personality Inventory (MMPI). Smith selected subjects from the entering freshman class at the University of Alabama who had "abnormal" MMPI clinical scale scores of contrasting types, and compared their self-disclosure scores with those obtained from subjects with "normal" MMPI clinical scale scores. He found no significant differences in self-disclosure between his "normal" males and females (subjects with no clinical scale T-score over 60) and subjects with abnormal (T-score beyond 70) Pd and Ma scales, called "94" code-types; and subjects with abnormal Sc and Pt scales, called "78" code-types.

Smith noted, however, that his "normal" control groups could not be regarded as typical of the parent population; he found valid MMPI profiles with T-scores below 60 in fewer than 10% of the 1820 MMPI records that he examined. Hindsight indicates that this might be expected, since the MMPI was standardized, not on college students, but rather on visitors to University of Minnesota hospitals who were representative of the urban area around that university. Consequently, it is possible that Smith's "normal" control group was not only unrepresentative of a college population on MMPI scores, but also on self-disclosure patterns.

The present study was undertaken (*a*) to compare the self-disclosure scores obtained by a more randomly chosen group of college subjects with those obtained by Smith's "normal" MMPI group, and (*b*) to compare self-disclosure scores of Smith's "abnormal" MMPI groups with those found in a more random selection of college students.

METHOD

Hypotheses

1. Subjects whose MMPI clinical scale T-scores fall below 60 (so-called "normals") will differ in self-disclosure pattern from randomly chosen control subjects in the same age range.

2. Subjects with MMPI scores in the range thought to betoken maladjustment will manifest less self-disclosure to "significant others" than randomly chosen control subjects within the same age range.

Subjects

A total of 54 males and 54 females were selected for the study, as outlined below.

The MMPI-selected subjects were obtained by Smith (1958) from the freshman class in the year 1957–58 at the University of Alabama as follows: (*a*) 9 males and 9 females with T-scores greater than 70 on Sc and Pt clinical scales, (*b*) 9 males and 9 females with T-scores greater than 70 on the Pd and Ma clinical scales, and (*c*) 9 males and 9 females with all clinical scale T-scores below 60. The first two groups were combined for this study to make up a male and female "MMPI-abnormal" group. The last mentioned group is termed "MMPI-normal" in subsequent discussion. Mean age of Smith's total sample was 18.8 years, with an SD of 1.23.

The control groups for these subjects were chosen at random from among a collection of self-disclosure tests that had earlier been administered to several hundred undergraduates in the same age range as the MMPI-chosen groups, at Birmingham-Southern College, Alabama College, and the University of Alabama. The only restrictions observed in drawing the control sample were that the subjects be unmarried, have both parents living, and fall within the age range of 18 to 21. Mean age of the total control sample was 19.2, SD 1.80.

Materials and Procedure

The 60-item self-disclosure questionnaire shown in Appendix 1 had been administered to all subjects. Entries were summed, with X's counted as zeros. Odd-even reliability coefficients for the target subtotals and for grand total had previously been found to be in the .90's.

RESULTS

Comparison of MMPI-"Normals" and Controls on Self-Disclosure

Analysis of variance showed significant differences between Smith's "MMPI-normal" groups and the control groups, as well as significant F-ratios for all interactions that included these group comparisons.

Inspection of Panel 1 in Figure 13 reveals that Smith's "normal" males disclosed significantly less to each target-person than did the control group of males ($P < .01$ for mother, father and same-sex friend, and $P < .05$ for opposite-sex friend). Smith's "normal" females tended to disclose more than control subjects to both parents than did the control

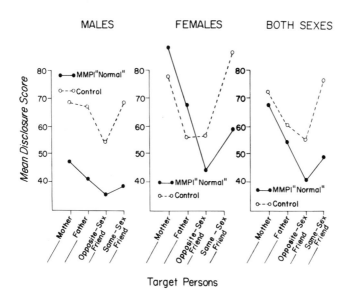

Figure 13. Self-disclosure scores of subjects with "normal" MMPI scores versus random control subjects.

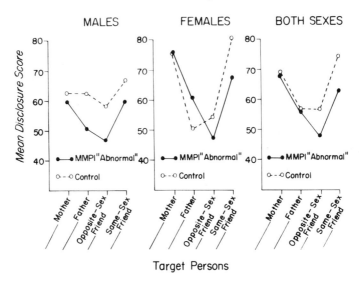

Figure 14. Self-disclosure scores of subjects with "abnormal" MMPI scores versus random control subjects.

subjects, and less to same-sex and opposite-sex friends, as shown in Panel 2. Only the difference for disclosure to same-sex friend, however, was significant ($P < .01$). Panel 3 shows that when the sexes were combined, the MMPI-normals differed most sharply from the control subjects on amount of disclosure to same-sex and opposite-sex friend.

It may be concluded that the subjects who obtained "normal" scores on the MMPI (i.e., no clinical scales with T-scores higher than 60) differed in self-disclosure pattern from a randomly chosen control group, especially with regard to disclosure to peers of both sexes. This suggests that when college students obtain "normal" MMPI profiles, it does not necessarily predict modal or average patterns of interpersonal behavior.

Comparison of MMPI-"Abnormals" and Controls on Self-Disclosure

Analysis of variance showed that, of all the F-ratios comparing the "abnormals" and controls on self-disclosure, only that for the triple interaction among "adjustment-level," target-persons, and sex reached significance.

Considering males alone, Panel 1 in Figure 14 shows that the MMPI-abnormal subjects disclosed less than the control group to all four target-persons. For disclosure to father and opposite-sex friend, the difference between groups was significant at the .05 level of confidence.

Panel 2 in Figure 14 shows that the control females disclosed more than the abnormals to same-sex friend ($P < .05$), but they did not differ significantly in disclosure to parents and to opposite-sex friend (P for the difference between MMPI-abnormals and controls on disclosure to father and to opposite-sex friend, however, was .10).

Obliteration of the sex-difference highlights a trend similar to that noted in the MMPI-normal versus control comparison. Panel 3 in Figure 14 shows that the combined control groups closely resembled the "abnormal" groups on disclosure to parents, but differed most sharply on amount of disclosure to peers of both sexes. This suggests that college students with "abnormal" MMPI scores find their greatest difficulty in establishing close interpersonal relationships with their peers.

Further Interaction Effects. Figures 13 and 14 are adequate to portray differences between groups in amount of disclosure to various target-persons, but they mask certain effects which become apparent when disclosure-means are plotted in the manner shown in Figure 15.

These graphs list the MMPI-normals, MMPI-abnormals, and the control groups along the abscissas, and they show sex differences in each group for disclosure to the four target-persons. A trend among the males becomes readily apparent; in the case of all four target-persons, a rank-order is seen, with MMPI-normals disclosing least, MMPI-abnormals an intermediate amount, and male controls disclosing most. Among the

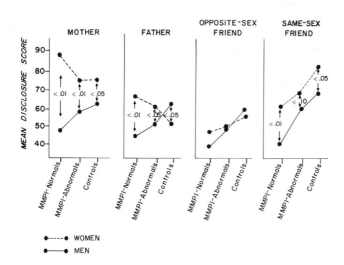

Figure 15. Mean self-disclosure to four target-persons of male and female subjects with "normal" and "abnormal" MMPI scores, and random controls.

females, a different pattern is apparent; for disclosure to mother and father, the MMPI-normal females disclose more than either the MMPI-abnormals or controls. For disclosure to peers, the control females disclose most, followed in rank order by MMPI-abnormals and MMPI-normals.

A trend in sex difference is highlighted sharply in Figure 15 as well. It may be seen that all groups of women disclose more than men to mother and same-sex friend. For disclosure to father, the MMPI-normal and MMPI-abnormal females disclose more than the males, while the control males are higher disclosers to father than the control females. For disclosure to opposite-sex friend, the males and females in all three groups did not differ sharply. Probabilities for the obtained sex-differences are shown in each panel of Figure 15.

DISCUSSION

The sharp difference between the MMPI-normals and controls on self-disclosure was perhaps to be expected. College students with "normal" MMPI profiles are certainly not typical of college students in general, either in MMPI scores or in pattern of self-disclosure. Indeed, if we regard the self-disclosure scores of the control groups as an index of average interpersonal adjustment of college students, there seems to be some warrant for proposing that college students with "normal" MMPI scores may well be or become maladjusted in the college environment. There is good reason to suppose that the ability to establish close relationships with peers is an indicant of personal adjustment, and the MMPI-normal groups differed most strikingly from controls in that respect. These findings, then, may be adduced as further evidence to support Cronbach's observation (Cronbach, 1949, pp. 320):

Although the (MMPI) test has been used successfully with clinical patients, it has not been found trustworthy with college students. Many college students earn scores which would usually be indicative of abnormality, although these students are known to be adequately adjusted. This is a further example of the undesirability of blindly applying a test validated on one population to a different type of group.

We would add to his remarks the observation that while some college students earn MMPI scores which would usually be indicative of "normality," other indicants lead us to suppose that these subjects are less than optimally adjusted.

Smith (1958) found that the "78" and "94" abnormal clinical groups did not differ significantly from one another or from MMPI-normals in self-disclosure pattern, but the present data show that the combined MMPI-abnormal groups do differ from more representative controls, chiefly in amount of disclosure to peers. Our data suggest, then, that subjects with "abnormal" MMPI scores likely are maladjusted in the sense that they do not establish relationships with peers that are as "close" as those found among control subjects.

The open question in the present study, of course, is whether the MMPI-chosen groups are in fact maladjusted. Doubtless, a more sensitive test of the hypothesis relating self-disclosure to adjustment would entail a comparison of psychological or psychiatric clinic patients with appropriate control groups.

Provisionally, we may suggest that all of the subjects included in the present study on the basis of their MMPI scores would be likely to encounter difficulties in living in a college milieu, at least if it be true that the ability to establish close, confiding relationships with others is a requisite to "healthy personality." The MMPI-selected groups could be characterized as less "accessible" to others or more "alienated" from others. Some writers have regarded alienation from the self (Horney, 1950) and from one's fellow man (Fromm, 1955) as the "sickness of our age." Self-disclosure scores seem to reflect, at the least, the degree of alienation of a person from significant others in his life. It is for this reason that we are tempted to regard both the MMPI-normals and -abnormals as "sicker" than the more randomly chosen control groups, in the absence of more direct, confirmatory data.

The sex difference in disclosure to the four target-persons that was shown differentially by the three groups of subjects warrants some comment. In several of the preceding chapters, we reported that women are higher disclosers than men. The present study forcibly calls our attention to the fact that, while women may in general be higher disclosers than men, it is meaningful to regard the sex difference itself as a dependent variable, and to investigate the conditions under which women will or will not be higher disclosers than men. For example, data in the present study show that men rather than women (from our control sample) are the higher disclosers to father.

It is also apparent that there can be no simple linear relationship postulated between amount of disclosure and quality of adjustment. Rather, it would seem that one's role and status, and the identity* of

---

* Charles Truax showed me (1970) some data which demonstrated that subjects with the most "disturbed" MMPI scores disclosed *most* to target-persons who had been rated as *least* empathic, accepting, and transparent in their relationships with the subjects. Subjects who confided most in target-persons who were most empathic, accepting, and transparent had MMPI scores betokening better "adjustment."

the closest confidant must be taken into account. Obviously, there is such a thing as being too close to one's parents, and not being close enough to one's age mates of both sexes, as seemed to be the case with all subjects in the MMPI-chosen groups.

SUMMARY

Eighteen male and 18 female subjects with MMPI T-scores in the abnormal range, and 9 male and 9 female subjects with "normal" MMPI profiles were compared with randomly chosen control groups on self-disclosure to four "significant other" target-persons. The MMPI "abnormal" and "normal" groups differed from controls, primarily in manifesting less disclosure to peers of both sexes.

Significant sex differences were noted, with women from all three groups disclosing more than males to mother and to same-sex friend. For disclosure to father, the MMPI-normal and -abnormal females disclosed more than the comparable males. Control males, however, disclosed more to father than control females. There were no significant sex differences for disclosure to opposite-sex friend.

Postscript

Later, I found an r of —.62 in a sample of 50 nursing students between total self-disclosure score for 4 target-persons, and the "Si" (social introversion scale) of the MMPI. Dutton (1963) and Himelstein and Lubin (1966) reported some low but significant correlations between self-disclosure scores and selected scales of the MMPI.

Self-Disclosure and Rorschach Productivity*

Although subjects do not always realize it, when they respond to the Rorschach inkblots, they are actually engaging in a form of self-disclosure or self-revelation. Indeed, one of the reasons why projective tests are utilized in diagnostic work is to facilitate the disclosure of subject's "private world" without his awareness—sneaking past his defenses, as it were. The possibility arises, however, that even on such a test as the Rorschach, subjects who are reluctant, consciously or uncon-

* S. M. Jourard, "Self-disclosure and Rorschach productivity," *Perceptual and Motor Skills*, 13, (1961), 232. Reprinted with permission from the publisher. The writer is indebted to Mary Hevener, who conducted the testing, and to Carol Currier, who undertook some of the tabulation of the data.

sciously, to make themselves known can implement this defensiveness by a low output of responses. The present study was undertaken to explore whether subjects who have disclosed little to their mothers, fathers, closest male and closest female friends (or spouses) give fewer responses to the Rorschach plates than subjects who are higher disclosers.

Method

Accordingly, the 40-item self-disclosure questionnaire was administered to a graduate education class of 25 male and 20 female students. Mean age of the combined group was 33.31 years, SD, 10.56. At a later class meeting, Rorschach was administered to the group, using the standard plates and an opaque projector. Three minutes were allowed for subjects to write their responses to each card. Product-moment correlations were calculated between the total number of responses to the Rorschach cards and (a) disclosure to mother, (b) disclosure to father, (c) disclosure to opposite-sex friend (or spouse), (d) disclosure to same-sex friend, and (e) total disclosure score, based on the sum of the 4 subtotals.

Results

Productivity on the Rorschach was correlated .37 ($P < .05$) with total disclosure score; .44 with disclosure to father ($P < .01$); and .35 with disclosure to same-sex friend ($P < .05$). The correlations with mother and with opposite-sex friend (or spouse) were .26 and .03, respectively, neither r being statistically significant.

These results show that there is a low but real correlation between productivity on the Rorschach test and a measure of the extent of self-disclosure to selected significant others. Low productivity on the Rorschach is regarded as one of many possible indicants of defensiveness in a subject. By the same token, it seems appropriate to regard low disclosure of self to significant others as a sign of defensiveness, that is, an unwillingness to be known. The present data may thus be regarded as evidence in support of the "construct validity" of the self-disclosure test.

Self-Disclosure and the Self-Concept

This study was undertaken to determine whether a person's view of himself—his self-concept—was a factor in his disclosure to the people with whom he is involved.

METHOD

Subjects

Fifty-two unmarried female undergraduates, mean age 19 years, served in the study.

Materials and Procedure

The subjects were tested on two separate occasions, in group meetings, with the 40-item self-disclosure questionnaire (Appendix 4), and the Tennessee Department of Mental Health Self-Concept Scale (Fitts, 1969). This questionnaire lists 90 items, each of which is classified in the following ways: positive-negative; kinds of content (physical characteristics, primary-group membership, moral-ethical characteristics, psychological characteristics, and secondary-group membership); and frames of reference (abstract description, self-satisfaction, and functioning).

Responses to the items are made according to a 5-point scale ranging from 1 (completely false) to 5 (completely true). Subscores and a total score are obtained for the questionnaire, high scores signifying a positive, accepting attitude toward the dimension of self under consideration. The scale has been shown to have satisfactory reliability, and there is evidence that scores correlate with outside criteria (Fitts, 1969).

RESULTS

Product-moment correlations between the self-disclosure scores and the self-concept test subscores are shown in Table 10. Significant r's ($P < .05$) were found between disclosure to mother and the self-concept total score, and all subscores except that for secondary group membership. Significant r's were found between scores for disclosure to father and the total self-concept score, self-satisfaction score, and the score for primary-group membership. None of the r's between the self-concept scores and scores for disclosure to male friend and female friend were significant.

DISCUSSION

The data show that the attitudes of these young women toward themselves are related to their disclosure to their parents, but not to disclosure to peers.

Table 10 Correlations between Self-Disclosure Scores and Self-Concept Scores.

	Total	Self-Satis-faction	Abstract Descrip-tion	Function-ing or Behavior	Physical Charac-teristics	Moral-Ethical Charac-teristics	Psycho-logical Charac-teristics	Primary-Group Mem-bership	Secondary-Group Mem-bership
Mother	.49†	.56†	.35†	.41†	.31*	.30*	.40†	.59†	.24
Father	.27*	.35†	.15	.21	.08	.09	.21	.36†	.25
Male friend ˙	− .03	.23	.17	.06	.19	.05	.19	.00	− .11
Female friend	.17	− .04	.05	− .01	− .04	.01	− .07	.26	.13

* $P < .05$.
† $P < .01$.

75

If we regard amount of self-disclosure to a given person as an index of interpersonal "distance," then we can say that "closeness" to one's mother is a correlate of self-esteem or self-acceptance among young females, while distance or estrangement between mother and daughter is associated with lower self-regard. To a lesser extent, this statement holds true in the case of the father as well. This correlation between parental "distance" and attitude toward the self does not explain which is cause and which effect; likely, both phenomena derive from something more basic, namely, the quality of the overall parent-child relationship. Other evidence strongly suggests that if the parents have been accepting and loving toward their children, the latter will be both secure and self-accepting, loving toward their parents, and quite free in disclosing themselves to their parents.

Support for this view is provided by the relatively high correlation between disclosure to parents, and scores on the "primary-group relationships" subscale. Analysis of the items that comprise this subscale show that they represent judgments about the quality of the family relationships, specifically: Item 55: I have a family that would always help me in any kind of trouble; Item 58: I am not loved by my family.

A provisional general theory to account for the obtained correlations may be staged as follows: a person's self-esteem derives, in large measure, from the experience of having been accepted by his parents (Jourard and Remy, 1955). The more that a person accepts himself, the less readily is he threatened by the experience of being known by others. Consequently, he will be better able to establish close relationships with others than a person who rejects much of his real self. This theory does not help us to understand why there was no relationship between self-concept scores and disclosure to peers, however. Possibly, the aspects of self which a person would be reluctant to disclose to his parents could be disclosed without threat to peers, and vice versa.

SUMMARY

A self-disclosure questionnaire and the Tennessee Department of Mental Health Self-Concept Scale were administered to 52 college females. Significant correlations were found between scores for disclosure to mother and father, and both total scores and selected subscores of the Self-Concept Scale. The data were construed as evidence to support the hypothesis that attitudes of self-acceptance are a factor in self-disclosing behavior.

The Next Chapter

I have long been interested in people's experience of their bodies. In 1952, Dr. Paul Secord and I began a series of studies inquiring into the attitudes people held toward various parts and functions of their bodies. We found correlations between attitudes of liking toward one's body and personal security, and the degree to which one's body dimensions approach one's concept of the ideal body. Remy and I found (Jourard and Remy, 1955) that a person's attitudes toward his body paralleled the attitudes which subjects believed their parents held toward their children's bodies. Then, I postponed further investigation for some time.

But as the research in self-disclosure was continued, I became fascinated with *touch*. To touch another person is to reduce the distance between you and him to zero. And self-disclosure is another way of making contact and reducing distance. To disclose oneself is to "unveil," to uncover one's subjectivity before another. I wondered if verbal self-disclosure and making one's body accessible to the sight and touch of another person were related, or independent dimensions for reducing distance.

Accordingly, in 1964 I designed a technique for measuring the degree to which people reveal their bodies to the sight and touch of selected target-persons, and demonstrated that it could show patterns and differences. A paper on this study was published in a British journal, and reprinted in *Disclosing Man To Himself* (1968). Between 1964, when I did that study, and the present time, there has been widespread interest in body experience through touching and massage (Gunther, 1967; Schutz, 1967). The next chapter presents a study which I did in collaboration with Jane Rubin, to determine whether self-disclosure to other people and making oneself accessible to their touch are correlated.

11. Physical Contact and Self-Disclosure*

If contemporary Western man lives alienated from his fellows, his body, and nature, it behooves psychologists to investigate alienation in any of its manifestations, including its opposite—encounter. To encounter another person means, among other things, to confirm him as a being who *experiences*. This means seeking to experience his experience. I can experience your experience most directly if you disclose it to me. You can, if you wish, conceal or misrepresent your self, in which case my experience of you will be autistic. I will then believe things about your being that you know are untrue. But if you wish me to know you as you know yourself, you will have disclosed your experiencing authentically to me, in dialogue, throughout the duration of our relationship.

A more direct, even literal, way for us to encounter one another, is for us to touch—my hand on some part of your body, and yours on mine. In touching you, I perceive you "haptically," as Gibson puts it (1966, pp. 132–133). I know that you *exist* in a way that hearing you or seeing you cannot confirm. I may not know much about you and your experiencing in touching you, but I surely know that you *are*, that you are there in the flesh, so to speak. Indeed, Professor John Macmurray (1957, pp. 107–126) has provided an astute analysis of the way in which we of the West, since Descartes' time, have come to use the visual field as a model for knowing, while neglecting the kind of knowing that comes from direct touching. Visual knowing is contact

* This chapter was first published in the *Journal of Humanistic Psychology*, **7**, 1968, 38–48, and is reprinted here in slightly altered form with permission from the publisher.

at a distance. You have to be near to touch, taste, or smell another person. It would probably be appropriate to change the old saw, "Seeing is believing," into the more fundamental source of truth about existence: "Touching is believing."

Indeed, if it is true that modern man lives out of his body, in a state of relative "unembodiment"—as Laing (1960) insists—then I can surely awaken your experience of your body by touching you. And if being discloses itself to our consciousnesses via our several sensory channels, then I can inquire into the means by which you disclose your being to me. How do you let me perceive you? Via my eyes? Ears? My touch receptors? Truly, for you to let me know you by touching you, you have let me get "closer" to you than if you limit yourself to verbal disclosure. When you let me touch you, you are disclosing your embodied being to my consciousness, by means of my tactual sense.

Yet, verbal self-disclosure is also a very direct means of decreasing distance between us, at least in a metaphoric sense. And much evidence attests that authentic verbal disclosure of experience to another person is or can be threatening. I have argued (1963, pp. 341–354) that full, reciprocal disclosure of self is the essence of relationships of love or deep friendship. If self-disclosure is a means of reducing distance between persons, and establishing or sustaining contact, we should expect that measures of self-disclosure and of physical contact will be related.

Such a prediction must be qualified, however, in view of the fact that there are strong societal norms that regulate who will touch whom and under what conditions. Most probably, these norms have arisen because of the intimate connection between physical contact and sexuality. In American society, it appears that touching is maximal among young adults in the heterosexual dyad. In same-sex pairs, or in relationships between young adults and their parents, physical contact is drastically curtailed (Jourard, 1966). We might predict, then, that in a sample of unmarried college-age men and women, correlations would be found between amount of self-disclosure to the closest friend of the opposite sex, and the amount of physical contact that is exchanged; and lower or nonsignificant correlations between self-disclosure and physical contact would be found in the relationships of college students to their parents and closest same-sex friend.

The present investigation was undertaken, in part, to explore these relationships. Additional aims of the research were to replicate and extend the earlier study of sheer frequency and locus of physical contact (Jourard, 1966). Thus, we shall report data comparing college men and women on such factors as the number of regions of their bodies on which they have been touched; the amount of touching exchanged in the different relationships; and the correlations between touching and self-disclosure.

METHOD

A questionnaire for measuring body contact, and the 40-item self-disclosure questionnaire (Appendix 4) were administered to 54 male and 84 female students enrolled in the author's class in Personality Development at the University of Florida. The purpose of the study was explained to the students, and the importance of frankness in reporting their experience was emphasized. Since participation in psychological research is a course requirement, and credit is given for such participation, those students who did not wish to disclose their experience to the researchers were given the option of receiving credit for participation while returning a blank questionnaire. Only about a dozen students out of the entire class chose this alternative.

Body-Contact Questionnaire

The body-contact questionnaire developed for this project was a modification of one employed in an earlier study (Jourard, 1966). An outline of the human figure, in front and rear view (see Figure 16), was marked off into 18 regions. Below the diagram the following instructions were printed:

In the diagram above, the human figure has been marked off into 18 areas. We want you to map out which regions of the body are touched, and which are not touched, in one's relationships with parents and closest friends of each sex. In the spaces below, you will make entries as follows: If the area is never touched meaningfully and purposefully (e.g., to express affection, anger, or to attract attention, etc.) enter the letter A. If contact occurs, but only rarely—not as a regular part of your relationship—enter a B. If contact is a regular part of your relationship with the person, enter the letter C. Note that for each person, you are asked to indicate, in the left-hand column, if that person touches you; in the right-hand column, you are asked to indicate if you touch that person.

For "opposite-sex friend," please indicate whether this person is someone whom you only date or see occasionally (less than once a month), frequently (up to once a week), or more frequently, as in "going steady" or "being engaged" (a space was given for this information).

Below these instructions, four sets of columns each with 18 rows were provided, one row for each of the numbered body regions. The subjects were to indicate, then, whether or how frequently touches were ex-

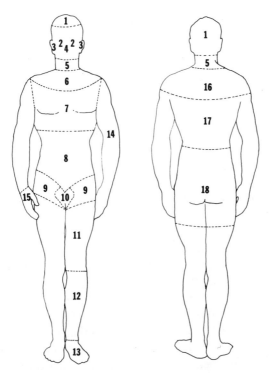

Figure 16. Diagram of front and rear view of the body as demarcated for the body-contact questionnaire.

changed with mother, father, closest same-sex friend, and closest opposite-sex friend.

The questionnaire was scored by counting A as zero, B as 1, and C as 2. The entries were then summed to yield totals that were employed in the various statistical analyses reported below. Odd-even reliability coefficients were calculated for the responses of 50 of the male and 50 of the female students, in order to ascertain the internal consistency of the questionnaire. Since the scores for touching and for being touched were correlated around .98 for each of the four target-persons, it was deemed adequate to compute r's only for the being-touched scores. The odd-even r's were .81 and .80 for males and females, respectively, for being touched by mother. For being touched by father, same-sex friend, and opposite-sex friend, the respective r's were (the r in parentheses is for the female students): .84 (.80); .87 (.91); and .89 (.89). It was concluded that the questionnaire, like the one developed for the earlier study, had adequate reliability to warrant its being used.

RESULTS

In order to facilitate the several statistical analyses that were performed, the scores from 50 of the males and 50 of the females were considered—the same subjects for whom the reliability coefficients had been calculated. All subjects were unmarried, and ranged in age from 19 to 22 years.

Body Contact

Means and SD's for the touching and being-touched scores are shown in Table 11. Analysis of variance of each of these sets of scores yielded the following: for being touched, an F-ratio of 3.87 ($P = .07$) was obtained for the between-sexes comparison (df 1/98); an F of 345.69 for between-targets ($P < .001$, df 3/294); and an F of 3.19 for the sex-by-target interaction ($P < .025$, df 3/294). For the touching scores, the F-ratios were of comparable magnitude, save for the between-sexes comparison, where the F-ratio fell short of the .10 level. Below Table 11, "critical difference" values are indicated, so that one can make comparisons between pairs of means by inspection, in order to ascertain which of the various differences reach statistical significance at the .05 and .01 levels.

It may be seen that, for the being-touched scores, the women's mean total score is higher ($P < .10 > .05$). In further comparisons between the sexes, the women are seen to be touched significantly more than the men by their fathers, but not by any of the other target-persons. Among the men, it is the mother who does the moust touching, followed

Table 11 Means for Touching and Being Touched

	Target-Persons									
	Mother		Father		Same-Sex Friend		Opposite-Sex Friend		Total	
Subjects	Touch	Touched by	Touch	Touched by	Touch	Touched by	Touch	Touched by	Touch	Touched by
Males	8.90	9.99	5.96	6.34	6.44	6.36	26.16	24.72	47.47	47.30
Females	10.58	10.96	9.78	10.62	7.16	7.22	25.26	25.86	52.78	54.66

* Critical difference for comparing mean scores in this table is 2.40, for $P = .05$, and 3.50, for $P = .01$ ($N = 50$ males, 50 females).

in rank order by same-sex friend and father. The latter two targets both touch the male subject less than do the subjects' mothers. For the women: opposite-sex friend is the one who touches them most. They are touched by each parent in comparable amount, which is significantly more than they are touched by their girl friends.

The touching scores follow a nearly identical pattern, which is not surprising, since touching is almost necessarily a reciprocal phenomenon comparable to the "dyadic effect" noted in self-disclosure (Jourard, 1964, p. 179). Thus, both men and women touch their opposite-sex friend nearly three times as much as they do the other target-persons; the men touch their mothers to the next highest degree, followed by same-sex friend and father—but the differences between scores for father and same-sex friend are not significant. The women touch their parents about equally, and their girl friends significantly less. The women touch their fathers more than do the men.

Touchability by Bodily Regions

Table 12 shows the extent to which the men and women were touched by the respective target-persons on each of the 18 body regions. The percentages were calculated as follows: the total possible score was determined, and of this total, for each body region, the actual entries for being touched were expressed as a percentage. It may be seen that the men and women reported being touched over most of their bodies, in their heterosexual friendships. In the other relationships, it is primarily the hands, arms, the face, and the upper region of the back which are most often contacted. These findings are comparable to those obtained in the earlier study (Jourard, 1966).

Correlations among Being-Touched Scores

Table 13 shows intercorrelations among the scores from being touched by the four target-persons. Among the men, it is apparent that the degree to which they are touched by their mothers predicts the degree to which they will allow their fathers and men friends to touch them, but that the extent to which they are touched by their girl friends is relatively independent of these other touching relationships. The same pattern holds for the women subjects. From these data, it may be said that a clear differentiation is made by unmarried college students in their receptivity to being touched; the relationship within which sexuality is possible is special. In nonsexual relationships, accessibility to touch, or receptivity to another's touch, appears to be a general personality

Table 12 Percentage Entries Showing Frequency with Which the Regions of the Body Are Touched by the Various Target-Persons

Body Re-gions*	Target-Persons							
	Mother		Father		Same-Sex Friend		Opposite-Sex Friend	
	Males	Females	Males	Females	Males	Females	Males	Females
1	43	46	23	42	16	34	72	76
2	62	56	16	64	5	25	84	88
3	18	18	10	15	6	9	68	73
4	56	40	12	43	5	7	94	97
5	20	21	15	21	12	13	75	80
6	27	26	23	25	27	21	72	78
7	12	2	7	0	10	2	62	55
8	11	13	9	9	15	8	68	64
9	2	2	2	2	3	2	53	47
10	1	1	2	0	1	0	48	42
11	14	13	9	12	11	12	61	66
12	9	12	7	9	6	13	31	43
13	10	15	7	14	8	13	36	41
14	50	59	40	53	44	46	80	89
15	55	58	68	57	65	46	95	95
16	49	52	43	51	43	40	79	89
17	37	50	23	37	26	33	75	87
18	7	22	7	17	6	10	43	74

* See Figure 16 for the body regions designated by the numbers.

characteristic. Since the touching and being-touched scores were well-nigh identical, and roughly correlated, it is reasonable to state that the same observations could be made about the subjects' touching practices in relation to the target-persons.

Self-Disclosure

The means for self-disclosure to the four target-persons, classified by sex of the subjects, are shown in Table 14. No significance tests were made, and it will be noted here that the trend was for the women to disclose more than men to mother, father, and same-sex friend, and slightly less than males to opposite-sex friend. For total scores, the

Table 13 Intercorrelations among Scores for Being Touched by the Four Target-Persons (Scores for Females in Parentheses)

	Target-Persons			
	Mother	Father	Same-Sex Friend	Opposite-Sex Friend
Mother	—	.69†	.67†	.31*
		(.79)†	(.68)†	(.23)
Father		—	.59†	.16
			(.92)†	(.20)
Same-sex friend			—	.23
				(.41)†

* $P < .05$
† $P < .01$

women appear to be the higher disclosers, a finding that is consistent with those reported elsewhere (Jourard, 1964).

Relation of Body-Contact to Self-Disclosure

Table 15 shows correlations between the scores for being touched by each of the target-persons, and the amount that the men and women disclose to those people. For the men, the only significant correlation found was between the contact and disclosure scores to same-sex friend. This r of .31, while statistically significant, is quite low, showing only a slight tendency for the men to have physical contact with their male friends in proportion to the amount they disclose themselves to them. It is interesting to note that being touched by girl friend, and disclosing

Table 14 Means for Self-Disclosure to the Four Target-Persons

Subjects	Target-Persons				
	Mother	Father	Same-Sex Friend	Opposite-Sex Friend	Total
Male	45.88	42.32	51.70	51.42	191.12
Female	48.60	42.50	53.40	50.72	195.22

Table 15   Correlations between Self-Disclosure and Being Touched

| Subjects | Target-Persons | | | |
	Mother	Father	Same-Sex Friend	Opposite-Sex Friend
Males	$-.01$	.12	.31*	.18
Females	.07	.11	.24	.38†

* $P < .05$
† $P < .01$

to girl friend, are clearly independent among the men, the r being only .18.

For the women, the only significant r (.38) is for the male friend: they indicate a low but significant tendency to equate the two kinds of intimacy: they allow a man to touch them in the context of a verbally disclosing relationship.

Again, it should be repeated that it does not matter whether we correlate the touching or the being-touched scores with the self-disclosure scores. Since they are virtually interchangeable, it can as well be said, for example, that the men may touch a girl whom they have not disclosed to, and they may disclose themselves to a girl whom they have not touched. The women, in the heterosexual dyad, appear to show more inclination to touch the fellow they disclose themselves to. Perhaps this empirical difference confirms the woman's oft-repeated lament: "You men are all alike."

Another curious sex difference appeared when the total self-disclosure score was correlated with the total being-touched score: for the men, the obtained r was only .12. For the women, by contrast, a low but statistically significant r of $-.34$ (P .05) was found. This latter result implies that, as a general trait, the women tend to establish contact with others verbally *or* physically. It is likely that this is an artifact, however, since a positive correlation of similar magnitude was found for the opposite-sex friend among the women.

DISCUSSION

The present results support, in the main, the findings obtained in the earlier investigation of body accessibility (Jourard, 1966). Women show a slightly greater accessibility to physical contact than men, but this is accounted for by their relationship with their fathers. The men and women touch and are touched by their mothers, same-sex friends, and opposite-sex friends in equivalent degree, differing in their relationships to their fathers.

The fact that the greatest amount of physical contact occurs in the subjects' relationships with opposite-sex friend attests to the equation of physical contact and sexuality in our culture. It further implies that, unless a young person has an intimate friend of the opposite sex, he is unlikely to experience his body as it feels when it is touched or caressed. If it is true that touching and being touched are ways of acknowledging one's embodied being, then the present data tend to support our earlier findings and the impressions of Laing (1960) that we tend to be somewhat unembodied in our usual, nonsexual interpersonal relationships.

The virtual independence of self-disclosure and body contact in the subject's relationships to parents and peers perhaps reflects the role of body contact in our American society. The authors' view is that touching is equated with sexual intent, either consciously or at a less-conscious level. The fact that it is the opposite-sex friend with whom the most widespread (over the body) physical contact is exchanged points to that interpretation. What is curious to note is the very weak, virtually nonexistent correlation between two modes of interpersonal relatedness: self-disclosure and touching. It appears that we *do* separate the two ways of "being close." The fact that the women show at least a slight tendency toward equating physical contact and self-disclosure suggests they may be better integrated then the men, who show a similar slight tendency in relation to their same-sex friends, but not to their girl friends. Evidentally, the men can establish physical intimacy with a girl, yet keep their "selves" (their subjectivity) concealed, and vice versa. The women appear more disposed to "give" themselves physically and in the mode of verbal self-disclosure. Perhaps this integrity likewise makes them more vulnerable to hurt and deception.

Research in physical contact—its frequency, experienced meaning, and its correlation with other aspects of being human, such as health and illness—is yet in its infancy. Frank (1958) reviewed much of the literature on the communicative meanings of touch, and we have made a bare beginning at systematic study of touching as such. Glazer (1967) completed an experiment studying the effect of being touched upon one's performance of a manual dexterity task—it tended to produce decrements in rate of improvement in a complex interaction with the subjects' attitudes toward their own bodies. But it may be hoped that these researches will encourage further work in a much-neglected area.

SUMMARY

A body-contact questionnaire and a self-disclosure questionnaire were administered to 84 female and 54 male college students, all unmarried, and all between the ages of 19 and 22 years.

The main findings were the following:

1. Women and men show similar patterns for the exchange of physical contact except in relation to their fathers, where the women touch and are touched more than the men.

2. Both men and women show nearly three times more physical contact exchange in relation to their closest opposite-sex friends than they do in relation to their parents or their closest same-sex friend.

3. In these latter three relations, it is mainly the hands, arms, face, and shoulders that are touched, perhaps an expression of touch taboos in all relationships save those frankly sexual in their implication.

4. Men and women alike tend to show a consistent trait of "touch-ability" and readiness to touch in their relationships with parents and same-sex friend—if they touch one target-person a lot or little, they are likely to show the same pattern in relation to the other persons. The amount they touch their opposite-sex friend cannot be predicted from their pattern of touching in the other relationships.

5. The two measures on intimacy, self-disclosure and body contact, are virtually independent in the present samples. A low but significant correlation was found among men in relation to same-sex friend, and among the women in relation to opposite-sex friend, signifying slight tendencies toward equating these two modes of intimacy. But the most striking finding was the fact that these two ways of being are not strongly or markedly correlated.

The Next Chapter

In the study just described, we showed that in the relationships of young men with young women, physical contact and reciprocal self-disclosure are practically independent of one another. The research reported in the next chapter looks, not at self-disclosure per se, but at a young man's reputed *readiness* to disclose information about himself on a first date with a young woman. An additional factor under study is the importance of a young man's physical attractiveness as a factor in a young woman's desire to go on a "date" with him.

12. Self-Disclosure, Physical Appearance, and Interpersonal Attraction

One of my graduate students hit upon an ingenious way of reconciling my interest in self-disclosure with his interest in what women found attractive in men. Mark Lefkowitz (1970) designed an experiment in which it would be possible to compare and contrast a man's physical appearance with his reputation for readiness to be self-disclosing, as factors in a woman's desire for a date with him.

METHOD

Lefkowitz selected facial pictures of male college students from university yearbooks and asked a group of 100 college girls to rate the pictures on a 7-point scale for physical attractiveness. On the basis of the girls' ratings, three pictures were selected upon which there was maximum agreement for degree of attractiveness, namely, a "good-looking," an "average-looking," and a "bad-looking" man.

Next, Lefkowitz asked another group of 87 girls to list topics of self-disclosure which they would consider important for a man to discuss on a first date in order that they might get to know him. They were also asked to list topics of male self-disclosure which they regarded as trivial and unimportant. From these lists, Lefkowitz constructed "disclosure profiles" for different types of hypothetical male "dates." The profiles covered five levels of "disclosingness": high, high-medium, medium, low-medium, and low. Each such profile contained 24 statements of a significant and/or trivial nature, as follows: high: 24 significant disclosures; high-medium: 18 significant, 6 trivial disclosures; medium: 12 significant, 12 trivial; low-medium: 6 significant, 18 trivial; and low: 24 trivial disclosures. The statements, both significant and trivial, are shown as Appendix 22.

With the pictures as stimulus materials, and the disclosure profiles to serve as information about the men who were pictured, it was possible for Lefkowitz to create 15 combinations of pictures associated with different degrees of disclosure-readiness: for example, the bad-looking man could be portrayed as ready to disclose himself at each of the five levels of significance.

Subjects and Procedure

One hundred and fifty female undergraduates, mean age 20 years, all unmarried, served as subjects. These were divided at random into 15 groups, 10 girls to a group. Each group was presented with one picture-disclosure-profile combination. The subjects were requested to study the picture and its associated disclosure-profile, and try to imagine herself on a first date with this man. After she felt she had a good "feel" for her date, the subject was asked to make ratings of the man and her reactions to him, as follows:

1. *A Positive Description Scale:* This comprised 10 bipolar adjectives, separated by a 7-point scale, viz: sincere-insincere; immature-mature; inconsiderate-courteous; unintelligent-intelligent; dull-interesting; tense-relaxed; selfish-thoughtful; withdrawn-sociable; affected-natural; and dishonest-honest. A total score was obtained by summing the entries, a high score signifying a positive attitude.

2. *Semantic Differential Score:* Six evaluative dimensions were taken from Osgood's semantic differential test (Osgood, Suci, and Tannenbaum, 1957) and a sum score was obtained, as above. The dimensions were worthless-valuable; unpleasant-pleasant; distasteful-tasteful; ugly-beautiful; awful-nice; and bad-good.

3. *Liking Score:* Each subject was asked to assign a number from 1 to 100 to indicate how much she liked her date.

4. *Desire to Date Score:* The subjects were told that the profile of her hypothetical date represented an actual male student at the University of Florida who expressed an interest in meeting new girls. Assuming she was available to date other people, each subject was asked to assign a number from 1 to 100 to signify her willingness to accept a date with this person.

Table 16   Analyses of Variance of Dependent Measures

Dependent Measure	Source of Variance	F	P	Omega^2
Positive Description Score	Self-disclosure	14.81	.01	.25
	Attractiveness	7.32	.01	.06
	Interaction	.79		
Semantic Differential Score	Self-disclosure	9.18	.01	.14
	Attractiveness	28.99	.01	.23
	Interaction	.94		
Liking Score	Self-disclosure	6.83	.01	.11
	Attractiveness	23.91	.01	.21
	Interaction	.69		
Desire to Date Score	Self-disclosure	5.02	.01	.07
	Attractiveness	33.53	.01	.29
	Interaction	.56		

Scores for each of these measures were subjected to analysis of variance as shown in Table 16.

Results

Highly significant F-ratios ($P < .001$) were found for comparisons between levels of attractiveness and levels of disclosingness in each of the four analyses that were conducted. In none of these was there a significant interaction between attractiveness and disclosingness. Figure 17 shows the results for the Liking Score and the Desire to Date Score for attractiveness (panel 1) and disclosingness (panel 2). The curves are closely parallel. Lefkowitz computed Omega^2 on his analysis of variance results and was able to show that, for *liking*, physical attractiveness accounted for 21% of the variance, as compared to 11% for disclosingness. For *desire to date*, the respective findings were 29% and 7%. Clearly, for the girls of this sample, physical attractiveness was deemed twice as important as disclosingness as a factor in liking, and four times as important as disclosingness as a factor in the desire to date. Omega^2 for the Positive Description Scores showed a different hierarchy of importance. Disclosingness accounted for 26% of the variance, as compared to 6% for attractiveness, suggesting that, with the more molecular analysis of attitude provided by this scale, the girls would weight a man's readiness to disclose himself significantly as a more important determiner of her attitude than appearance alone. With the

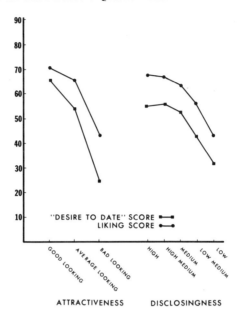

Figure 17. Liking (L) score and desire-to-date (DTD) score as a function of level of physical attractiveness and level of self-disclosure.

Osgood Semantic Differential evaluative score, the greater importance of appearance again was revealed.

Discussion and Conclusions

Lefkowitz's study offers an experimental analogue of the situation encountered by many young women who are asked to consider whether they would like to date a man on the basis of information that is provided by a matchmaker. It is interesting to note that, for the young women who were tested, beauty was not seen solely as skin deep, but was tempered by some concern for the kind of person the hypothetical date might disclose himself to be.

From the point of view of our research program, we can note that reputation for readiness to disclose oneself is a factor in interpersonal attraction.

The Next Chapter

The various questionnaires for measuring self-disclosure were developed in rough-and-ready fashion, simply listing topics that I thought were important if one were to make himself known to another, and then asking subjects to indicate the extent to which they had revealed this information to others. I had done item analyses and tests of consistency of measurement, but I wanted a further test of the 40-item questionnaire I was using. Toward this end, I obtained the cooperation of Dr. Wilson Guertin, a master of factor analysis and of the computer, and we did the study reported in the next chapter. Factor analysis revealed that significant proportions of the total variance in self-disclosure scores were attributable to a "parent" factor, a "boy friend and girl friend" factor, and several other factors grounded in interaction between target-persons and subject matter. The questionnaire data thus show that "openness" is a complex quality for a person to possess, depending as it does on the confidant, and the content of the disclosure.

13. Factor Analysis
of a Self-Disclosure
Questionnaire

What is the underlying "factor structure" of questionnaires which aim at measuring self-disclosure? In our first study (Chapter 1), responses were obtained from various samples of subjects on a 60-item self-disclosure questionnaire that classified personal content into 6 general areas. Analysis of variance showed significant proportions of the total variance were attributable to sex and race differences between groups of subjects, between target-persons, between categories of subject matter, and all interactions among these variables save one, the exception being a lack of significant interaction between groups of subjects and the subject matter of disclosure. In other words, different groups agreed in disclosing some kinds of subject matter in high degree, and other kinds to a lesser degree, demonstrating the effect of social norms pertaining to the overall disclosability of varying types of personal subject matter. This study suggested that group membership, targets, and content were likely factors in self-disclosure, in the factor analytic sense of the term. The present study was undertaken with one homogeneous group of subjects to verify the importance of target-persons and content in the factorial structure of a self-disclosure questionnaire.

METHOD

Materials, Subjects, and Procedure

The 40-item questionnaire had been administered to 300 unmarried female students of nursing, ranging in age from 17 to 22 years. The instructions requested each subject to indicate on an answer sheet the extent to which she had revealed information bearing on each questionnaire item to her mother, father, closest male friend, and closest female friend. Responses were made according to a scale whereby *zero* signified no disclosure, *1* signified that she had revealed a limited amount of information to the target-person in question, and *2* signified that she had told the other person enough about that item to permit the other person really to know her in that regard.

Individual target-by-item subscores were obtained by selecting the entry for every fourth item. Thus, the item scores for disclosure to mother were obtained from questionnaire items 1, 5, 9, 13, 17, 21, 25, 29, 34, and 38. For father, male friend, and female friend, every fourth response was selected beginning with items 2, 3, and 4, respectively. Four 10-item questionnaires with differing content were thus produced, each with a different target-person as recipient of disclosure.* From another point of view, it may be seen that there were 40 separate measures of the self-disclosing behavior of the 300 subjects, each measure varying through a 3-point range, from zero to 2. Tetrachoric r's were computed between each item score and all others. The 3-point scores were dichotomized by establishing the cutting line at the point closest to the median for that item. The resulting 40-by-40 correlation matrix was then factor analyzed by the complete centroid method. The factor matrix was rotated by the computer employing the quartimax criterion, thus retaining the orthogonal structure.

RESULTS

Table 17 shows the rotated factor matrix, with the sums of squared factor loadings along the margins. Eight factors in all were extracted, the first three accounting for 67.4% of the communality, with the fourth factor adding only an additional 8.5%.

The communality of the test item intercorrelation matrix accounted for 51.18% of total variance. This is reasonably large and indicates that

---

* The sums for each of these 10-item questionnaires were obtained, and means and sigmas calculated. They were 12.29, *SD* 4.27 for mother; 8.47, *SD* 4.29 for father; 10.75, *SD* 4.26 for opposite-sex friend, and 12.27, *SD* 3.90 for same-sex friend. This array of means, when plotted on a graph, yields a profile that has been consistently found in all unmarried female college samples, employing self-disclosure questionnaires differing in content and length: e.g., 60 items, 40 items, and 25 items. Though each of the four target questionnaires had different content, the results suggest that each was an equivalent sample of the longer list of 40 items.

Table 17 Rotated Factor Matrix for Self-Disclosure Items

Target	Item	I	II	III	IV	V	VI	VII	VIII	$\Sigma a_{ij}{}^2$
Mother	1	70	−07	18	01	−01	−13	14	02	56
Father	2	48	−07	05	30	10	09	−07	05	36
Boy friend	3	08	51	−03	−15	14	−29	−35	−02	44
Girl friend	4	25	08	54	05	−02	−05	−02	11	37
Mother	5	40	−07	15	03	−01	−13	07	−22	26
Father	6	43	19	−09	14	−06	00	−03	−48	49
Boy friend	7	−06	55	−09	01	10	07	−32	−16	45
Girl friend	8	10	11	75	14	02	09	07	10	63
Mother	9	63	−03	−19	−14	27	07	−09	11	57
Father	10	41	01	03	69	08	03	−03	04	66
Boy friend	11	−09	45	00	09	27	−05	−10	−41	47
Girl friend	12	19	−02	49	02	37	−27	−14	02	50
Mother	13	55	−03	16	04	03	−05	38	09	49
Father	14	53	03	15	65	13	12	01	−10	77
Boy friend	15	05	70	05	10	24	08	−01	03	57
Girl friend	16	08	05	16	18	68	−01	00	01	54
Mother	17	80	10	−18	05	02	03	12	14	72
Father	18	43	00	41	24	−04	−16	−14	13	48
Boy friend	19	10	45	39	−19	05	−03	26	−20	51
Girl friend	20	25	24	42	06	32	−23	07	−04	47
Mother	21	78	−02	20	−01	−14	14	00	−02	68
Father	22	41	11	10	07	01	09	−33	−02	31
Boy friend	23	−24	65	−06	−26	14	18	−18	−06	65
Girl friend	24	07	06	26	−02	46	21	05	−06	34
Mother	25	59	11	19	−11	22	04	10	00	46
Father	26	57	13	12	32	12	20	−09	−08	52
Boy friend	27	20	74	17	−01	−15	−25	07	04	71
Girl friend	28	17	10	52	−03	28	06	13	−19	45
Mother	29	57	−01	17	01	−09	11	−09	−36	52
Father	30	65	09	06	20	−09	11	−24	−18	57
Boy friend	31	07	81	15	10	−20	05	20	05	78
Girl friend	32	06	36	51	11	07	−06	−07	07	42
Mother	33	42	12	23	03	−02	57	−03	09	58
Father	34	24	−09	20	34	04	05	14	−03	25
Boy friend	35	07	49	30	20	11	27	−04	19	50
Girl friend	36	19	22	56	−10	04	28	−05	00	49
Mother	37	38	03	43	00	−28	17	15	−20	51
Father	38	27	03	08	32	−01	47	−03	−18	44
Boy friend	39	24	45	25	−03	−09	−20	−01	−29	46
Girl friend	40	27	04	55	04	01	03	−22	−25	49
$\Sigma a_{ij}{}^2$		6.21	3.94	3.65	1.75	1.56	1.34	.94	1.10	20.47

most of the item variance could be attributed to the operation of the obtained multiple-group factors.

The Parent Factor

Factor I depended mainly upon the mother target, since 9 of the 10 items with the mother as target were loaded .40 or higher. Eight of the 10 father target items also showed loadings of .40 or higher, but while the average loading for the mother target was .58, that for father target items was only .44. The first factor thus appeared to depict confiding in parents, but the better items for evaluating it were those with the mother as target.

The Boy Friend Factor

Factor II clearly depended upon the opposite-sex friend as target, since all 10 relevant items were loaded .40 or higher. None of the items with other persons as targets were loaded this highly on the factor.

The Girl Friend Factor

Factor III was readily identified as dependent on the same-sex friend as target, since 8 of the pertinent items were loaded .40 or higher. Only one mother target item was loaded this highly on the factor.

A Father by Content Interaction Factor

Factor IV was a small factor depending upon two father target items for identification. This was the first of the factors extracted to indicate that the actual content of the item was important in the correlational analysis. The two items which identified this factor (10 and 14 in Appendix 3) both have unusually intimate character. This factor, though weakly sampled in the test, seemed to depend upon the choice of one's father as a confidant with whom highly intimate personal matters might be discussed.

Other Factors

Factor V, like Factor IV, seemed to represent a target-content interaction, but it too was small. Only two items (16 and 24) had loadings greater than .40, and both referred to the disclosure of highly personal material to the female friend target.

Factor VI was small, related primarily to disclosing humor interests (items 33 and 38) to parents. Only two items were loaded beyond .40 on this factor. Factor VII did not load any items to the degree of .40 and is hence difficult to interpret. Factor VIII loaded two items higher than .40 but it is similarly difficult to interpret. One item in Factor VIII (6) was concerned with disclosure of one's religious activity to father, while the other (11) concerned disclosure of the facts about one's sex life to male friend. The only common element in these two items seems to be that they entail disclosure to a person of the opposite sex.

DISCUSSION

The most salient outcome of the overall analysis was the demonstration of a relatively strong factor implying degree of closeness of the confiding relationship between these female subjects and their parents, especially their mothers. The factors which loaded items of disclosure to the female and male friends were relatively independent of the parent factor, suggesting that, if self-disclosure is a general trait, it is not markedly so.* Openness to one's mother may be a fair forecaster of openness to the father, but it is poor as a predictor of the degree to which these young unmarried girls would confide in their closest male or female friends.

The fact that several of the "weaker" factors that were extracted (viz: Factors IV through VIII, excluding VII) loaded items for disclosure to one given target-person and not another demonstrates that item-target interaction exists in measurable degree. Stated another way, it implies that there are some kinds of disclosure that are reserved for one target-person and no other. This makes psychological sense and confirms the finding noted in our first study where a significant F-ratio was reported for the content-by-target interaction. It further suggests that when a questionnaire of sufficient length and with sufficient diversity of content is employed in self-disclosure investigation, the content-by-target interaction provides an empirical definition of self-other role relationships. That is, a defining characteristic of a mother-daughter relationship, or a hus-

---

* Intercorrelations among the target subtotals of 100 of the subjects were computed. The r's were .55 between mother and father; .09 between mother and opposite-sex friend; .29 between mother and same-sex friend; .23 between father and opposite-sex friend; .36 between father and same-sex friend; and .32 between opposite-sex friend and same-sex friend ($r = .20$ for the .05 level, and .26 for the .01 level with $df = 98$).

band-wife relationship, is that some kinds of personal information are shared, but not other kinds.* For example, in the first study, unmarried subjects were found to have disclosed little information about their money situation to their opposite-sex friends. Comparable married subjects not only disclosed more about money to their spouses than unmarried subjects did to the comparable target, but the husbands seemed to discuss money with their wives more than any of the other categories of information.

The present findings also imply that in studies of the relationship between self-disclosure and other variables, differential correlations may be expected, depending upon which target-persons are considered. In one such study (Chapter 8), significant correlations were found between scores for disclosure to mother (and female friend) and nursing students' grade-point averages in nursing college. The correlations between grades and disclosure to male friend and father were significantly lower.

The question may be raised whether it is justifiable to utilize total scores based on the target subtotals as a variable in research. This is particularly germane, since the factor structure thus far discerned appears to be rather complex. The use of total scores may be justified on the premise that the diverse target scores obtained from the questionnaire can be viewed as a special case of representative sampling of the item-universe. The argument has some empirical support, in that previous studies have shown that the total score based on the sums for disclosure to four target-persons differentiated in predicted and meaningful ways between various groups (viz: between sexes, between races, between nationalities), and between levels of rated interpersonal competence, while the target subtotals did not consistently discriminate.

SUMMARY

A 40-item questionnaire measuring amount of self-disclosure to both parents and to the closest friend of each sex was administered to 300 female students in a college of nursing. Ten-item questionnaires, one for each target-person, were prepared by scoring every fourth entry on the answer sheet for each of the four target-persons. The intercorrelation of each target-by-item entry with every other entry was obtained by the tetrachoric method, and the resulting intercorrelation matrix was factor analyzed by the complete centroid method.

Eight factors were extracted. One of these, called the "parent" factor, loaded most of the items included in the mother and father subscales.

---

* See also the study of Block (1952) cited in Chapter 1.

Another factor, called the "boy friend" factor, loaded all the items included in the opposite-sex friend questionnaire. A similar "girl friend" factor was found.

The remaining 5 factors all were of small order and were interpreted as indication of interaction between subject matter and target-person. The findings confirmed results obtained in an earlier investigation of factors in self-disclosure in which analysis of variance was employed.

14. Summary, Conclusions, and Prospects of Self-Disclosure Research with Questionnaires

All "self-report" questionnaires provide the person who completes them with an opportunity to disclose something of himself *to somebody*, the person who tabulates and interprets the "results." Obviously, if the person does not trust the researcher or the clinician who studies the questionnaire findings, he will misrepresent himself in his answers to the queries posed on the questionnaire.

I recognized the possibility that the people whom we tested with our questionnaire might be reluctant to disclose personal data to me, and so I devised the technique which we employed in the studies reported above. Anyone completing our questionnaires was simply asked to tell us *how much* of the personal data that is listed he has revealed to certain other people. He was asked, in short, to make a judgment or estimate of the degree to which he has let others know him. I did not find any people who found this kind of disclosure to a researcher threatening though, of course, there is always the possibility that some did misrepresent their disclosure patterns. Accordingly, the findings we obtained must be viewed with the caution that investigators are accustomed to assume when they do research with questionnaires.

What have we found, thus far, in the series of explorations that have been completed? Here are the main findings.

1. There are large individual differences in self-disclosure scores, indicating that people differ widely in willingness to be known. The presence

of such large standard deviations always intrigues students of personality.

2. Various groups have characteristic levels of self-disclosure. We found, for example, that females disclose more than males; blacks disclose less than whites; American college students disclose more than do comparable students from Britain, the Middle East, Puerto Rico and Germany; Jewish male college students disclose more than do Protestant and Catholic students; women receive more disclosure than men. Police officers are lower disclosers than college students, and nursing students who are rated best at relating to patients are higher disclosers than students with poorer ratings at this skill.

3. There are various situational and personality correlates of self-disclosure to various target-persons: among women, liking for a target-person is a strong correlate of disclosure to that person, whereas among men, knowledge of the other person is a stronger correlate of disclosure. For both sexes, disclosure-output to a target-person is most strongly correlated with disclosure-input received from that person—a phenomenon we named "the dyadic effect." Some relationships between scores on the MMPI, the Tennessee Self-Concept Test, and the Rorschach test, on the one hand, and self-disclosure scores on the other, were found.

4. Physical contact with others and self-disclosure to others are virtually independent measures of the "closeness" of a dyadic relationship.

5. Readiness to be self-disclosing was found to be a factor in interpersonal attraction.

6. There are wide differences in person's readiness to disclose various kinds of personal data. Some classes of information are readily revealed to most target-persons, while others are deemed more "private" and are disclosed selectively if at all.

7. There are marked interactions among group-membership of subjects, targets, subject matter, and personality characteristics in self-disclosure.

The questionnaire approach has its advantages and its limits for research. We did the kinds of things one does to reduce error in measurement, such as test for reliability, ensure that the content of the questionnaire was representative of a person's experience, simplify the instructions, and explore some of the dimensions of validity (see Chapter 22). Fiske (1966) found that our first questionnaire compared quite favorably with many other personality-measuring devices in precision and reliability. But a questionnaire always remains a record of what a person is willing to let an experimenter know about him (see Chapter 15). Our studies are actually research into what subjects are willing to disclose to *us* about their past disclosure to *others*. It could be that the thousands of questionnaires are a record of thousands of lies which the subjects told me regarding what they had disclosed of themselves to others. If this is so, and it could be—then at least the subjects lied with some consistency, because we did get some substantial differences and correlations in our various studies.

Of course there is room for improvement in the construction of self-disclosure questionnaires. Taylor and Altman (1966) did a commendable job in scaling several hundreds of self-disclosure topics for intimacy value. A Guttman-type (Guttman, 1944) scaling of content might likewise improve the precision and unidimensionality of measurement in future questionnaire research. But even with our first instruments, we were able to make a start at significant research.

One area I would like to see investigated by large-scale survey with questionnaires is the relationship between patterns of self-disclosure and health—both physical health and psychological well-being. Elsewhere (1964) I asserted that chronic self-concealment and duplicity are factors in breakdown. Certainly clinical experience points to this correlation; but no definitive studies have yet confirmed this hypothesis. I continue to believe that the stress engendered by chronic false-self-being is a factor in just about every form of physical illness, even including cancer (cf., Bakan, 1966); and Mowrer (1961) has documented the part played by self-concealment and misrepresentation in psychosis. Now let us turn to our studies of self-disclosure in the laboratory.

PART II

Self-Disclosure in the Laboratory

One trait that separates an investigator from more "reasonable" men is the tendency to mull, fiddle, ponder, and play with an idea long after others have sickened with boredom. A research idea, like a painter's vision, becomes an obsession. I became obsessed with self-disclosure, and thought I could see connections between self-disclosure and health, interpersonal competence, marital felicity, personal growth, and all manner of other good things. I recorded these views in *The Transparent Self* (1964). In numerous speeches and papers, I proposed that professional people whose work entails interviewing—psychologists, psychiatrists, physicians, counselors, nurses, teachers, social workers, personnel men—should reverse their usual interviewing procedures, and disclose themselves to their clients as fully as they expect the latter to reveal themselves. I also had, and retain, a robust concern for privacy (*cf.*, Jourard, 1967). To me, it is important to have the ability to be utterly open when the circumstances call for it, and utterly mysterious and unknown, when that is called for. The man who can "swing" both ways is in a better position than Candide, or a compulsive dissembler.

At the conclusion of *The Transparent Self*, I wrote,

. . . How curious it has seemed to me that our textbooks in psychology are written about man as an habitual concealer of himself. I am beginning to think that we, as researchers, have actually fostered self-concealment and inauthenticity in our human subjects, and then reported that human subjects are notoriously duplicitous (Jourard, 1964, pp. 154–155).

The dyadic effect seemed to me to prevail as much in the laboratory as it did in everyday life. I began to play with the idea that if a researcher misrepresents himself to his subject, the subject would probably reciprocate with "play-acting" his responses. I knew that many psychologists lied to their subjects, in order to conceal their purposes in conducting their studies. And I knew that many subjects falsified their performances in psychological experiments (Jourard, 1968, pp. 9–12). And so the hypothesis occurred to me that, perhaps all of published psychology is grounded on the false disclosure (in words, test-responses, and behavior in the laboratory) of people who are treating the researcher the way he treats them—behavior evokes its own kind. I wondered what kind of behavior and disclosure we would invite from human subjects if we, the researchers, presented ourselves in truth to our subjects. Would the latter show different facets of themselves than they had done up to that time? Would we produce an experimental science of man that was grounded on man's *willingness to show himself,* rather than on the assumption that he had to be tricked and bribed to reveal himself to an observer?

Accordingly, I proposed we should commence "Project Replication"—that psychologists should do *all* the research that has been done to date over again. The researcher should present himself once more as a relatively anonymous, high-status stranger to his subjects, in the traditional way, then do the same experiment, preceding it with the effort to let his subject know him in all relevant ways. My hypothesis was that if researchers thus presented themselves in good faith to their subjects, the latter would reciprocate by dropping their defenses and their desires to appear "normal," and would show themselves as they knew themselves to be.

From many lecture platforms, I invited my colleagues to commence "Project Replication." Quite properly, there were no takers. Indeed, many colleagues invited me to start it. And so, with the help of my students I did. In *Disclosing Man To Himself* (Jourard, 1968), I reported the first of the exploratory studies that we did at Florida. Several of the studies reported in this part are continuations of the investigation of what happens to the outcome of a psychological experiment when the experimenter lets his subjects know him more fully than has traditionally been the case in research.

The Next Chapter

In the first experiment to be presented, Mrs. Lee Drag was able to show that a brief (20-minute) period of mutually revealing dialogue undertaken with her subjects before the experiment proper affected the subjects' willingness to disclose themselves to her, and to another subject at a later session. Of no less importance was her discovery that self-disclosure questionnaires completed by her subjects before the experiment forecasted their actual behavior when the experimenter was anony-mous and impersonal, but not when the experimenter had engaged in the pre-experimental dialogue.

Linwood Small's study explores interactions among the personal value orientation of the subjects, and their readiness to disclose themselves to an interviewer when he is "open" and self-disclosing, and when he is not.

Mrs. Jaffe's study picked up the idea that an experimenter provides a model for the way a subject is expected to behave. With exquisite clarity, her findings show a dyadic effect in two ways—the subjects disclosed themselves in depth and intimacy comparable to the example she set (and more intimately than they had earlier declared themselves willing to), and the very duration of the subjects' self-disclosing utterances was affected by the duration of her statements.

These studies, like those of Rosenthal (1967), show that an experi-menter is not just a passive recorder of the phenomena he studies, but is rather a powerful influence on these very phenomena.

15. The Effects of Experimenters' Disclosure on Subjects' Self-Disclosure*

Experiment-Subject Interaction: A Situational Determinant of Differential Levels of Self-Disclosure

We developed this study in a brainstorming session, culminating from some exploratory work that Mrs. Lee Drag (1968) had done with a disclosure game we called "Invitations." Two years earlier, two of our students, Michaeline Mylet and Morgan Worthy, did a Thurstone-type scaling of nearly 100 disclosure topics, asking judges to rate them for degree of intimacy, or reluctance to let others know this information about them. The reason for doing this was to produce an interview schedule such that an interviewer could measure a respondent's "depth" of trust of an interviewer. The schedule was employed in several exploratory studies.

Mrs. Drag modified this depth-scaled schedule and began to conduct interviews, first by simply asking the subject to answer the questions they felt comfortable answering, then, she would disclose true personal information on the topic after the subject had answered. The response was staggering. Interviews with subjects—college students of her casual

* The material in this chapter, as well as Chapters 16 through 19, was first published in C. Spielberger, ed., *Current Topics in Clinical and Community Psychology*, Academic Press, New York, 1969, pp. 109–150, and is reproduced here in slightly altered form.

acquaintance—sometimes lasted 3 to 5 hours, with complete mutual disclosure taking place.

Out of this experience, we devised a procedure akin to a game. A subject would be given a list of topics, half of high, and half of low intimacy value, and would be invited to ask the interviewer to disclose on any topics that interested her, *but to ask a question signified willingness to reveal that information oneself.*

The procedure for Mrs. Drag's experiment was as follows: 4 groups of female college undergraduates, 12 in each group, were selected from the "subject-pool." These groups were matched on their responses to a specially designed 40-item self-disclosure questionnaire (see Appendix 8) that asked them to indicate on which topics they had disclosed themselves in the past to somebody, and which topics they would be willing to disclose to a stranger of the same sex. Half the items were of high-intimacy value, and half were low-intimacy, based on median ratings given by an independent group of judges.

The first group was treated as follows: the experimenter first spent 20 minutes in mutually revealing dialogue with each subject, in an individual session. The next phase of the experiment called for the experimenter and the subject to play "Invitations" (see Appendix 9). Out of the 40 scaled disclosure topics, the subject was asked to pick 5 which she wanted to ask the experimenter, signifying thereby her own willingness to disclose that information. The experimenter had already chosen 5 high-intimacy topics, mostly dealing with aspects of sexual experience, as the ones she would ask each subject (and on which she was also willing authentically to disclose this information about herself). Of interest here is the intimacy level of the 5 topics which the subject chose to ask the experimenter to discuss and which the subject was herself willing to reveal. The "game" was then played.

At a second session, the subjects in Group I—who had all experienced the 20-minute mutual disclosure session with the experimenter and had played the game with her—were paired with each other at random, the only stipulation being that the subjects not be previously acquainted with each other. They were asked to spend 20 minutes getting acquainted in any way they chose, then to choose 5 questions from the "Invitations" list of disclosure topics, and play the game. Again, the intimacy level of the topics they chose to ask and answer to one another was the focus of interest.

This, then, was the complete procedure for the first group. The independent variable was the nature of the experimenter-subject interaction before playing the game of Invitations, first with the experimenter and then with a peer. The dependent variables were as follows:

1. *Trust:* A 15-item questionnaire dealing with the respondent's attitude toward the experimenter and the other subject, administered after the 20-minute introductory acquaintance session. This questionnaire is reproduced as Appendix 10.

2. *Perceived Risk:* This score was based on the difference between the number and the intimacy level of topics that each subject said she would be willing to disclose to a same-sex stranger, and the number she indicated she would willingly disclose to the experimenter (a same-sex stranger of a special kind) *after* the 20 minutes of mutual disclosure. A similar Perceived Risk score was obtained when the subject was paired with another subject in the second stage of the experiment.

3. *Experimenter-Subject Depth of Disclosure:* This score was simply the number of high intimacy questions asked by Mrs. Drag which the subject answered.

4. *Subject-Experimenter Depth of Disclosure:* This score was the number of high-intimacy value questions which each subject chose to ask the experimenter, signifying thereby her willingness to disclose this information herself.

5. *Subject-Subject Depth of Disclosure:* This score was the number of high-intimacy value questions which each subject chose to ask her fellow subject (and to disclose) in the second phase of the experiment.

After having outlined the procedure and the measures taken from members of Group I in detail, it will be simpler to outline the procedure for the remaining three groups of 12 female subjects each. The independent variable was the nature of the get-acquainted session undertaken by the experimenter with each subject, before playing the game of Invitations. In Group I, the experimenter spent 20 minutes in mutual disclosure. In Group II, she interviewed each subject in this stage, asking a variety of personal questions comparable to those mutually discussed in Group I, but revealing nothing of herself. In Group III, she omitted the get-acquainted session and got involved with each subject in the Invitations game. Group IV was a further control group in which the first phase of the experiment was eliminated. Subjects were paired immediately and asked to go through the second stage of the experiment only. Groups III and IV were included for control and comparative purposes, and are not discussed further here (see Drag, 1968).

Here, in summary, are the main findings:

1. The girls with whom the experimenter entered into dialogue (Group I) showed more trust of experimenter than did the girls in Group II, whom the experimenter cross-examined. On 4 out of 14 items of the trust questionnaire, more subjects in Group I than in Group

II answered in the positive direction (Q-value $< .05$ Cochran's test).

2. The girls in Group I changed their willingness-to-disclose scores more in the direction of greater risk, both with the experimenter and with a fellow subject, than did the girls in Group II ($P < .027$, Friedman's analysis of ranks). That is, after being introduced to the experimenter in dialogue, the subjects in Group I indicated they would be willing to disclose topics to the experimenter that were more intimate than they had said they would disclose to a stranger, and they changed in this respect more than did the girls in Group II. Moreover, the girls in Group I maintained this willingness to risk more intimate disclosure with a fellow subject, in the second phase of the experiment, as compared with the girls in Group II. The latter maintained their reserve with a fellow subject and were willing to risk disclosure only on low-intimacy topics.

3. On the matter of actual depth of disclosure, the girls in Group I answered more of the experimenter's intimate questions, they asked her more intimate questions, and asked and answered more intimate questions when paired with a peer, than was true for the girls of Group II.

Here in Mrs. Drag's words, is a summary of these findings:

. . . [The] type of relationship established between the experimenter and subject is an important situational determinant of the subject's self-disclosing behavior, as reported in questionnaires and in actual dialogue. When the experimenter was transparent with subjects, subjects tended to trust her more, reported themselves to be more willing to be . . . open on intimate topics at a deeply personal level with her and with other subjects, than did subjects when the experimenter remained an impersonal interviewer, or an anonymous "other" (Drag, 1968, p. 54).

Interestingly enough, Mrs. Drag found something else bearing upon the predictive value of research questionnaires. The list of topics which comprised the instrument for selecting subjects for the experiment asked each subject to indicate how willing she would be to disclose herself on each topic to a same-sex stranger. She found that this questionnaire was a good predictor of the subjects' actual disclosure-behavior in Group II. The subjects in Group I, who met the experimenter through 20 minutes of mutual disclosure, changed their disclosing behavior, such that the questionnaire taken earlier did not forecast their actual behavior. *Thus, personality questionnaires may indeed forecast behavior in impersonal situations, but not where the situation involves people ready to be open, and thus spontaneous with each other.*

Mrs. Drag's study was complex, but it showed convincingly that even 20 minutes of mutual disclosure between an experimenter and a subject in an experiment has powerful effects. And since, in her study, we were concerned with disclosure of personal data, our hypothesis that mutual acquaintance between researcher and subject yields more authentic revelations of a person's being is provided further support. Now let us describe Peggy Jaffe's study, which shows another dimension of experimenter influence.

A Further Effect of Experimenter's Self-Disclosure on Subjects' Self-Disclosure*

If an experimenter functions like an exemplar to his subjects, the question arises, "How far, and in what ways, will the subjects follow the example of self-disclosure set by the experimenter?"

In Peggy Jaffe's (1969) study, subjects were asked to signify which topics of a personal nature they had disclosed to someone else in the past, and which topics they would be willing to reveal to Mrs. Jaffe, as in Mrs. Drag's study. In the conduct of the interviews, the experimenter asked personal questions of the subject, but answered these questions about herself, truthfully, *before* the subject responded. The experimenter was thus serving as a model for the subject to emulate. The subject could accept the invitation to disclose or not. Moreover, Mrs. Jaffe disclosed herself briefly under some experimental conditions, and at greater length under others. The questions under consideration were (*a*) would subjects disclose themselves on as many, more, or fewer topics than they had to others, and (*b*) would the duration of the experimenter's disclosures influence the duration of the subjects'.

Subjects and Procedure

The experiment consisted of two phases. Eighty female subjects from introductory psychology classes at the University of Florida were given the 40-item self-disclosure questionnaire (see Appendix 8) on which they were to indicate their past disclosure rate and their anticipated disclosure rate. In addition, the subjects were asked to rate the topics for intimacy value according to a 5-point scale. The subjects were unmarried, and the age range was from 19 to 21 years.

For the second part of the experiment, 40 subjects out of the original sample were assigned to four groups such that the groups were matched for past disclosure rate plus anticipated disclosure rate. These subjects were recalled to participate in individual interviews. The treatment for

* An expanded version of this study was published in the *Journal of Counseling Psychology*, **17**, 1970, 252–257, and is reproduced here with permission from the publisher.

the four groups differed only in the length of the interviewer's remarks over 20 disclosure topics. (See Appendix 11.) Among the 20 topics used, there was an equal distribution of items rated as highly intimate and impersonal. The topics were typed on cards which were shuffled for each interview. The interviewer's utterances were varied as follows:

1. Group AA: Experimenter disclosed herself on each topic for a maximum of 20 seconds.
2. Group BB: Each topic was discussed a minimum of 60 seconds.
3. Group AB: Experimenter disclosed herself on the first 10 topics for a maximum of 20 seconds, and on the remaining 10 topics, a minimum of 60 seconds.
4. Group BA: Same as Group AB, except the order of the condition was reversed.

The experimenter was Mrs. Jaffe. The following instructions were stated at the beginning of each session:

I have 20 topics I would like to discuss with you. I will first state the topic, then openly and truthfully express my thoughts and feelings regarding each of the topics. After I finish discussing a topic, you will have the opportunity to present your views and reactions to it. If, for any reason, you do not want to comment on a topic or feel that you cannot discuss a particular topic with complete honesty and openness, then simply say "I'd rather not discuss it." Please remember that I will always be honest with you, so that if you decide to discuss a topic, I will expect you to be the same way with me. Although this is being taped, what we say to each other will be kept in strictest confidence and the speakers' names will remain anonymous. Okay, the first topic is . . . .

Following the interviews, the duration of both the subjects' and experimenter's utterances were timed from the tapes.

RESULTS

Anticipated versus Actual Disclosure

Table 18 shows the mean number of topics that subjects in each of the groups indicated they had disclosed, and that they would be willing to disclose to the experimenter, and the number of topics which they actually disclosed to the experimenter during the experimental interviews. In the case of each group, the subjects disclosed themselves on significantly more topics than they said they would and more than they had disclosed in the past. It may be concluded that these two personality

Table 18 Comparison of Groups on Number of Topics of Past Disclosure, Anticipated Disclosure, and Actual Disclosure

Group	Past Disclosure	Anticipated Disclosure	Actual Disclosure
AA	15.1	15.2	19.5*
BB	15.3	15.1	19.7
AB	14.0	16.5	19.1
BA	15.2	15.1	19.3

* t-Ratios for the comparisons between past and actual disclosure, and between anticipated and actual disclosure were greater than 3.00($P < .01$) in all cases.

factors did not forecast extent of disclosing behavior in the present experimental conditions.

Experimenter-Modeling and Subjects' Disclosure

Figures 18 and 19 show the mean disclosure time in seconds on each of 20 topics for the experimenter and the members of each of the four groups. The subjects in all the conditions tended to match their speaking

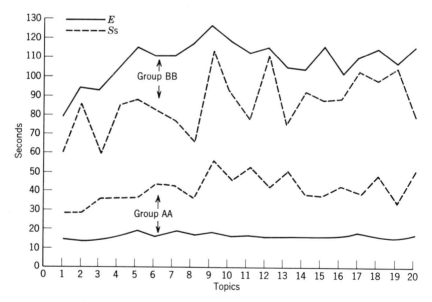

Figure 18. Mean number of seconds spoken by experimenter (E) and by subjects (Ss) in Groups AA and BB, on each of 20 topics.

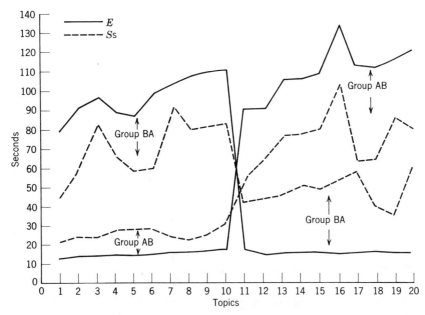

Figure 19. Mean number of seconds spoken by experimenter (E) and by subjects (Ss) in Groups AB and BA, on each of 20 topics.

time to that of the interviewer. When the experimenter spoke briefly on each topic, the subjects also spoke briefly; and when the experimenter spoke at length, the subjects spoke significantly longer. When the experimenter changed from long to short utterances, the subjects did likewise; and when the experimenter switched from short to long utterances, the subjects again followed suit.

A correlation coefficient of .75 was found between the experimenter's and subjects' mean disclosure time on each of the 20 topics under all four conditions ($n = 80$). The correlation coefficient between the duration of each of the experimenter's utterances and the length of time each subject spoke on each of the 20 topics was found to be .59 (significant beyond the .01 level with $n = 800$; i.e., the total number of possible experimenter-subject mutual disclosures).

Analyses of variance were conducted with these data. The duration of the experimenter's utterances significantly affected the length of time each subject spoke (F-ratio $= 17.48$ $P < .01$). Those subjects interviewed under the condition in which the experimenter limited her remarks to 20 seconds per topic talked considerably less ($\bar{X} = 40.8$ seconds) than subjects interviewed by the same experimenter who spoke a minimum of 60 seconds per topic ($\bar{X}$ = 85.9 seconds). A separate analysis of variance was conducted for Groups AB and BA, since it was expected that the main effects of the duration of the experimenter's utterances would cancel each other out. This was confirmed. Also in accordance with expectation, a significant F-ratio (21.92 $P < .01$) resulted from the change in the experimenter's disclosure time from short to long utterances, and vice versa.

Figure 18 shows that the mean disclosure time for Groups AA and BB remained relatively stable from the first to the second half of the interview; in Figure 19 it may be seen that mean disclosure time for Groups AB and BA shifted significantly from the first to the second half of the interview. No significant differences were found between the mean disclosure time on the first 10 topics of subjects in Groups AB and AA, nor between the mean disclosure time on the last 10 topics of subjects in Groups AB and BB. In addition, the differences in mean disclosure time on the first 10 topics of subjects in Group BA and Group BB and on the last 10 topics of subjects in Group BA and Group AA were nonsignificant.

To rule out a "warming-up effect," a comparison was made between the mean disclosure time in the first 10 topics and the second 10 topics for Groups AA and BB. It was found that for both groups there was only a slight increase in disclosure time between the first and the second halves of the interview.

Table 19 shows the mean disclosure time according to the intimacy level of the topics for each group of subjects. Contrary to expectation, subjects consistently spoke at greater length on topics of high intimacy value than of low intimacy value. However, in only the first half of condition AB did this difference reach significance.

Table 19   Mean Number of Seconds Spoken by Four Groups of Subjects on Topics of High and Low Intimacy Value

Groups	High	Low	t	p^*
AA	44.59	37.88	1.87	NS
BB	94.40	77.98	2.06	NS
AB (Topics 1–10)	26.44	20.96	2.08	NS
AB (Topics 11–20)	83.09	65.71	2.22	NS
BA (Topics 1–10)	83.16	59.38	6.85	.01
BA (Topics 11–20)	49.05	37.14	1.97	NS

* Critical value for $\alpha/2$ = .05 and 9 degrees of freedom is 2.26.

DISCUSSION

The most striking finding in the present study is that the subjects did indeed disclose themselves on a variety of personal topics, some of them quite intimate in nature. Moreover, the length of their utterances was obviously influenced by the duration of experimenter's disclosures. While the experimenter clearly invited the subjects to disclose themselves, and primed them by doing so herself, she did not explicitly set a time limit on the subjects' disclosure. They apparently followed her example unreflectingly. Moreover, the subjects disclosed themselves to the experimenter on more topics than they said they would on one of the selection instruments (the Anticipated Disclosure Questionnaire). The situation created by a self-disclosing experimenter does indeed override "personality" factors. This confirms the findings of Chittick and Himelstein (1967) and Himelstein and Kimbrough (1963).

The present findings also provide confirmation of Matarazzo's results (1965). But more generally, this experiment supports Rosenthal's (1967) well-documented thesis that one of the most powerful "determiners" of an subject's performance in an experimental setting is the experimenter himself.

SUMMARY

Forty female subjects were selected and randomly assigned to four groups matched for past and anticipated disclosure rate. The subjects in all groups were interviewed in the same manner. First the experimenter openly and truthfully discussed her thoughts and feelings regarding each of 20 topics, followed in turn by the subject's reactions. The treatment for the four groups differed only in the length of the interviewer's remarks over the 20 topics.

A significant relationship was found between the length of time the experimenter spoke and the duration of the subjects' utterances. When the experimenter spoke briefly, the subjects spoke briefly; and when the experimenter spoke at length, the subjects spoke significantly longer. When the experimenter changed from long to short utterances, the subjects did likewise; and when the experimenter switched from short to long utterances, the subjects again followed suit. A further indication of the effectiveness of a model in promoting self-disclosure was the significant increase found in the number of topics subjects discussed during the interview contrasted to the number they indicated they would be willing to discuss before the experiment. The effect of a topic's intimacy value on disclosure time was also considered. Contrary to expectation, the subjects tended to talk longer on topics of high intimacy value; but the difference in disclosure time between topics of high and low intimacy value was insignificant.

Personal Values and Self-Disclosure to an Experimenter

Linwood Small provides further evidence of the effect of the experimenter's self-disclosing behavior on a subject's readiness to disclose himself in the experimental situation.

Small wished to explore possible relationships between personal values and readiness to disclose oneself.

Method. Eighty-six female undergraduate students were administered Charles Morris' "Ways to Live" Scale (Morris, 1956) and a 21-topic self-disclosure inventory (Appendix 12) requesting the subjects to indicate which topics they had disclosed to someone in the past, and which they would be willing to discuss with a male experimenter.

From the initial sample of 86 subjects, Small selected 20 who responded to the Ways to Live Scale such that they could be classified as strongest in "Factor B", which Morris described as "enjoyment and progress in action," and another 20 whose scores loaded most heavily on "Factor E"—"sensuous enjoyment." Previous factor-analytic work by Morris had established 5 factors that accounted for the majority of the variance in subjects' responses to his questionnaire.

Thus, Small had chosen 20 girls whose Ways to Live scores indicated they "delight in vigorous action for the overcoming of obstacles . . . and in the initiation of change; . . . they have confidence in man's powers, and are oriented outward to society and nature" (Morris, 1956, p. 33). These were the Factor B subjects. His other group, Factor E, were girls who "stress sensuous enjoyment, either in the simple pleasures of life, or in adandonment to the moment . . . their reference point is to some state or activity of the self" (Morris, 1956, pp. 34–38).

Two scores were computed from the self-disclosure inventory which all subjects had taken, namely, a past disclosure score, and a willingness to disclose score. Analysis of variance showed the mean scores on these variables did not differ significantly for the two groups of subjects. The B-factor and E-factor subjects were thus fairly matched on these two measures.

Experimental Procedure. Small then interviewed each subject, without knowing from which value group she was drawn, according to the following plan:

All subjects in each group were asked to discuss 2 nonintimate self-disclosure topics, and 4 that were more intimate in nature. The nonintimate topics were "your hobbies: how you best like to spend your spare time" and "your favorite foods and beverages, and dislikes in food and drink." The intimate questions were: (1) "Describe a person with whom you have been in love." (2) "What are the aspects of your personality you worry about?" (3) "Who are the people with whom you have been sexually intimate: the circumstances of your relationship with each?" (4) "How satisfied are you with different parts of your body?" With half the subjects in each group, Small kept his participation to a minimum, revealing nothing about himself. With the other half, Small disclosed himself on each of the topics before asking the subject to disclose herself. Thus, there were two interviewing conditions—"open" and "closed."

Scoring. The interviews were tape-recorded. Adapting a technique described by Haymes (1969) (see Appendix 13), Small rated the subjects' disclosure for amount of actual disclosure on the 4 intimate topics as opposed to "mere talk." He had established inter-rater reliability at a level of .98 with another rater. From the tapes, a "tape-rated disclosure score" was obtained for each subject. In addition, each subject rated her own responses to each topic on a 3-point scale and these were summed to produce a "self-rated disclosure score."

Results. Analysis of variance of the Tape-Rated Disclosure scores showed that the B-factor group did not differ from the E-factor group in mean disclosure to the experimenter. When value orientation was discounted, the subjects interviewed by the "open" method obtained a mean disclosure score of 47, as opposed to a mean of 15 for those interviewed by a nondisclosing interviewer. The difference was significant well beyond the .001 level. It appeared that the situational impact overrode any influence on self-disclosure that might have been contributed by the subjects' value orientation.

But Small then calculated correlations between the questionnaire scores—past disclosure, and willingness to disclose—and the tape-rated disclosure scores. A startling discovery was made. The correlation (Spearman *rho*) between past disclosure, and tape-rated disclosure for the B-factor subjects, under the "open" interviewing condition was .75

($P < .01$). For the B-factor subjects interviewed by the "closed" method, the *rho* was $-.82$ ($P < .01$). For these subjects, their past disclosure forecasted their actual self-disclosure to an experimenter when he showed himself to be open and self-disclosing. When the experimenter did not disclose himself, the B-factor subjects *reversed* their behavior; subjects who had disclosed a lot in the past virtually clammed up in the presence of an impersonal interlocutor, while those who had disclosed little in the past increased their disclosure.

The E-factor subjects, by contrast, showed comparable *rho*'s of .60 and .71 ($P < .05$) between past disclosure, and disclosure to an "open" and "closed" experimenter, respectively. Their past disclosure predicted their level of disclosure in the experimental situation to a moderate degree, irrespective of the experimenter's way of presenting himself.

Discussion and Conclusions. An open, self-disclosing interviewer appears to invite equivalent amounts of disclosure from subjects, irrespective of their personal value orientation. This finding lends confirmation to the findings reported by Drag and Jaffe, and also demonstrates once again an "experimenter effect" (Rosenthal, 1967) that is of considerable power. The difference in value orientation of the two groups of subjects did not make a difference in *mean* self-disclosure to the experimenter. But when the past disclosure scores of the subjects in the two groups were used to predict actual disclosure in the experimental situation, a difference between the groups was found. Clearly, the Ways to Live Scale did portray a difference between the B-factor and E-factor groups, albeit a subtle difference. It can be concluded that the "dyadic effect" is a strong determiner of self-disclosure in an experimental situation, and personal value orientation imposes a subtle but definite effect.

A methodological comment is warranted here. The subjects' self-ratings of the extent of their disclosure of Small did not differ, either for the comparison between interviewing method or value orientation. The correlation (*rho*) between self-rated and tape-rated disclosure, for all 40 subjects, was .48 ($P < .01$), suggesting that the subjects were able to estimate their extent of disclosure with some accuracy; but the fact that the more objective measure did discriminate between interview conditions while the self-ratings did not suggests that the subjects may have overestimated the degree to which they disclosed themselves. Small noted that 23 of the 40 subjects gave themselves the maximum rating. In future interviewing research, the investigator would do well to ensure that he has objective indices of the subjects' disclosure as well as their self-ratings.

Small also found *rho*'s of .38 between past disclosure and tape-rated disclosure scores, and .52 for willingness to disclose and tape-rated disclosure ($N = 40$, $P < .01$). In this experimental situation, irrespective of conditions, the two questionnaire measures of disclosure did show modest predictive validity.

We may conclude by noting that the field for study of personality factors in past disclosure, and self-disclosure in laboratory situations is a fertile field for further investigation, in spite of the powerful influence of the experimental situation itself.

The Next Chapter

In Lee Drag's study, it was noted that a self-disclosure questionnaire inquiring into subjects' past disclosure and willingness to disclose in an experiment did not predict the subjects' behavior when the experimenter let the subject know something about her before the experimental interviews. When the experimenter commenced the experimental sessions *in the usual, impersonal way, the questionnaires forecasted their actual disclosing behavior.*

Other researchers (Himelstein and Kimbrough, 1963; Hurley and Hurley, 1969) had noted that self-disclosure questionnaires did not predict actual behavior in an experimental setting. This is not so suprising, since the investigators were expecting that a subject's report of past disclosure to parents and closest friends would forecast the extent of disclosure to strangers encountered in the psychological laboratory. While there is a tendency for people to be characteristically open or reserved, the influence of the situation and the identity and number of confidants* cannot be neglected. We were able to show that an experimenter can create situations where a personality trait of "disclosingness" manifests itself, and another where it is overridden. But a more general question about psychological testing is raised by these considerations. If the experimenter exerts such an influence on the subject's behavior, might we not expect a similar effect to appear when the subject is called upon to respond to any test of personality or ability? If a psychometrician affects the subject's performance by his way of relating to him, then uncritical use of psychological test scores to ground decisions affecting the testee's life is questionable.

A psychological test, after all, is a device that asks a person to disclose something of himself to the person who examines the test results. If the latter is neither known nor trusted, it should not be surprising to

---

* Richard Drag (1968) showed that the number of persons in a group-for-disclosure led by an experimenter influenced subjects' readiness to disclose themselves. Subjects disclosed more fully in a 4-person group than in groups of 2 or 8 subjects.

find that many people lie or misrepresent themselves on tests. In the two studies presented next, we were interested in simply ascertaining whether differences in the behavior of the tester would have any measurable effect on the subjects' test performance. In the first study, a widely used questionnaire for measuring "psychological needs"—the Edwards Personal Preference Schedule (EPPS) (1953), was examined. In the second, a "projective" personality test, the Rotter Sentence Completion Blank, was employed.

16. Experimenter-Disclosure and Performance on Psychological Tests

The Edwards Personality Preference Schedule (EPPS) *

The question under study here was: "Will subjects who have exchanged personal information with an experimenter change their responses on the EPPS significantly more than subjects who have taken the same test, but who have not interacted in this way with the experimenter?" The research was done by Leo Kormann for his master's thesis (1967).

Method. Thirty male and 30 female students enrolled in introductory psychology courses at the University of Florida served as subjects in the study. Each was administered the EPPS and the modified version of Rivenbark's (1965) Disclosure Target Scale shown in Table 20. This questionnaire requested each subject to rank 19 targets according to their value to him as persons or situations in which he would willingly disclose himself. The target, "this experimenter" (Kormann), was included.

Twenty-eight subjects, half of them male and half female, were chosen at random as the experimental subjects; they met individually with the examiner over the next two weeks for three 20-minute interviews. Two subjects were dropped because they could not meet the experimenter

* An expanded version of this chapter was published in the *Journal of Humanistic Psychology*, 8, 1968, 155–160.

Table 20   Disclosure Target Scale

Name.................   Date.................   Exp.................

Instructions:

Here is a list of nineteen "targets" to which you might disclose some personal information. Some of these you might be very willing to disclose to and others you might not wish to disclose to at all. Using the numbers 1 through 19 try to rank preferences from the target you would be most willing to talk to about yourself down to the target you would be least willing to talk to about yourself.

A radio or T.V. audience
A group of friends and strangers at a party
A stranger on a bus, train, etc.
Friends in a "bull session"
A clergyman
A psychotherapist or analyst
An interviewer for scientific purposes
Your closest parent
Your best opposite-sex friend or spouse
Your best same-sex friend
Write in an autobiography for publication
A secret diary
An application for a job or club membership
An *anonymous* questionnaire for scientific research
A letter to a friend
A favorite teacher or professor
A physician
An assembly in a class or club group
This experimenter

for subsequent sessions. Each subject was informed that the sessions were to allow him and the experimenter to become better acquainted. All interviews were held in a relaxed social atmosphere. A tape recording was made of each session with the subjects' permission. The remaining 23 subjects (the control group: 12 men, 11 women) were given no such sessions but simply returned two weeks after the initial testing. (Seven of the 30 subjects did not return.) At that time all subjects, experimental and control, took the same tests as before. Soon afterwards each subject was interviewed to determine whether or not he subjectively felt that he changed answers on the EPPS. A questionnaire was then administered to determine reasons for changing or not changing, depending on the subject's self-evaluation.

The measure of change on the EPPS for any one need category was defined as the absolute difference between the raw score for one of the 15 need dimensions at the first testing and the score for the same need at the second testing. All such differences for each of the 15 needs represented were summed to establish a measure of change for each subject. This sum was called the absolute difference score. The higher the absolute difference score the greater the number of changes made by the subject.

Table 21   Changes in Rank for Targets: "Interviewer," "Questionnaire," and "This Experimenter"

	Percent of Experimentals			Percent of Controls		
	−	0	+	−	0	+
Scientific interviewer	39.1	21.7	39.1	31.6	26.3	42.1
Questionnaire	37.5	12.5	50.0	36.8	21.0	42.1
This experimenter	33.3	16.7	50.0	21.0	52.6	26.3

− = target changed to a lower rank
0 = no change
+ = target changed to a higher rank

Results and Discussion. The subjects in the experimental group made a mean total of 36.00 changes in their response to the EPPS (*SD* 9.88), while the control group made 31.65 such changes (*SD* 8.01). This difference, while small, was significant ($t = 1.70$, $P < .05$, one-tail test). A one-tail test of statistical significance was legitimately employed because the prediction was that the experimental group would show *more*, rather than more *or* less change than the control group.

It was expected that ranking changes made by the experimental group would involve a more favorable rank for such targets as scientific interviewer, questionnaire, and "this experimenter" than would be true for the control group. Table 21 shows a trend in this direction, but only for the target designated "this experimenter."

In the questionnaire follow-up, those who felt they changed many answers on the EPPS at the second testing, in both experimental and control groups, reported difficulty in some of the choices, and their own variable nature as playing a major role in the changing. Among the experimental subjects who felt they changed, 20% listed their changes as due to the interaction with the examiner, and the feeling that they could be more truthful in disclosing their preference to him. None of the control subjects listed this as a reason.

Of course, in this type of research we may well become victims of the very phenomenon in which we are interested, namely, that subjects may not reveal themselves candidly in our research. However, if these people have been wholly truthful, our results lend support to the hypothesis that some subjects hesitate to reveal themselves with the intent to be truthful to an unknown experimenter. If our subjects have not been honest and our data represent false reports, then we simply come to the same conclusion.

A disconcerting implication of the present findings (if they prove in further study to be reliable) is that psychological test findings may not reflect the intent of the testee to portray himself to the examiner in the way he actually experiences himself. Indeed, some of the subjects in the experimental group produced EPPS scores that were as much as 70 percentile points different on the second administration from the percentile value obtained the first time. If decisions or counsel are grounded on such unreliable disclosure, then the decisions and counsel may not be very helpful. The most important implication which we draw from this little study, however, is that more systematic study needs to be done of the effect of the experimenter-subject relationship upon a subject's willingness to disclose himself veridically to an experimenter through the medium of a psychological test.

Experimenter-Subject Acquaintance and Performance on a Projective Personality Test

In the last section, performance on a widely used personality questionnaire was found to be affected by the nature of the experimenter-subject relationship. The question under consideration here was whether subjects' performance on a projective test of personality would likewise be affected when experimenter and subject became better acquainted than usually occurs in conventional psychometric practice.

The experiment to be was conducted by M. Heifitz (1967). His report is reproduced as he wrote it:

Thirty-eight students enrolled in introductory psychology courses were recruited to serve in the study. Of these 38 subjects, 18 were assigned to the experimental group, and 20 in the control group. An equal number of males and females was placed in each group.

Each subject was tested individually, with the experimenter and subject seated facing each other across a small table. This situation prevailed during the entire experiment. After being seated, the subject was given the Rotter Incomplete Sentence Blank (a widely used projective test of personality) and instructed to follow the directions at the top of the blank. These directions were: "Complete these sentences to express your real feeling. Try to do every one. Be sure to make a complete sentence." The subject was to complete each of the 40 sentence items on a separate sheet of paper, to allow him as much freedom as possible concerning the length of his responses.

After completing the blank, there was a 30-minute interval during which the experimenter talked with the subject if he was in the experimental group. The subject read or studied if he was in the control group. The experimenter attempted to create a friendly, receptive atmosphere when talking with members of the experimental group, and freely disclosed personal data comparable to that revealed by the subject. With subjects in the control group, the experimenter merely studied or read at the same table and engaged in as little conversation as possible during the interval. After the 30-minute interval, all subjects were given the Rotter Incomplete Sentence Blank and instructed to follow the same directions.

When the complete set of blanks had been collected, the experimenter compiled complete lists of paired responses to each incomplete sentence. Thus, for sentence #1 there was a list of 38 paired sentences, each pair representing the responses of one subject. There were 40 such lists (one for each incomplete sentence), containing both responses of every subject, the first and second response varied at random.

Three judges were asked to go through these 40 lists. All the judges were college students, and 2 of the 3 were males. They were instructed to pick out pairs in which one response seemed to reveal more to them about the responding person's personality, personal history, or values than did the other. The judges were cautioned that lengthy responses should not necessarily be regarded as more revealing (more open) than short responses.

When the judges had made their selections, a list was compiled containing pairs of responses which at least one of the judges had selected. The reason for this procedure concerned the extremely large number of pairs (1520) which each judge had to compare. The judges were of the opinion that fatigue, boredom, or loss of concentration might have caused oversights in judging the lists. In order to include as many potentially different responses as possible, all pairs in which at least one judge saw a difference in openness were used in a second list.

This list, consisting of 103 pairs, was given to the same 3 judges individually. They were instructed to indicate which response ("1" or "2") in a pair was more revealing. Thus, a rating of "2" would indicate that the second response was more open than the first. In other words, a "2" rating indicates a change toward "openness of response." If a pair showed no difference, this was indicated by a dash (—) on the answer sheet. Those pairs which 2 of the 3 judges rated either as "1" or as "2" were included in a new list.

This third list, containing 80 pairs of responses, was presented individually to 10 new judges. These judges were 5 male and 5 female college students. They were asked to pick out which response ("1" or "2") in each pair seemed to reveal more about the responding person's personality, personal history, or values. If neither response seemed more revealing, a dash (–) was to be put on the answer sheet. The judges were cautioned that lengthy responses are not necessarily more revealing than short responses. Only those responses which at least 9 of the 10 judges rated as either "1" or as "2" were included in the final data. The judges therefore had to agree on two things. First, they had to agree that one response in the pair was more revealing. Second, they had to agree on *which* response ("1" or "2") was more revealing.

Results. Of the 80 pairs of responses included in the final list, 57 pairs contained one response which was rated by at least 9 of the 10 final judges as more revealing than its paired response. Forty-six of these pairs came from the experimental group, a mean of 2.56 pairs per subject. The control group produced 11 pairs, or a mean of 0.55 per subject. The difference between these means was significant ($t = 2.54$, $df = 37$, $p < .02$). This finding indicates that the groups differed significantly in the degree of change exhibited, the experimental group showing a significantly greater variability of response (change in openness) than the control group.

The "direction of change" for a group (toward greater or less openness of response) was determined by substracting the sum of "1" ratings from the sum of "2" ratings. That is, the number of changes toward a more revealing response minus changes toward less revealing responses was a positive or negative number indicating more or less openness in a group's responses after the 30-minute interval. In the experimental group, 41 of the pairs had more revealing second responses, and 5 pairs had more revealing first responses. Therefore, the direction of change was +36, in the direction of greater openness. The mean change score for subjects in this group was thus +2. In the control group, 5 pairs had more revealing second responses, and 6 pairs had more revealing first responses. Therefore, the direction of change was −1, or slightly in the direction of less openness. The mean change score for subjects in the control group was −.05. The *t*-test was performed across means to determine the significance of these data and a $t = 2.77$, $df = 37$, $p < .01$ was found. This indicates that the groups differed significantly in the "direction of change" exhibited. The responses of the experimental group exhibited a significant change toward greater openness of response.

The data indicate a change toward openness of response in the experimental group, and no such change in the control group. The data also indicate a greater degree of variability in openness in the experimental group. However, these statements require qualification. In the experimental group, 4 subjects (out of 18 subjects) accounted for 67% of the total number of pairs showing a change in openness. There were 8 subjects in the experimental group showing no change in openness. This indicates that the effect of personal contact with the experimenter varied considerably from subject to subject.

From this experiment it is not possible to determine the cause of changes in openness. One may only say that "something" took place during the 30-minute interval when the experimenter and the subject talked to each other. It is not clear whether the change in openness of response was due to the subject talking to the experimenter, or the experimenter talking to the subject. The personalities of the experimenter and the subjects could prove to be an important factor. The effect might be related to the content of the conversation, or simply that a conversation took place. Jourard would suggest that subjects will tend to be more open to an experimenter that they trust. There are many possibilities, but discussion of these possibilities before further research is done would be unnecessary conjecture (Heifitz, 1967).

Heifitz' subjects in his experimental group produced more responses that impressed a judging panel as "more revealing," after the mutually disclosing conversations with him, than did the members of the control group. This certainly suggests that when people are tested by someone with whom they have become personally acquainted, they are less defensive, or more self-disclosing, than when the tester remains a stranger.

Parenthetically, I remember my experience as a clinical psychodiagnostician. I used to establish a rapport with the clinic patients through sharing personal experiences with them, thus letting them get to know me more personally than the various test manuals required. And I shared with them my findings and the inferences based on them. I found that the Rorschach, TAT, and other projective test protocols which the patients produced for me included more expressive, less "defensive" material than appeared in earlier testing undertaken by other clinicians. I cannot help but wonder if the psychodiagnostic test behavior of patients in clinics is not as much a response of the patient *to the person of the clinician* as it is to the stimulus material that is provided. If the tester actually perceives the patient as "one of Them," as the embodiment of a disease process, doubtless he will interact differently with the patients he is testing than if he perceives the patient as a person entitled to know who is testing him.

Some Concluding Remarks

Those who employ psychological tests for personality diagnosis and personnel selection have long recognized that the motive of the person who is tested affects his performance. If a person wishes to make a good impression on the test examiner, he will respond differently than when he wishes to appear sick or disturbed. If we regard any such tests as an idiom or vehicle for self-disclosure, the reason for misrepresenting oneself on tests becomes clear. The one disclosing himself has a vested interest in knowing who will receive his disclosures, and what will happen to him as a consequence. Kormann's and Heifitz's studies show that when the test-examiner makes himself known, even a little, the subjects vary their self-presentation on the tests. If the dyadic effect is applicable to the testing situation—and I believe it is—then those who wish to obtain authentic self-disclosure from subjects on psychological tests might best do so if they first make themselves known as *persons* rather than as professional *éminences grises* to the people they test.

The Next Chapter

Continuing "Project Replication," we wanted to ascertain if other aspects of human behavior and experience were affected by increased contact between experimenter and subject. In every study of learning, perception, and social interaction, the experimenter is assumed to be a neutral, or constant, presence whose subjective side is unknown to subject. We had shown that a self-disclosing experimenter elicits more disclosure from his subjects than does a more formal and reserved experimenter. The next family of questions to be considered is, "Do people learn, perceive, and perform differently in a laboratory with an experimenter who had made himself known than they do when he remains a stranger?" In the next chapter, a study of paired-associate learning conducted by Marshall Frey (1967) is presented. Frey served as the experimenter, and in one condition, he revealed something of himself to his subjects, while in the other, he presented himself as a typical experimenter.

17. Experimenter-Subject Acquaintance and Learning

The purpose of this experiment was to ascertain whether subjects would learn a list of 20 word pairs to a criterion of two successive trials without error more, or less, efficiently when the experimenter disclosed himself to the subject. Two other independent variables were also studied: "fantastic" versus "normal" associations, and "social reinforcement."

Method. The subjects were 40 students from the introductory psychology courses at the University of Florida who were randomly selected as they signed an experimental participation list.

Procedure. The experimental design called for 8 groups of 5 subjects each in a $2 \times 2 \times 2$ factorial arrangement of three independent variables. The effects of social reinforcement and prior interview were investigated in relation to the paired associate task.

The subjects were presented with a list of 20 word pairs (see Appendix 14) which appeared on a standard laboratory memory drum at the rate of 4 seconds per item. The method of anticipation was employed in learning the list; that is, the subject saw first the stimulus word, then on the following turn of the drum both the stimulus and response words. During the 4-second presentation period of the stimulus word, subjects were to respond by anticipating aloud the associated response word.

The list of paired-associates was presented to half of the subjects (Groups E_1, E_2, E_3, and E_4) with the instruction that they could learn each word pair in any manner they wished. They were told in addition that previous research had shown that the simplest associations one

131

could think of were usually best in memorizing word pairs of the type to be presented. These were designated the "normal" association groups.

The other four groups were required to learn the word list by forming "fantastic" associations in linking the two members of each pair. A fantastic association was operationally defined as "a connection or bond between two words which is formed by envisioning the objects that they may represent in a highly unusual physical relationship with each other; that is, a relationship which could not possibly exist if the objects were under ordinary circumstances." Any association that did not satisfy the definition for a fantastic association was termed a "normal" association. The subjects in groups E_5, E_6, E_7, and E_8 were instructed in the formation of fantastic associations and were given 4 word pairs on which to practice immediately before presentation of the 20 pair experimental list. During the practice trials, the experimenter discussed with the subjects the images which they had formed and suggested improvements in view of the definition. These subjects were told also that extensive research and testing had shown that their particular associative method was the most efficient in memorizing word pairs.

The subjects in Groups E_1, E_2, E_5, and E_6, upon entering the experimental room, were interviewed by the experimenter for a period of 25 minutes before participation in the learning task. The interview was aimed at developing a relatively intimate personal relationship between subject and experimenter through mutual self-disclosure. The interview centered around the topics in Appendix 16, all of which were discussed to some extent with each subject.

The subjects in Groups E_3, E_4, E_7, and E_8 were not interviewed by the experimenter before receiving the list of paired associates. To control for the difference in time spent in the experimental room between these subjects and those in the interviewed groups, the noninterviewed subjects, upon entering the experimental room were asked to occupy themselves with magazines or homework. This activity lasted for a period of time equal in length to the interview.

The remaining independent variable, social reinforcement, was given by the experimenter in the form of a sound or gesture of approval, such as "mm-hm" or a subtle nodding of the head after each correct response by subject during the learning task. The subjects in Groups E_1, E_3, E_5, and E_7 received this type of impersonal reinforcement. During the course of learning of the remaining groups, E_2, E_4, E_6, and E_8, the experimenter offered no gestures or signs of approval at the performance of subject.

After a subject had successfully mastered the list to a criterion of two successive errorless trials, he was given the entire list of pairs, each pair followed by a blank space in which he was instructed to briefly describe in writing exactly how he associated its two members. Later, the descriptions were classified by experimenter as belonging in either the normal or fantastic categories. Since a particular word pair might have had specific personal connotation for an individual, for which he would not have employed a fantastic association, subjects who described at least 16 of 20 pairs in accordance with the definition were classified in the appropriate category.

Any questions the subjects had about the experiment and its purposes were answered fully in a debriefing session which followed the task.

Materials. The 20 paired-associate words shown in Appendix 14 were used in the experiment. The words were nouns of varying length, chosen from among the thousand most frequent words appearing in the language, according to the Thorndike and Lorge (1944) word count. The list was typed in capital letters and appeared in three random orders on a continuous sheet of memory drum paper. It was presented on a standard laboratory memory drum to each subject.

In order to control for peculiarities that may have existed within any of the pairs, the response members of all of the pairs were reassociated with other stimuli on the list to generate three distinct lists of paired associates. Each of the pairs on the three lists were matched according to certain specifications: no two words of a pair began or ended with the same letter or combination of letters, nor did the same number of letters appear in both the stimulus and response members of any pair. The three lists were assigned in an arbitrary manner to the 40 subjects.

Results. The three independent variables were analyzed in a $2 \times 2 \times 2$ analysis of variance (see Table 22). The three independent variables, each of which had two conditions, were association, interview, and reinforcement, as previously noted. Means are shown in Figure 20. The reinforcement groups (mean number of trials, 8.15) did not significantly differ from the nonreinforcement groups (mean: 7.75). The two remaining main effects were found to be significant, however. The mean trials to criterion for these were 8.75 trials for normal, and 7.15 for fantastic associations ($P < .05$); the latter method was more efficient. Those subjects interviewed learned the list in 6.45 trials as compared to those who were not interviewed. Their mean was 9.45 trials ($P < .005$).

Mutual self-disclosure between experimenter and subject before the learning task led to significantly faster mastery of the list of words, as compared to no interview. None of the four possible interactions among factors were statistically significant at any level.

Table 22 Analysis of Variance of Learning Trials

Sources	SS	df	MS	F
Association (A)	25.6	1	25.6	4.53*
Disclosure (D)	90.0	1	90.0	15.94†
Reinforcement (R)	1.6	1	1.6	
A × D	4.9	1	4.9	
A × R	22.5	1	22.5	3.98
D × R	8.1	1	8.1	
A × D × R	.4	1	.4	
Error	180.8	32	5.65	
Total	333.9	39		

* $P < .05$.
† $P < .01$.

The results of this experiment demonstrated primarily that in an experimental setting such as the present one, subjects who have participated in an interview with the experimenter based on mutual self-disclosure show far superior performance on a pair-associate learning task than subjects who are not acquainted with the experimenter at all (Frey, 1968).

Frey showed that those subjects who had engaged in mutual disclosure with him, prior to the conduct of the learning experiment, took about one-third fewer trials to learn a paired-associate list to criterion than

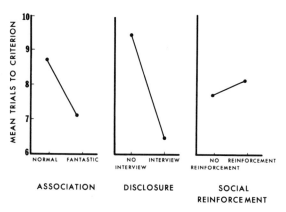

Figure 20. Mean number of trials to learn paired-associates under three experimental conditions.

did subjects with whom he did not get so acquainted. If there is value in rapid learning, then we can argue that, following the dialogue-like conditions of the acquaintance session, the subjects were better able to "show their stuff." Perhaps their motivation to learn was increased. It may not be too farfetched to propose that our image of human achievement capacities is imperfect; that when we study man under conditions where the subjects know who is studying them, and why, a broader depth and range of human potentialities will be unfolded.

The Next Chapter

When an experimenter discloses himself to a subject before an experiment, the subject behaves differently than he does when the experimenter remains unknown. Presumably, this is because the subject perceives the experimenter differently as a function of the latter's disclosure. In the next studies to be described, we go beyond the simple measure of subjects' trust of the experimenter that was employed by Lee Drag (see Chapter 5), and measure subjects' actual perception of the experimenter, and empathy with the experimenter.

18. Experimenter's Disclosure and Subject's Perception of the Experimenter

Self-Disclosure and Impression-Change

When I appear before you undisclosed, you develop a concept of me. As I disclose myself, the new information affects your beliefs and assumptions, changing them in many possible ways. Jane Rubin's (1968) study demonstrates this empirically.

Briefly, Rubin selected 80 female undergraduate subjects, and composed 40 dyads, where each participant was hitherto unknown to the other. In the experimental group, comprising 20 dyads, the subjects were asked to fill out a 30-item polar-adjective impression scale (see Appendix 15) upon first being introduced to each other by the experimenter. Then the subjects, in the experimenter's presence, were asked to disclose to each other and discuss 10 topics of personal relevance, as shown in Appendix 16.

Twenty minutes were to be devoted to this. Then, the subjects completed the impression scale again. The dyads who comprised the control group were asked to discuss, for 20 minutes, the possible solutions to two human relations problems that were printed on a piece of paper. They were to confine their discussion to the facts presented. After this time, the subjects again indicated their impression of each other.

Rubin counted a "Basic Shift Score," which was simply the number of items on the impression questionnaire for which ratings in both administrations were made at the same step of the 7-point scale. This number was subtracted from 30, the total number of scale items. The group of dyads that engaged in self-disclosure between administrations obtained a mean basic shift score of 19.98; the group that engaged in less personal discussion had a score of 15.60. The t-ratio for the difference was 3.65 ($P < .01$) indicating greater impression change in the mutual disclosure group.

It seems to me that in future research, investigators can inquire into the subjects' impressions of them as they present themselves in various ways, and ascertain whether the outcome of the research is related to the way in which the experimenter is perceived.

The degree to which two persons in relation, like experimenter and subject, have empathy with one another may be another factor influencing subjects' performances in psychological experiments. The following study presents a promising technique for an experimenter to measure subjects' empathy with him. The researcher was Mrs. Diane Skafte, who did the work under my supervision.

Self-Disclosure and Empathy

Mrs. Skafte tape-recorded a 20-minute autobiographical statement, telling of her past, childhood experiences, and current status. A co-worker presented this tape to a group of judges (college undergraduates), with the instruction:

You are going to hear a tape-recording of someone talking about herself. When it is over, write a description of how this person seems to feel about herself, about others, about life. Try to write your description so that someone who had not heard the tape would sense how the speaker thinks and feels about things.

One hundred male and 101 female students heard the tape, and wrote out their descriptions. Mr. and Mrs. Skafte read each description and independently rated each according to a 5-point scale developed by Truax (1961), called "Scale for the measurement of accurate empathy." The Skaftes attained inter-rater agreement of 94% in rating the judges' descriptions. By disclosing herself to a group of judges, Mrs. Skafte was able to discern which of them "grasped" her subjectivity most astutely; and since she had disclosed herself quite fully, over time, to her husband, she had another rater available to meet the requirement of inter-rater reliability.

Who is better equipped to assess another's empathy into me than me? There is the possibility of new inroads into our understanding of factors in empathy, by varying the amount and kind of self-disclosure in which the person to be "empathized-with" engages, and then one can test all kinds of groups of people, to see what group and personality factors account for variance in empathy. Of more direct relevance, I see the point of an experimenter asking subjects to state their views of him either in free expression or by means of appropriate questionnaires. The experimenter can then assess these, perhaps rate subjects' empathy, and see whether the empathy scores are related to subjects' performance in the experiment.

The Next Chapter

It becomes apparent that if we wish to make subjects' behavior in our experiments more fully intelligible, we will have to intensify our study of how a subject experiences the experimenter. Since the subject's experience of the experimenter is affected by the experimenter's behavior, then the experimenter will have to study his own behavior as well as that of his subjects. But the subjects' experience of the experimenter is quite researchable. Drag employed a simple measure of the degree to which the subject trusted the experimenter. I described (Jourard, 1968) a questionnaire method to measure trusting behavior on the part of the subject, by ascertaining what the subject was willing for the experimenter to know of him *besides* the behavior under study in the experiment. In Friedman's studies (see next chapter), measures of subjects' experience of the experimenter are used to good advantage. Two experiments concerned with the effects of reduced distance between experimenter and subject on subjects' disclosure are next to be reported.

19. Experimenter-Subject "Distance" and Self-Disclosure*

Distance between persons has phenomenological dimensions. People who exchange mutual eye contact may be "closer" to one another than when they are not looking into one another's eyes. Moreover, two people who are discussing the weather or baseball scores are not as "close" as a pair who are disclosing their problems, joys, sorrows, and plans to one another.

People differ in the distance between themselves and another which they find comfortable, whether distance is measured physically or in its interpersonal dimensions. Thus, Anglo-Saxons find that people from Latin cultures stand too close to them when they are speaking, and they touch them more frequently than is welcomed (Hall, 1966). Cultural differences have also been found in modal self-disclosure patterns (Chapter 5). The late Harry Stack Sullivan was sensitive to the discomfort of his schizophrenic patients on being looked at, so he was careful to keep his gaze directed, not into his patients' eyes, but at the wall and ceiling (Sullivan, 1954, p. 6). These observations all suggest a kind of "territorial imperative" (Ardrey, 1967) operative among humans, but in a manner more complex than occurs among baboons or stickleback fishes.

It is in the light of this modified territorial imperative that we can view the "distance-equilibrium" phenomenon postulated by Argyle and Dean (1965) in their study of some vicissitudes of eye contact. These workers reported that subjects in an experiment tended to sustain mutual

* Adapted from a study published in the *Journal of Personality and Social Psychology*, **15**, 1970, 278–282.

eye contact with an experimenter so long as he remained at a comfortable distance. If he walked closer to the subject, the subject tended to
react by withdrawing from eye contact. Argyle and Dean proposed the
hypothesis that as distance between experimenter and subject was reduced along one dimension, subjects would tend to increase it along
another dimension, presumably to maintain a sense of comfort. But the
experimenter in Argyle and Dean's experiment was a stranger to each
subject. One wonders whether the subjects would have withdrawn from
mutual eye contact if they were better acquainted with the experimenter.

In human affairs, a distinction is usually drawn between inter-role
relations, where the participants can be unknown one to the other, and
personal relations, where each lets the other know something about
him as a unique individual (Jourard, 1963, pp. 341–354). Mutual self-
disclosure is the most direct means by which strangers performing roles
in relation to one another transmute their relationship to one that is
more "personal" where increased "closeness" is tolerated if not welcomed.
Previous research (Chapters 2, 3, 4, 12) has shown that a person is
most willing to disclose personal information to another person who
has shown willingness to reciprocate.

The next two experiments were conducted by Robert Friedman to
determine whether subjects who are "approached" by an experimenter
(in the phenomenological sense) will respond by decrements of self-
disclosure (increasing distance) or increments of disclosure (reducing
distance).

Experiment I: The Look of an Experimenter

In his first study, Friedman sought to test the effect of an experimenter
looking into a subject's eyes upon the latter's self-disclosing behavior.
We saw this type of relatedness as a step along a continuum from
absence to presence, or great distance to slight distance between experimenter and subject. In an ultimate design, we would have wished to
test a subject's willingness to disclose to an experimenter who varied
in perceptual presence to the subject in various ways, for example, seen
but not heard, heard but not seen, at varying physical distances, up
to complete embrace and mutual dialogue, contacted via telephone or
closed circut TV, and various combinations of these conditions. However,
practical considerations made it necessary to limit ourselves to that which
was feasible.

Method. Three degrees of presence-to-the-subject of the experimenter
were arranged. Level I: the experimenter (Friedman) introduced him-

self by name to a subject, gave instructions as to what was expected of the subject—he was to disclose himself on the topics listed on a sheet of paper, speaking into the microphone of a tape recorder—and then he left the room. Level II: the experimenter introduced himself to the subject, gave instructions as in Level I, after which the experimenter sat, at about a 45-degree angle away from direct face-to-face, with his gaze continuously averted from the subject's face. Level III: the experimenter introduced himself, gave instructions, and asked the subject to look into the experimenter's eyes throughout the duration of the interview. Much of the time experimenter and subject were in direct mutual eye contact as the subject proceeded to disclose himself.

In conditions II and III, the experimenter confined his verbal participation to nods and grunts to convey only that he was listening to what the subject was saying.

Following Simmel (1921, pp. 356–358), we regarded mutual eye contact as another means of decreasing distance. We predicted that when eye contact was introduced in a self-disclosure situation: (1) the amount of self-disclosure should diminish: (2) it should diminish more for female subjects than for males, when the experimenter was male; and (3) it should decrease self-disclosure on intimate topics more than on superficial topics.

The subjects were 24 male and 24 female college students who signed up for the experiment on a paper which announced it by number in the introductory psychology course. Eight males and 8 females were assigned at random to each of the three experimental conditions described above. All subjects were given identical instructions, which Friedman read to them: they were asked to answer questions about themselves which were typed on a sheet of paper. The questions were taken from a self-disclosure questionnaire and had been earlier rated for intimacy level by a group of student judges who employed a 5-point scale, from high intimacy (rating of 1) to low intimacy (rating of 5). The topics are shown in Appendix 12.

The subjects were free to take as much or as little time discussing as many of the topics as they wished, but the experimenter stopped the subject after 30 minutes had passed. After the subject had finished, or was stopped, he was given a questionnaire entitled "The Experience of Being a Subject" (see Appendix 17). Friedman obtained a "trust," or "positive attitude" score from this by counting the number of times which each subject answered in a positive direction and dividing it by the number of items which he answered.

There were, thus, two dependent variables: the trust or positive attitude score; and the measure of self-disclosure engaged in by the subject in the interview. This latter was simply the length of each subject's self-disclosure, measured in seconds from the tape-recording of the interview. The disclosure scores were classifed as high, medium, or low, depending upon whether they were in response to questions of high, medium, or low intimacy. Analyses of variance were conducted, between groups, on the ratio scores for trust of experimenter, and for the disclosure time scores, with three conditions of being interviewed, three levels of intimacy, and the two sexes. Finally, Spearman correlations were calculated between the trust scores and the disclosure time scores.

Results. The three groups did not differ in the mean scores betokening trust of, or positive attitude toward, the experimenter. Analysis of variance conducted with the disclosure time scores showed no significant differences attributable to the three conditions of interviewing. There were significant differences in length of disclosure attributable to the intimacy level of the topics, and to subjects' sex. Finally, a significant sex-by-interview condition interaction was found.

Table 23 shows that when the sexes and the interviewing conditions are combined, the high intimacy topics produced significantly less disclosure than the medium or low topics. Table 24 for the sex-by-interview condition interaction, shows that when the men and women were speaking only into the tape recorder, with Friedman out of the room, their mean disclosure time for all topics was roughly similar—around 1000 seconds of disclosing talk. But for the next two conditions, the sexes differed. The men talked longer when the experimenter was present, but not looking in their eyes, and still longer when he was looking in their eyes. The women, by contrast, cut their disclosure time nearly 50% when the experimenter was present. Under conditions II and III, the men talked nearly twice as long as the women. These data are shown graphically in Figure 21.

Table 23 Mean Disclosure Time, in Seconds, on Topics at Three Levels of Intimacy

Intimacy Level	Mean Disclosure Time
Low	372.81*
Medium	314.67*
High	216.35

* Do not differ significantly ($p < .05$) as determined by the Duncan New Multiple Range Test (DMRT).

Table 24 Mean Disclosure Time, in Seconds, for Males and Females in Three Interview Groups

Group	Males	Females
I	992.45*	1086.90†
II	1055.07*	563.89†
III	1154.59*	576.89†

*,† Means having a common superscript do not differ significantly ($p < .01$) as determined by the DMRT.

The number and intimacy value of the topics on which the subjects refused to disclose themselves was then determined (they were free to talk or not talk on any of the topics). Again, analysis of variance showed no overall interview group differences, but the main effects for sex and intimacy value of the topics were significant, and there was a significant sex-by-intimacy value interaction. Table 25 shows the expected trend—no low intimacy topics refused; a mean of .08 medium intimacy topics declined, and .73 of the high intimacy topics refused by the combined group of 48 subjects. For the sex difference—the women declined more medium and high intimacy topics than the men (see Table 26).

The last analysis was of the correlation between the measures of subjects' attitude toward the experimenter, and the subjects' disclosure times summed over all topics discussed. Under Level I, where the subjects spoke into a tape recorder, with Friedman out of the room, significant

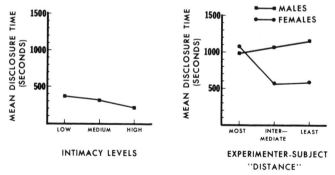

Figure 21. Mean disclosure time as a function of intimacy-value of topics (left panel) and experimenter-subject "distance" (right panel).

Table 25   Mean Number of Disclosure
Topics Refused at Each Intimacy Level

Intimacy Level	Mean
Low	.00*
Medium	.08*
High	.73

* Do not differ significantly $(p < .01)$ as
determined by the DMRT.

rhos of .71 and .66 were found, for males and females, respectively. With the experimenter present, but not looking at the subjects, the *rhos* were .78 and zero for men and women, respectively. Evidently, attitude toward Friedman affected the men's disclosure to him, but not the women's. When experimenter was exchanging eye contact, the men's *rho* dropped to .60, which fell short of statistical significance, and the women's increased from zero to .51, which was still below statistical significance. From this, we can tentatively conclude that, for the men, attitude toward the experimenter is a factor in their willingness to reveal personal information to him whether he is out of the room, in the room but not looking in their faces, or in the room and exchanging eye contact. Under the latter condition, the correlation is attenuated somewhat. For the women, attitude toward the experimenter, or toward a stereotype of experimenters, is a correlate of willingness to disclose to him, when he first appears and then vanishes from sight. If he is visually present, however, attitude has no relationship to disclosure. It is as if by being physically present, Friedman inhibited the girls' disclosure, and knocked out any significant relationship between positive attitude toward him

Table 26   Mean Number of Topics Refused by
Males and Females at Each Intimacy Level

Intimacy Level	Males	Females
Low	0	0
Medium	0	.17*
High	.46ª	1.00

ª Do not differ significantly $(p < .01)$ as determined by the
DMRT.

and willingness to confide. When he exchanged eye contact with the girls, there was a tendency for attitude and disclosure to covary.

Experiment II: Experimenter-Disclosure, Touching, and Subjects' Self-Disclosure

In this second study, subjects were asked to disclose personal information to the experimenter at four degrees of phenomenological distance (Friedman, 1969). In the first two of these, the experimenter was to remain unknown as a person; in one, he would touch the subject in a minimal, socially appropriate way. In each of the second pair of conditions, the experimenter would disclose some true information about himself; in one of these two, he would also touch the subject, as he did in the first pair of anonymous conditions. The hypothesis was that disclosure from an experimenter would have the most powerful effect upon the subjects' disclosure; that touch unaccompanied by self-disclosure from an experimenter would not have a facilitating effect upon subjects' disclosure, but that a touch from an experimenter who discloses who he is will result in even more disclosure from the subjects than self-identifying disclosure from the experimenter alone.

We proposed this hypothesis because a touch from an unknown person may be experienced as an unwanted invasion of one's personal space; but a touch received *from a stranger who has revealed personal data* may be experienced as an acceptable invitation to reduce distance still further. In short, the "dyadic effect" found in other studies of self-disclosure may override a persons' need to maintain his usual distance from an unknown stranger. Our expectation was that the distance-equilibrium phenomenon postulated by Argyle and Dean (1965) would not apply in the experimental situation that we contrived.

METHOD

Selection of Subjects, Materials, and Procedure. One hundred undergraduate students from introductory psychology courses at the University of Florida, half male and half female, between the ages of 18 and 21, were asked to react to 21 self-disclosure items (see Appendix 12) indicating their willingness to disclose information about themselves to Friedman, who served as experimenter. They also were asked to record their impression of him, using the form shown in Appendix 15. At the time of the study, Friedman was 22 years of age.

Thirty-two males and 32 females were assigned to four groups, each with 8 males and 8 females, such that their mean scores for reported willingness to disclose to the experimenter were matched.

All subjects, before assignment to one of the esperimental conditions, were interviewed and tested singly by Friedman.

Interviewing Procedure. Each subject was given 8 cards, on each of which was typed one of the 8 self-disclosure topics encircled in Appendix 12. Four of the topics had been rated as low intimacy, and four as high intimacy value.

Four degrees of "distance between experimenter and subject" were arranged, as follows:

Group 1. Greatest Distance. The subject was asked to read each question aloud, and answer it or not, as he chose. The experimenter limited his responding to nods and grunts, and saying "yes," "I see," to show he was listening. He told nothing about himself.

Group 2. Less Distance. The procedure for this group was identical with Group I, except that the experimenter touched the subject by putting his hand in the center of the subject's back as he entered the room, guiding him to the chair with a light but noticeable pressure.

Group 3. Still Lesser Distance. For this condition, the experimenter spoke to the subject about himself for 3 to 5 minutes, after the subject was seated. His stated purpose was that, since he would not be able to say anything while the subject was disclosing himself, he would let the subject know something about him. The experimenter gave a similar account of himself to each subject, telling the subject truthfully about his academic interests, professional plans, hobbies, and some of his personal views about school, religion, and music. The experimenter did not touch these subjects. After this introduction, the subjects were instructed to proceed as in the first two groups.

Group 4. Least Distance. The experimenter touched each subject as in Group 2, and disclosed himself as in Group 3.

Forty-five minutes were allowed for subjects in all groups to discuss the 8 disclosure topics, though none was informed about this limit. No subject exceeded the time allowed. The interviews were recorded with the knowledge of the subjects. Time spent in talking on each disclosure topic, in seconds, was measured from the tapes. These times were employed as the measure of subjects' self-disclosure.

Measurement of Subjects' Feelings. After being interviewed, each subject was asked to indicate how he experienced the session, employing a 10-point scale for each of the following feeling-dimensions:

1. Being at ease.
2. Liking for the experimenter.
3. Trust of the experimenter.
4. Feeling understood by the experimenter.
5. Feeling liked by the experimenter.
6. Overall satisfaction with experimental situation.

The ratings were summed to yield a feeling score. High totals signified more positive feelings toward experimenter and the situation. A longer questionnaire for measuring these feelings, comprising 50 items, was also administered to the subjects, but since the scores were highly correlated with the above feeling-dimensions, only the results for the shorter questionnaire are reported here.

Measuring Impression Change. Each subject again completed the Impression Sheet shown in Appendix 15 following the interview. Impression change was measured by noting differences in subjects' rating of the experimenter on each trait, between the first and second administrations. The differences were summed. High scores indicated greatest impression change. This was the procedure which Rubin followed (see Chapter 17), and this phase of the experiment represents a replication of her study.

RESULTS

Experimenter-Subject Distance and Self-Disclosure

The number of seconds subjects spent talking about each of the 8 disclosure topics was subjected to analysis of variance. A significant between groups F-ratio (43.00, df 3/112, $P < .01$) was found. The Duncan New Multiple Range Test was employed to determine significant differences between pairs of means, the means of Groups I through IV being, 88.81^a; 121.72^a; 372.53^b; 455.43^c seconds. The means with different superscripts differ at or beyond the .05 level of confidence. While Groups I and II did not differ from one another, all other comparison showed significant differences. There were no significant differences in disclosure time attributable to sex of subjects, topics, or interactions.

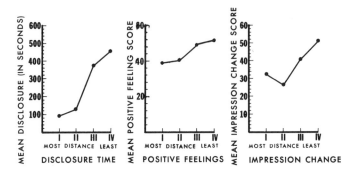

Figure 22. Effects of reduced experimenter-subject distance on subjects' disclosure time, reported feelings, and impression change.

Feelings

Analysis of variance of subjects' reported feelings, as measured by the feelings questionnaire yielded an F-ratio significant beyond the .01 level (40.50, df 3/336) for the between groups comparison. The mean total scores for Groups I through IV were, respectively, 39.06[a]; 40.98[a,b]; 48.72[b,c]; and 52.20[c]. As above, means with different superscripts differ significantly beyond the .05 level of confidence. Groups III and IV reported more positive feelings than Group I. Group IV differed significantly from Group II, while Group III did not.

Impression Change

A significant F-ratio was found for the comparison of total impression change scores between groups ($F = 23.76$, df 3/56, $P < .01$). The comparisons between the sexes and the sex-by-group interaction did not produce significant F-ratios. Means for Groups I through IV were 32.25[a]; 26.31[a]; 41.25[b]; and 50.75[c]. Groups III and IV differed in mean impression-change score from each other, and their scores were higher than the scores obtained for Groups I and II. Clearly, self-disclosure from the experimenter resulted in more impression change than did nondisclosure. The disclosure plus touching from experimenter produced more impression change than did disclosure alone. The above results are shown graphically in Figure 22.

DISCUSSION

The experimental findings confirmed our expectations. Subjects to whom the experimenter revealed something of himself disclosed themselves at greater length than did subjects to whom he did not so reveal himself. Touching the subjects, in combination with experimenter's self-disclosure, resulted in more disclosure from the subjects than either touching alone, or experimenter's disclosure alone.

The decreases in phenomenological distance initiated by the experimenter were evidently welcomed by the subjects. They showed significant increases in positive feelings toward the experimenter and the experimental situation as the experimenter moved from impersonality (Groups I and II) to lesser personal distance (Groups III and IV). The minimal touch that the experimenter applied to the subjects in Group IV did not produce significantly more positive feelings than did disclosure from experimenter to subject, without touching. Apparently it was only the disclosure from the experimenter which had a significant effect upon positive feelings reported by the subjects.

The measure of impression change as a function of increased experimenter-subject contact was included in the present study as further test of the effect of reduced distance between experimenter and subject. Here, the inclusion of a touch from the experimenter along with his self-disclosure (in Group IV) was reflected in a significant difference in mean impression-change score. Touch without disclosure from experimenter did not produce a significant change in subject's perceptions of experimenter (Group II vs. Group I). Experimenter's disclosure, and his disclosure plus touching were differences that made a difference in subjects' perceptions.

The effect of distance-reduction was opposed to the distance-equilibrium phenomenon postulated by Argyle and Dean. Our subjects did not increase "distance" from the experimenter as the latter "approached" them through his self-disclosure and touching. Instead, subjects liked and trusted him, and disclosed themselves at greater length than they did when the experimenter was at the greater distances from them.

Clearly, a distinction needs to be made between those situations in which the distance-equilibrium phenomenon occurs, and those in which it does not. Comparison of the Argyle and Dean study with the present work suggests that subjects' withdrawal as a response to experimenter's approach is most likely to occur when experimenter and subject are mutual strangers. If the experimenter takes the initiative and reveals something of himself (i.e., moves closer), the subject responds by moving even closer. The mediating factor here is the subjects' feelings and perceptions of the experimenter and the experimental situation. Here, the experimenter's distance-reduction was associated with increases of positive feelings, of subjects' self-disclosure, and subjects' impression change. We may propose that if an experimenter moves "close," and the subject discovers he likes and trusts him on such closer contact, he will respond by further decreasing the distance between them. If the subject does not like the experimenter, he may "move back." We did find a correlation of .73 between the positive-feelings score, and the time each of the 64 subjects spent in disclosing themselves to experimenter.

It is as if the subject in a psychologist's experiment, like the baboon or the stickleback fish, wants to know who is invading his "territory." If it is someone with whom he can feel at ease, someone trustworthy, he may invite him still further into his "home." If the approaching experimenter is not perceived in this way, the subject may not chase him away, since the experimenter is usually of higher status than the subject. But the subject may then express his distrust and lack of ease by various withdrawal and self-concealing maneuvers.

The Next Chapter

All the experiments described so far in Part II may be viewed as further tests of the dyadic effect. We concentrated on the relationship between experimenters and subjects because it seemed a crucial area to investigate. In the laboratory situation, a situation is created where one person, the experimenter, is of higher status than the subject, and we have shown much evidence that the experimenter is a source of influence on the subject—indeed, he may be viewed as a kind of model who subtly invites the subject to comply with the example he sets. To round out the picture, I want to present a study where the experimenter's overt influence was minimal, and the question under consideration was the following: If persons who are characteristically high-disclosers are paired with low-disclosing peers for mutual interviewing in the laboratory, will the "highs" follow the example of the "lows" and reduce their level of disclosure in that situation? Or will the "lows" follow the example of their more highly self-disclosing peers?

20. High versus Low
Disclosers: A Contest[*]

This experiment was conducted by Jaquelyn Resnick. We wanted to determine whether high-disclosing subjects influence low-disclosing subjects, or is there a reverse effect? The experiment was conducted to answer the question.

METHOD

Subjects

Eighty unmarried female undergraduates ranging in age from 18 to 20 years at the University of Florida were invited to participate in the study. They all were administered a 40-item self-disclosure questionnaire (see Appendix 19) which asked them to indicate which of the topics they had fully revealed to somebody in their lives, and which topics they would be willing to discuss fully with a same-sex partner whom they would first meet in the course of the study. Of the 80 subjects, the 12 with the highest pooled scores were chosen to form the high-disclosure group, while the 12 lowest scores were assigned to the low-disclosure group. Mean disclosure score of the high group was 149.00, with the low group at 42.08. For the difference between means P was beyond the .001 level. The two groups did not differ in mean age: the highs, 19.25 years; the lows, 19.33 years.

[*] This experiment was first published in the *Journal of Humanistic Psychology*, **10**, 1970, 84–93, and is reprinted here with permission from the publisher.

Instruments and Scoring

The subjects' disclosure output with respect to 20 topics was measured by a single self-report technique. These self-disclosure topics were selected from items used by Taylor and Altman (1966) and Drag (1968); they had been rated by college students for their intimacy value. Five of the topics were of low-rated intimacy, 5 of intermediate, and 10 of very high intimacy value. Each topic was printed on a 4" × 4" index card and randomly ordered from 1 to 20 (see Appendix 20).

After both members of the dyad had considered a topic and discussed it or declined to do so, each reported her experience of what had transpired. An answer sheet requested each subject to rate her response to the topic, her perception of her partner's response, and her own feelings about discussing the topic. The subject's rating of her own response, confirmed by the partner, provided the self-report measure of the dependent variable.

The answer sheets were scored in two ways: unweighted and weighted with respect to the intimacy value of the item. In the unweighted method, each item was simply rated by subject on the following scale:

X: declined to answer (0)
1: withheld some relevant things; did not disclose fully (1)
2: withheld nothing relevant; disclosed *fully* (2)

The numbers in parentheses reflect the numerical value assigned to each rating. These were summed for each subject, yielding unweighted self-disclosure output scores.

For weighted scores, the intimacy value of the topic was taken into account, with the following numerical weights assigned as indicated in parentheses:

L: low intimacy (1)
M: medium intimacy (2)
H: high intimacy (3)

A weighted score for each item was obtained by multiplying the subject's rating by the intimacy value of the item. For example, if a subject reported that she disclosed a highly intimate item *fully*, her weighted score for that item would be 2 × 3, or 6. If she answered a low-intimacy item *fully*, her weighted score would be 2 × 1, or 2. These weighted scores were summed for each subject, yielding total self-disclosure output scores for the weighted self-report data.

Procedure

In the first experimental session, the members of the high-disclosure group were paired with each other at random, and similarly, lows were paired with lows. The only stipulation was that the members of each dyad did not know each other. The subjects were contacted by telephone by the experimenter and notified of the time and place of their appointment. All the experimental sessions were scheduled during the daytime, with both high and low dyads appearing on the same day, in an attempt to make the experimental conditions comparable. The initial session lasted about 10 days, and constituted the "same" condition, where subjects were paired with others of their own disclosure category. This yielded 6 dyads composed of high disclosers (highs with highs), and 6 dyads of low disclosers (lows with lows).

The second experimental session took place about two weeks later, with the same procedure being followed with one major exception. In this session, high disclosers were paired at random with low disclosers, yielding 12 dyads composed of members from opposite disclosure categories (highs with lows). This second session constituted the "different" or "mixed" condition.

The instructions to the subjects were identical in both sessions. The two members of each dyad were introduced to each other by the experimenter. They were requested to enter into dialogue with one another, with regard to the 20 topics on the cards before them (placed face down). Each subject had the option to speak on a topic if she wanted to, or decline to discuss it. She then handed the topic to her partner, who either spoke on it, or declined to do so. After each topic was considered by both partners, the subjects rated their experience of what had occurred on the answer sheet. The process was repeated until all 20 topics had been considered by the subjects. In an effort to account for ordering effects, the members of each dyad alternated going first on an item. This meant that one member of a dyad always spoke first on an odd-numbered topic, and the other on an even-numbered one.

The experimenter emphasized that the subject should respond to an item only if she wanted to, and that she could disclose as much or as little about the topic as she felt comfortable doing. The subject was reminded that there was no penalty for declining to disclose herself fully on an item. The subjects were assured that information obtained during the experimental sessions was confidential and would be destroyed once the experimental data were gathered. After answering any questions, the experimenter turned on a tape recorder and left the room.

No time limit was placed on the interviews. The sessions on the average lasted 65 minutes, but ranged from 20 to 100 minutes. The average length of time for the second session was the same as for the first.

After subjects had completed both sessions of the experiment, they were asked to write down any comments about the experiment.

RESULTS

Means for the weighted and unweighted disclosure output scores are shown graphically in Figure 23. Analysis of variance of the two sets of scores yielded significant F-ratios for all comparisons. Inspection of Figure 23 shows that:

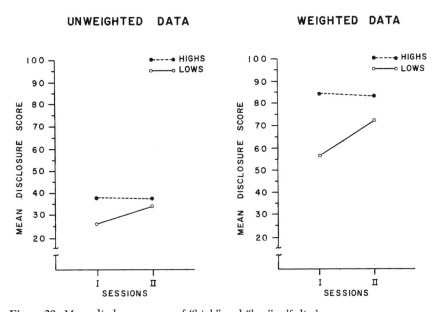

Figure 23. Mean disclosure scores of "high" and "low" self-disclosers.

1. Low-disclosing subjects, when paired with lows, disclosed less ($\bar{X}$ = 26.33, unweighted score; 56.17, weighted) than did high-disclosing subjects who were paired with highs ($\bar{X}$ = 37.83, unweighted score; 84.25, weighted). The difference between each pair of means was significant beyond the .01 level of confidence. The self-disclosure questionnaires employed for the allocation of the subjects to the low and high

groups thus predicted actual behavior, and hence may be regarded as validated for this purpose.

2. Low-disclosing subjects, when paired with high-disclosing subjects, disclosed *more* ($\bar{X}$ = 33.00 unweighted score; 72.08, weighted) to the latter than when they were paired with lows ($P < .05$, weighted and unweighted scores). Clearly, the lows changed their disclosing behavior, contrary to what would have been predicted from their scores on the selection instrument.

3. The high-disclosing subjects did not reduce their disclosure output when they were paired with lows, but remained at the higher level of self-disclosing behavior.

4. The lows did not differ from the highs at a statistically significant level in mean disclosure output when they were paired with the highs.

DISCUSSION

When low-disclosing women were paired for mutual interviewing with similarly low-disclosing peers, they did indeed disclose relatively little about themselves. When more highly disclosing women were paired with similarly self-revealing peers, they disclosed a lot about themselves, and more on the average than occurred in the low-disclosing dyads. What is of greatest interest is that when highs were paired with lows, and when all subjects were of equivalent social status, it was the low-disclosing women who changed in the direction of greater openness. The possibility was present for the high-disclosing women to become more inaccessible but they did not do so. The research of Shapiro (1968) yielded similar outcomes—low disclosers changed their behavior when paired with more highly disclosing partners for mutual interviewing.

One might argue that to be more "open" is more rewarding or less of a "strain" for a person than remaining in a self-concealed state, and that, given the appropriately safe setting, people will abandon the mode of interpersonal reserve. Conformity with the face-to-face example of a higher status researcher has been found to influence subjects to change in the direction of greater self-disclosure (cf. Powell, 1967; Drag, 1968) and even to have some limited carry-over value (Drag, 1968). In the present study an effort was made to minimize any direct influence from the experimenter, so that a fairer "contest" between highs and lows might be conducted. In this contest, it was the highs who appeared to prevail, and the lows who dislodged themselves from their characteristic, low-disclosing interpersonal "position." These findings thus lend further support to the hypothesis of a dyadic effect in self-disclosing behavior that was first noted in earlier questionnaire studies (Jourard, 1959; Jourard and Landsman, 1960; Jourard and Richman, 1963). It appears that when status differences are controlled and disclosure readiness is varied, disclosure prevails over reserve.

It is of some methodological interest to note once more that the self-disclosure questionnaires predicted actual behavior in a differential way. Women with low-disclosure histories did behave consistently with their pasts when relating to women just like them; the questionnaire forecasted behavior in that situation. But when introduced to a situation where a high-disclosing peer was included, low disclosers behaved contrary to their past performances, and contrary for that matter to their own self-expectation. The highs confirmed their past behavior and their self-expectation when paired with highs and lows alike. Drag and Jaffe likewise found differential predictive value of self-disclosure questionnaires for subjects' performance in their experiments. When the experimenter was impersonal with subjects, prior to the conduct of the experiment, the subjects behaved consistent with the scores obtained on the self-disclosure questionnaire used to select subjects. When the experimenter was more open and personal with subjects, the latter's scores did not predict self-disclosing behavior in the experiment.

Comments of the subjects which were written at the conclusion of the experiment indicate that most preferred dialogue with a partner from the high group, no matter which category the subject belonged to herself. Sample comments were: "My first meeting was much easier than this last dialogue, I think it was easier to talk to my first partner" (comment from a high subject); "It was easier to discuss with someone who discussed also . . . " (a low subject).

SUMMARY

Twelve women designated high disclosers and 12 low disclosers were selected from a sample of 80 female undergraduate students, on the basis of scores on a self-disclosure questionnaire. A two-part experiment was conducted, inquiring into (a) the predictive value of the selection instrument at forecasting self-disclosure in a dyadic situation, and (b) whether a subject would increase or decrease her predicted level of self-disclosure when paired with a partner who differed from the subject in usual self-disclosure. The low-disclosing subjects disclosed less to their partners than did the high-disclosing subjects when dyads were formed with like-disclosing pairs. When lows were paired with highs, however, the latter remained high disclosing and the lows showed a significant increase in self-disclosure to their partners.

The Next Chapter

In Chapter 15, we showed that self-disclosure questionnaires differentially forecasted the extent of subjects' disclosure to experimenter. In Drag's study, measures of past disclosure and willingness to disclose were correlated with actual amount of disclosure to experimenter when the latter presented himself impersonally; not when experimenter preceded the experimental interview with 20 minutes of self-revealing dialogue. Small showed an interaction among past disclosure and willingness to disclose to an experimenter, on the one hand, and personal values and actual disclosure on the other. Personality factors have thus been shown to be related to self-disclosure in a specific situation.

In the next study to be reported, Sharon Graham explored the question of whether or not another personality factor—attitude toward one's death—was related to willingness to disclose oneself to others.

21. Attitude toward Death and Self-Disclosure

According to the existentialist view (Heidegger, 1962), authentic existence does not begin until a person realizes his years and days are numbered, that he will die. Until that fact is confronted, a person postpones full involvement in the world, compromises his integrity, and acts as if he would live forever. He thus "puts off" living in the present and engaging in dialogue with his fellows.

Sharon Graham became fascinated with this aspect of existentialist thought, and investigated (Graham, 1970) the relationship between a person's attitude toward his own death, and the nature of his involvement in one aspect of living, namely, self-disclosure. It was her contention that authentic disclosure involves a sort of death while the person is alive—he must be willing to "kill" his self-concept, or let it die, in order to let growth and change take place. In this way, self-disclosure is quite risky, and so it seemed appropriate to Miss Graham to inquire if persons who accept their finitude differ from those who reject the finality of death, in the depth and "targets" of their past disclosure, and their willingness to disclose themselves to another person who is himself open and self-disclosing.

METHOD

The first task Miss Graham addressed was that of measuring a person's attitude toward his own death. She proceeded directly enough; a Death Attitudes Questionnaire adapted from previous work by Middleton (1958), was administered to 197 male and female undergraduates. Subjects were asked whether they believed in some sort of future existence after death. Those who answered in the affirmative were classified as

"Non-Acceptors of Death" if they were (1) able to describe this existence, and (2) were unable to describe, or were resistant about, describing the process of physical decay after death. Subjects who answered in the negative were classified as "Acceptors of Death" if they were (1) able to describe the process of physical decomposition occurring after death and (2) were able to describe the possibility of their own imminent and personal death. Two graduate student judges rated the subjects' responses on these secondary criteria; inter-judge agreement was 90% in the case of Acceptors, and 70% in the case of the Non-Acceptors for 20 subjects tested in a pilot study.

Both judges agreed in identifying 66 Non-Acceptors and 23 Acceptors. Fifteen subjects in each of these two groups, 7 males and 8 females, were chosen at random and completed the second part of the experiment.

Measures of Self-Disclosure

Subjects were seen individually by the experimenter for further testing without knowledge of the group to which they belonged. Upon arrival at the interviewing room, the experimenter (Miss Graham, a 24-year-old woman) asked each subject:

1. To complete a self-disclosure inventory inquiring into past disclosure to parents, closest friend of each sex, and willingness to disclose to a female experimenter. (The 35 items of this questionnaire are those shown in Table 27.)

2. To participate in a "disclosure interview," in which the subject was asked to disclose or to decline to disclose himself on 5 topics, after the experimenter had first truthfully disclosed herself on each of these topics. The topics were: (1) your hobbies, (2) describe a person with whom you have been in love, (3) the aspects of your personality you worry about (4) the people with whom you have been sexually intimate; the circumstances of your relationship with each (5) how satisfied you are with different parts of your body.

3. To complete a self-disclosure sentence-completion blank (SDSB) developed by Greene (1964). This questionnaire consists of 20 sentence stems to be completed by the subject with statements about his personal world (see Appendix 21).

The self-disclosure inventory was scored by summing the number of 2 responses (indicating full disclosure), 1 responses (partial disclosure), and zeroes (signifying no disclosure) entered by the subject with regard to each of the given target-persons. The total past disclosure score (PD) was obtained by summing entries for parents and friends.

The willingness-to-disclose score was the sum of the entries for "female experimenter."

Scores for the disclosure interview were obtained by the method developed by Haymes (1969); Miss Graham adapted this technique for the present purposes in collaboration with Linwood Small, and her procedure was identical with that described on pp. 166–167. Briefly, this technique called for judges to rate 30-second segments of talk as recorded on the tape recorder, such that a score of 3 was assigned if the subject made a self-disclosing, first-person reference in the present tense; a score of 2 was assigned if the reference was in the past tense, and a score of 1 was allotted if the subject was making a self-disclosing statement with regard to a third person (see Appendix 13). A total tape-rated self-disclosure score was obtained by summing the scores for all 30-second segments. Inter-rater reliability for this technique was .98.

The Greene Self-Disclosure Sentence-Completion Blank was scored by two undergraduate judges whose inter-rater agreement was .91 over 10 subjects. The judges rated each completion on a scale from 1 (most disclosing) to 5 (least disclosing). A composite score for the 2 judges was calculated by experimenter. Total SDSB score was the sum of the composite scores for the 20 sentence stems.

In summary, then, a total of 30 subjects were first classified as Non-Acceptors or Acceptors of the reality of their own death. Four measures of disclosing behavior were then obtained from them: (1) a measure of past disclosure to parents and closest friends; (2) a measure of willingness to disclose oneself on 5 topics to a female experimenter; (3) a measure of their actual disclosure to experimenter, obtained from a tape-recording of the interview she conducted with them; and (4) a "projective" measure of subjects' self-disclosure to the experimenter, from a special sentence-completion blank.

Miss Graham had proposed that Acceptors would obtain higher scores for disclosure than Non-Acceptors on all measures except that for past disclosure to parents. She reasoned that the Non-Acceptors would be less emancipated from their parents than the Acceptors, and would show higher scores for disclosure to those target-persons, and lower scores for disclosure to peers.

RESULTS

Past Disclosure and Willingness to Disclose

Figure 24 shows the mean scores for past disclosure to each parent, closest friend of each sex, and the score for reported willingness to

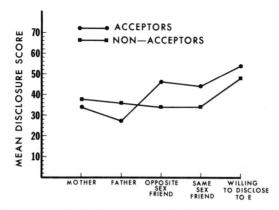

Figure 24. Mean scores of death-acceptors and Non-Acceptors for past disclosure and willingness to disclose to experimenter (*E*).

disclose to a female experimenter. Analysis of variance showed significant F-ratios for the comparison between target-persons ($F = 13.73$, df 4/96, $p < .01$), and for the interaction between target-persons and attitude toward death ($F = 5.12$, df 4/96, $P < .01$). Significant differences ($P < .01$) were found among the Acceptors' scores for disclosure to the several target-persons; they disclosed more to peers than to parents. The Non-Acceptors did not show this pattern. The Acceptors did not differ significantly from Non-Acceptors on willingness to disclose themselves on the questionnaire topics to a female experimenter, and may be regarded as matched on this variable. It is interesting to note that though the groups did not differ to a statistically significant degree, both groups declared themselves willing to be more open to an experimenter they had not yet encountered than they had been to either parent or to their closest friends.

Self-Disclosure in the Interview

The mean disclosure score of the Acceptor group measured from the tape-recorded interview was 74.00 while that for the Non-Acceptors was 34.60 (see Figure 25, left side). The difference between groups, as tested by the Mann-Whitney test, was significant beyond the .001 level. The difference between the sexes was not statistically significant. Clearly, the subjects who accepted the reality of their own death disclosed themselves more fully and freely to Miss Graham than did the Non-Acceptors, thus lending further confirmation to her hypothesis.

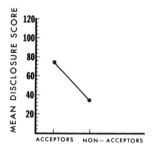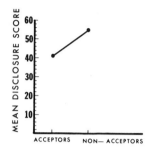

Figure 25. *Left:* Mean self-disclosure scores rated from interviews. *Right:* Mean self-disclosure scores rated from Sentence-Completion Blank (high scores signify low disclosure, and vice versa).

Sentence-Completion Test

Mean self-disclosure scores (see Fig. 25, right side) as rated from the Greene Sentence-Completion Blank were 41.13 for the Acceptors, and 55.33 for the Non-Acceptors. The difference between these means was significant beyond the .001 level ($t = 4.79$). It will be recalled that a low score on this test signifies high disclosure, and vice versa. The Acceptor group thus showed themselves more willing to be self-revealing in this projective test than did the Non-Acceptors. (The sexes did not differ in mean scores on this measure.)

It may be concluded from these comparisons that those subjects who fully acknowledged the finality of their death entered more fully into self-disclosing relationships with their peers, and showed themselves readier to be self-revealing to a female experimenter than subjects who denied the reality of their death. Miss Graham's predictions were nicely borne out in this experiment.

Correlations Among Measures of Self-Disclosure

Miss Graham then studied the relationships among the several self-disclosure measures which she employed, both to determine whether Acceptors differed from Non-Acceptors in direction and magnitude of the relationships, and also to determine the predictive validity of the questionnaire measures of past disclosure to parents and peers, and willingness to disclose to experimenter. A significant *rho* of .59 ($P < .05$) was found in the Acceptor group between the score for past disclosure to both parents, and the disclosure score obtained from the interviews. The *rho* for the Non-Acceptors was —.02, which was not significant. The scores for past disclosure to friends were not significantly correlated with the interview scores in either group. The total past disclosure score (parents and friends combined) was significantly correlated with the interview scores ($rho = .51$, $P < .01$) in the Acceptor group, but not in the Non-Acceptor group.

The score for willingness to disclose to a female experimenter was correlated .73 ($P < .01$) with actual disclosure in the interview among the Acceptors, and only .33 among the Non-Acceptors (not significant).

The subjects who accepted the reality of death were thus found to be rather consistent in their total past disclosure, and their self-disclosing behavior to parents, and to Miss Graham, and they behaved in the interview with her in a manner consistent with their declared intention.

The scores for the Sentence-Completion Blank correlated .54 ($P < .01$) with interview scores for the combined group of Acceptors and Non-Acceptors, showing some validity of this instrument, but the *rhos* between these two measures for each group considered separately fell short of statistical significance (.31 for Acceptors, .16 for Non-Acceptors). The Sentence-Completion Test disclosure scores were not significantly correlated with the past disclosure scores, or the willingness to disclose score in any consistent way. Among the Non-Acceptors, a *rho* of −.48 ($P < .05$) was found between past disclosure to parents and the Sentence-Completion Test scores, signifying that the more they had disclosed to their parents, the more open they were on the other test. A *rho* of .34 ($P < .05$) was found between Sentence-Completion Blank scores for both groups combined and past disclosure to friends.

DISCUSSION

This was an ingenious study, and it yielded clear-cut differences. Frankly, I was skeptical when Miss Graham presented her initial proposal to compare people who do accept the fact that they will die with those who do not. Her method for selecting exemplars of each group seemed rather flimsy to me: simply asking subjects to state whether or not they believed in a future personal existence, and then asking 2 further questions just to ascertain whether the subjects were serious about it. Yet, the groups did differ in self-disclosure in the ways that she predicted. Her findings cannot easily be attributed to any subtle "experimenter effect" (Rosenthal, 1967) because she tested and interviewed her subjects without knowing to which group they belonged. She seems to have hit upon a crucial personality variable that merits further study.

If her present findings hold up, then substantial experimental support will be afforded the existentialist thesis about the effects upon a person's life of the realization that he will die. Certainly, her findings are consistent with this hypothesis. But since this book is primarily concerned with the experimental analysis of self-disclosure, I feel most justified in asserting that Miss Graham demonstrated the effect of a personality variable upon self-disclosure in an experimental interview. Moreover, she provided further evidence of the predictive validity of self-report questionnaires for measuring self-disclosure.

I was also interested to note that the Sentence-Completion Blank had some validity, in that it correlated significantly with actual disclosure to the experimenter for the combined group of subjects.

Unlike Lee Drag or Linwood Small, Miss Graham confined her method of interviewing her subjects to the "open" way; we wonder what might appear if she had added further groups of Acceptors and Non-Acceptors and simply asked them to disclose themselves to her without reciprocal or exemplary disclosure on her part.

SUMMARY

Fifteen subjects designated Acceptors of personal death were compared with 15 subjects found to be Non-Acceptors of personal mortality on four measures of self-disclosure:

1. A questionnaire measure of past disclosure to parents and peers.
2. A questionnaire measure of subjects' willingness to disclose to a female experimenter.
3. Self-disclosure scores obtained from a tape-recorded interview conducted by the experimenter who served as an exemplar of openness on the topics of the interview.
4. A projective test of self-disclosure, the Greene Sentence-Completion Blank.

The Acceptors were found to have disclosed more to peers than the Non-Acceptors (who disclosed more to parents); they were more willing to disclose themselves to experimenter, they actually did disclose themselves most fully to experimenter, and obtained scores signifying fuller self-disclosure on the Sentence-Completion Blank. Some predictive validity was found for the questionnaire measure of past disclosure.

The Next Chapter

Every one of the studies thus far reported can be viewed as an exploration of the validity of self-disclosure questionnaires, because some version of a self-report questionnaire was employed in most of them. In the next chapter, I draw together some of the evidence that we have gathered which shows wherein the questionnaires do show "predictive" validity, and where they do not. Other kinds of validity (e.g., content validity, construct validity, concurrent validity) are touched upon in Part I of this book.

PART III

Some Implications of Self-Disclosure Research

In this last section of the book, I explore some ramifications of the research that has been reported.

One question that I address is that concerned with the validity of questionnaires for the measurement of self-disclosure. I offer a progress report on this question, and I expect from time to time to bring the answers up to date.

I also present a game that can be employed both as a research instrument, and as a means whereby two or more persons can radically alter their relationships and their lives.

Finally, I explore some of the implications of transparency, or self-disclosure, for the living of life.

22. Are Self-Disclosure Questionnaires Valid?

The various questionnaires which we developed ask the subjects to indicate, usually by means of a 3-point scale, how much personal data they have disclosed to various people in the past. I have viewed the scores obtained in this fashion as an index of a person's "openness," or demonstrated readiness to disclose to the given target-persons. This view rests on the assumption that, within limits (to be discovered), a person's past performance is a fair estimate of how he will behave in the present and future. In the area of "psychometrics," this is a matter of the validity of the test or questionnaire under consideration.

Psychologists recognize different kinds of validity. One speaks for example of "construct" validity, "concurrent" validity, and "predictive" validity. Of these three, the last-named is deemed the most powerful evidence that a test indeed measures what its designer hopes or claims it will.

It is appropriate to ask about the validity of self-disclosure questionnaires. What are they valid *for?* Himelstein and Kimbrough (1963) showed that one of our questionnaires did not forecast self-revealing behavior in a classroom situation, where students who had been tested with our questionnaires were asked to stand up and speak about themselves to their classmates. Hurley and Hurley (1968) demonstrated that disclosure-questionnaire scores did not predict self-disclosing behavior of participants in encounter groups. Himelstein and Lubin (1966) demonstrated a failure of our questionnaires to predict scores on the MMPI "K-scale"—which presumably measures openness and concealment.

Clearly, our questionnaires do not predict the above-named classes of behavior. But this is not to say that they are not valid. The question, to repeat, is "What are self-disclosure questionnaires valid *for?*"

168

Part I of this book provides abundant evidence that our 60-item, 15-item, 25-item, and 40-item versions of this test enjoy "construct" and "concurrent" validity. Other workers (see bibliography) have provided even more evidence along these lines.

The matter of predictive validity, however, remains the strongest test of any measuring instrument. Here, I would like to assemble our evidence, as well as point to a bit of evidence from other workers, which shows that self-disclosure questionnaires do indeed forecast actual self-disclosing behavior, as well as behavior related to openness.

First, I mention my study of nursing students (Chapter 9), where we not only showed correlations between self-disclosure scores obtained 2 years earlier, and grade-point averages in nursing courses at the University of Florida College of Nursing; but were also able to demonstrate that students rated as superior at "entering into communicative relationships with patients" obtained higher self-disclosure scores in an earlier test than fellow students who were inferior at this interpersonal skill.

Moving into Part II of this book, we first note in Lee Drag's study (Chapter 15) that self-reports of "willingness to disclose" forecasted actual disclosure to an experimenter and to a fellow-subject, when the experimenter related to the subject in the impersonal mode. The disclosure scores did not predict actual self-disclosing performance when the experimenter interacted with the subject before the actual experiment in a way that approximated mutually revealing dialogue.

Perhaps the strongest validity check in Part II was provided by Resnick's experiment (Chapter 20). She selected subjects with the highest and the lowest scores for "past disclosure" and "willingness to disclose to a peer." When she paired low disclosers with low disclosers, and compared their performance on a self-disclosing interview with that produced by high-disclosing pairs, she found that the former did indeed disclose much less to one another than did the latter. Evidently, the questionnaires predicted actual behavior in this precisely defined situation. D. Taylor's study (1965) likewise confirmed the predictive value of the questionnaires.

Small's experiment (Chapter 15) showed differential validity of questionnaire measures of past-disclosure and willingness to disclose. It will be recalled that his subjects, who were characterized as "B-factor" scorers on Morris' Ways to Live Scale, showed a positive correlation of .75 ($P < .01$) between past disclosure and actual disclosure to an experimenter who was himself quite self-revealing in the experimental interview. When the experimenter was "closed" and only interrogated these subjects, their past disclosure scores were negatively correlated with their actual disclosure to him ($rho - .82, P < .01$). Subjects with a different value-orientation, designated "E-factor," obtained positive correlations between past disclosure, and disclosure to the experimenter when he was "open" ($rho = .60$, $P < .05$) and when he was "closed" ($rho = .71$, $P < .05$). Again, questionnaires forecasted self-disclosing behavior, in this case, in a complex way, because of the interaction with the personality dimension of values.

Sharon Graham (Chapter 21) showed even stronger evidence for the predictive validity of measures of past disclosure to others, and actual disclosure to an open, self-disclosing experimenter, when the personality factor she was exploring (attitude toward death) was taken into account. She found a significant rho (.59) among subjects who accepted their own mortality, between amount of past disclosure to parents, and amount disclosed to the experimenter in an interview. The total past disclosure score of both Acceptors and Non-Acceptors was correlated .51 ($P < .01$) with actual disclosure to the experimenter. Again, among Acceptors, a pre-interview measure of willingness to disclose to a female experimenter was correlated .73 with actual disclosure, while a nonsignificant rho (.33) was found between these variables in the Non-Accepting group.

Lee Drag's doctoral dissertation (1971) provided yet another demonstration of predictive validity for a self-disclosure questionnaire. In this study, 16 female college students in one group were paired first with their roommates, and in a second session with a friendly stranger (a confederate of the experimenter) who was an open and freely disclosing person. In the other group, 16 college women had their first interview with the friendly stranger, and their second session with their roommate. In all, 32 college women served as subjects in this study, with 8 dyads formed for each group. A modified game of "Invitations" (see Appendix 9) was employed in this experiment. All subjects had been closely matched on a measure of past disclosure, and for willingness to disclose to their roommate as well as to a same-sex stranger. It should be noted that at the time this study was begun, the roommates had been acquainted for only three days.

The purpose of this study was to determine whether a "bus rider" phenomenon could be found; that is, it was predicted that the subjects might disclose themselves more fully to the friendly stranger than to their roommate, with whom they expected to live throughout the academic year. Drag found that the subjects did disclose more to the stranger (23 items) than they did to their roommates (18 items), when they played the disclosure game with their roommate first. When they interacted with the stranger first, the numbers of items disclosed to the stranger and then to the roommate were identical—23 items to each.

She concluded that the experience of talking to a friendly stranger carried over to the more enduring relationship with the roommate.

More germane to this chapter, however, were the correlations Mrs. Drag found between the measures of willingness to disclose and actual disclosure to roommate (.77 and .78 for each of the 2 groups, $P < .01$). The comparable correlations between willingness to disclose and actual disclosure to the stranger were .26 and .04, neither of which is statistically significant. Clearly, the subjects predicted their level of disclosure to their roomate with more precision than they did to the stranger, who appeared to invite more disclosure from the subjects than they had anticipated.

Outside our own laboratory, we can point to the study of Shapiro and Swensen (1969), of self-disclosure and mutual knowledge between spouses. These workers were able to show strong correlations between what one spouse claimed to know about the other, and what the other spouse had said he had disclosed. Their paradigm followed that employed in the studies described in Chapters 2 and 3 in this book. This is not so much predictive validity, however, as it is concurrent validity; yet a change in frame of reference makes it possible to state that study of one spouse's self-report of disclosure forecasts statements by the other spouse of how much he knows about the first.

This brief overview of evidence for the validity of our questionnaires is by no means exhaustive. I have included it, however, to show that validity is a precise matter. Measures that are valid forecasters of one kind of behavior in one kind of situation may be quite useless and invalid ways of predicting behavior in other types of situations.

While scores for past disclosure to parents and peers have been found to be intercorrelated—suggesting a more general factor of openness or transparency—situational factors have also been shown to override personality factors in self-disclosure (cf. Chapter 15). I was not surprised, for example, when Himelstein and the Hurleys failed to find relationships between past disclosure to significant others, which took place in a dyadic relationship, and the "broadcasting" type of self-disclosure which was called for in the classroom or in an encounter group.

As more research is done, we will doubtless obtain a broader and yet more precise view of the situations for which self-disclosure questionnaire scores are valid as prognosticators of self-disclosing behavior.

The Next Chapter

Growing numbers of Americans are participating in "encounter groups" where they can disclose themselves to other group members in the hope of gaining self-awareness, discovering new possibilities for growth and self-actualization, and where they can simply enjoy the sometimes intense interaction that occurs. Many leaders of such groups have developed techniques for overcoming initial reserve and shyness among the group members, so that they can get right down to honest, spontaneous disclosure with polite preliminaries by-passed.

Lee Drag and I developed a game, based on self-disclosure questionnaires, that has proven to be not only a useful research tool (see Chapter 15), but also an effective means of getting pairs of people deeply acquainted with one another in a hurry. The next chapter describes the game.

23. A Disclosure Game

The game is really a structured way for two people to become acquainted with one another through mutual disclosure on assigned topics. The topics are roughly graded for intimacy. Participants in the game take turns disclosing themselves to their partner on the given topic. The rules of the game are simple enough—complete honesty is called for, including an honest statement of unwillingness to disclose the subject matter in question. The other rule calls for complete respect on the part of the listener, who must avoid pressuring and probing, unless the other person expresses a willingness to be pressured or probed.

Table 27 and Appendix 9 show long versions of the game, which is also designed in such a way that an investigator might gather useful data on the "depth" to which two players have permitted themselves to be known by their partners. In encounter groups, I have experimented with different kinds of initial acquaintance processes before playing the game (see Instruction 3 on p. 240), for example, having the partners give each other a back-rub, or engaging in ordinary social chit-chat.

I have also used short versions of the game, as shown in Table 28 eliminating the more complicated instructions shown in Table 27 and Appendix 9—simply inviting pairs of people to begin getting acquainted by disclosing themselves to one another on just 5 or 10 topics, such as hobbies, attitudes toward their own bodies, problems and satisfactions in work, and personal satisfactions and problems with members of their own family. What nearly always happens is that, after initial embarrassment, at the artificiality of the situation, the partners become intensely involved in mutual disclosure, spending sometimes as much as 7 hours at it.

I include the game in this book so that others may play with it, or use these versions as research tools. If they are employed in research, the investigator is advised to pre-test the items, so that they may be assigned an intimacy value appropriate for the groups or individuals whom he is testing.

I have observed that many people do not know how to become acquainted with others. It is also true that on large campuses, in dormitories, and other places where crowds of people reside, they live in mutual ignorance and misunderstanding. I believe that a step in the direction of increased mutual understanding between black and white, young and old, man and woman, foreigner and American might be

Table 27   A Disclosure Game for Two Players

A Study in Self-Disclosure

Your name_____ Age____ Occupation_____
Religious Denomination_____ Your Partner's Name_____

INSTRUCTIONS

This is a "game" I am asking you to play for serious scientific purposes. I want you to participate in a kind of "dialogue" with a stranger. You will have an illuminating kind of experience, and I will obtain valuable scientific data.

Procedure

1. Read the 35 topics listed below in Part 1. Check those topics that you have disclosed fully to *somebody* in your life. If there is nobody to whom you have *fully* revealed that aspect of yourself, leave the space blank.

2. In Part 2 check the topics you are willing to discuss *fully* with the partner to whom you have just been introduced, when once the dialogue between you begins. If you are reluctant for any reason to discuss a topic fully, leave that space blank.

3. After you have completed the above procedure, go through the fuller acquaintance process, as instructed by the investigator.

4. After the acquaintance process, turn to Part 3 and check on the left side of the page the topics you feel willing to disclose to your partner.

5. Now flip a coin with your partner. Whoever wins the toss asks the first question. The other person answers or declines, according to his intent. He then asks the same question of the other, who answers or not, as he wishes.

If the other person has answered the question you asked, place a check mark on the right-hand side of the page. Otherwise, do not check.

Take turns asking each question first, throughout the entire list.

At any time during the dialogue, you can change your mind. If you intended to speak on a topic, and in the course of the interview you find you would rather not, then simply decline that topic. And if you intended not to disclose on a topic but decided you will, go ahead and do so. Encircle the items on which you changed your mind.

Part 1

Check those topics on which you have disclosed yourself *fully to somebody.*

1. Your hobbies; how you like best to spend your spare time.
2. Your favorite foods and beverages, and chief dislikes in food and drink.
3. Your preferences and dislikes in music.
4. The places in the world you have traveled, and your reactions to these places.
5. Your educational background, and your feelings about it.
6. Your personal views on politics, the presidency, foreign and domestic policy.
7. The aspects of your body you are most pleased with.
8. Aspects of your daily work that satisfy and that bother you.
9. The educational and family background of your parents.
10. Your personal religious views, nature of religious participation if any.
11. Your views on the way a husband and wife should live their marriage.
12. The names of the people who helped you significantly in your life.
13. Your present financial position: income, debts, savings, sources of income.
14. The occasions in your life when you were happiest: in detail.
15. The worries and difficulties you experience now, and in the past, with your health.
16. Habits and reactions of yours that bother you at present.
17. Your usual ways of dealing with depression, anxiety, and anger.
18. The features of your appearance you are most displeased with and wish you could alter.
19. Your favorite forms of erotic play and sexual lovemaking.
20. Your most common sexual fantasies and reveries.
21. The names of the persons you have significantly helped, and the ways in which you helped them.
22. Characteristics of yourself that give you cause for pride and satisfaction.
23. The unhappiest moments in your life: in detail.
24. The circumstances under which you become depressed, and when your feelings are hurt.
25. The ways in which you feel you are most maladjusted or immature.
26. The actions you have most regretted doing in your life, and why.
27. The main unfulfilled wishes and dreams and failures in your life.
28. Your guiltiest secrets.
29. What you regard as the mistakes and failures your parents made in raising you.
30. How you see and evaluate your parents' relationship with one another.
31. What you do to stay fit, if anything.
32. The sources of strain and dissatisfaction in your marriage (or relationship with the opposite sex).
33. The people with whom you have been sexually intimate; the circumstances of your relationship with each.
34. The persons in your life whom you most resent; the reasons why.

Part 2

Check those topics you are willing to reveal to your partner.

1. Your hobbies; how you like best to spend your spare time.
2. Your favorite foods and beverages, and chief dislikes in food and drink.
3. Your preferences and dislikes in music.
4. The places in the world you have traveled, and your reactions to these places.
5. Aspects of your daily work that satisfy and that bother you.
6. Your educational background, and your feelings about it.
7. The educational and family background of your parents.
8. Your personal views on politics, the presidency, foreign and domestic policy.
9. Your personal religious views, nature of religious participation if any.
10. What your personal goals are for the next 10 years or so.
11. Your present financial position: income, debts, savings, sources of income.
12. Habits and reactions of yours that bother you at present.
13. Characteristics of yourself that give you cause for pride and satisfaction.
14. Your usual ways of dealing with depression, anxiety, and anger.
15. The unhappiest moments in your life: in detail.
16. The occasions in your life when you were happiest: in detail.
17. The circumstances under which you become depressed, and when your feelings are hurt.
18. The ways in which you feel you are most maladjusted or immature.
19. The actions you have most regretted doing in your life, and why.
20. The main unfulfilled wishes and dreams and failures in your life.
21. Your guiltiest secrets.
22. What you regard as the mistakes and failures your parents made in raising you.
23. How you see and evaluate your parents' relationship with one another.
24. Your views on the way a husband and wife should live their marriage.
25. The worries and difficulties you experience now, in the past, with your health.
26. What you do to stay fit, if anything.
27. The aspects of your body you are most pleased with.
28. The features of your appearance you are most displeased with and wish you could alter.
29. The sources of strain and dissatisfaction in your marriage (or relationship with the opposite sex.
30. Your favorite forms of erotic play and sexual lovemaking.
31. Your most common sexual fantasies and reveries.
32. The people with whom you have been sexually intimate; the circumstances of your relationship with each.
33. The persons in your life whom you most resent; the reasons why.
34. The names of the persons you have significantly helped, and the ways in which you helped them.
35. The names of the people who helped you significantly in your life.

Part 3

Check the topics you *intend to reveal* to your partner on the *left* side of page. On the right side, check those topics your partner fully discussed.

1. Your hobbies; how you like best to spend your spare time.
2. Your favorite foods and beverages, and chief dislikes in food and drink.
3. Your preferences and dislikes in music.
4. The places in the world you have traveled, and your reactions to these places.
5. Aspects of your daily work that satisfy and that bother you.
6. Your educational background, and your feelings about it.
7. The educational and family background of your parents.
8. Your personal views on politics, the presidency, foreign and domestic policy.
9. Your personal religious views, nature of religious participation if any.
10. What your personal goals are for the next 10 years or so.
11. Your present financial position: income, debts, savings, sources of income.
12. Habits and reactions of yours that bother you at present.
13. Characteristics of yourself that give you cause for pride and satisfaction.
14. Your usual ways of dealing with depression, anxiety, and anger.
15. The unhappiest moments in your life: in detail.
16. The occasions in your life when you were happiest: in detail.
17. The circumstances under which you become depressed, and when your feelings are hurt.
18. The ways in which you feel you are most maladjusted or immature.
19. The actions you have most regretted doing in your life, and why.
20. The main unfulfilled wishes and dreams and failures in your life.
21. Your guiltiest secrets.
22. What you regard as the mistakes and failures your parents made in raising you.
23. How you see and evaluate your parents' relationship with one another.
24. Your views on the way a husband and wife should live their marriage.
25. The worries and difficulties you experience now, in the past, with your health.
26. What you do to stay fit, if anything.
27. The aspects of your body you are most pleased with.
28. The features of your appearance you are most displeased with and wish you could alter.
29. The sources of strain and dissatisfaction in your marriage (or relationship with the opposite sex.
30. Your favorite forms of erotic play and sexual lovemaking.
31. Your most common sexual fantasies and reveries.
32. The people with whom you have been sexually intimate; the circumstances of your relationship with each.
33. The persons in your life whom you most resent; the reasons why.
34. The names of the persons you have significantly helped, and the ways in which you helped them.
35. The names of the people who helped you significantly in your life.

Table 28   A Shorter Disclosure Game

Interpersonal Yoga

The immediate object of Hatha Yoga is to master the various *asanas*. Each of these is a specific position which one leads one's body to assume. A beginner commences to assume one of these positions and finds that his muscles "protest." The means by which one fully enters an *asana* is by entering it up to one's limit, and then press gently at that limit. There can be no forcing, no cheating. The novice enters a position no further than he has "earned."

One can view authentic dialogue as a kind of interpersonal *asana*. The ultimate in dialogue is unpremeditated, uncontrived, spontaneous disclosure in response to the disclosure of the other. The following is an exercise aimed at helping a person discover his limits to ongoing dialogue. The first person discloses himself on the first topic until he and his partner are satisfied there is no more to be said. Then, the other person does likewise. Then, on to the next *asana*, or topic. The rule is— complete honesty, respect for one's own limits (as they are experienced in the form of embarrassment, anxiety, etc.) As soon as this point is reached, the person declares he is at a limit. The partners can then discuss reasons for the reserve, and the person may overcome it.

Part I: Disclosure

1. My hobbies, interests, and favorite leisure pursuits.
2. What I like and dislike about my body—appearance, health, etc.
3. My work—satisfactions, frustrations.
4. My financial situation: income, savings, debts, investments, etc.
5. Aspects of my parents I like and dislike; family problems encountered in growing up.
6. Religious views, philosophy of life, what gives meaning to my life.
7. My love life, past and present.
8. Problems in my marriage, or in my dealings with opposite sex at present.
9. What I like and dislike about my partner, on the basis of this encounter.

Part II: Physical Contact

(The same rules of respect for one's own limits, and one's partner's, apply.)

1. Massage the head and neck of the partner.
2. Massage the shoulders of the partner.
3. Give a back rub.
4. Rub the stomach of the partner.
5. Massage the partner's feet.

---

taken if places to play the disclosure game were set up, and people were encouraged to participate every day or so with a stranger. My impression is that people find the two-person situation more comfortable than a group setting for personal disclosure.

The Next Chapter

The first chapter in Part III is a theoretical analysis of how self-disclosure can be viewed. I wrote it from the perspective of "existential phenomenology," the disciplined effort to make sense out of behavior by consideration of the experience which it discloses.

24. The Transparent Way[*]

To be transparent is a twofold action, with consequences for self and others. It is to let the disclosure of the world, including our own embodied being, stand forth before our consciousness. It is to be accepting and nonselective toward the ceaseless disclosure *of* the changing being that is the world. And it is to be an active discloser *to* the world, which includes one's fellow beings. If I make myself transparent, I suspend my concepts, my expectancies as to how things and people are, and let myself perceive (that is, receive the transmissions of) their being. I suspend my concept of my own being (my self-concept) and let my changing being present itself to my experience, thus necessitating a changed concept of myself, with attendant changes in my behavior. I will suspend my concepts under special conditions: when my goal-seeking fails, when it becomes apparent my concepts are radically out of touch with the changed reality to which they refer (cognitive dissonance, surprise). And if it happens that my usual projects and needs are in abeyance, and I am doing nothing in particular—then I will let the world present itself to me like a many-faceted gem, turning first one side, then another to me, as in the playful perceiving and conceptualizing that Maslow (1962) has called B-cognition. This aspect of transparency I can practice and perfect—instructors of art are good at teaching it to their pupils. It makes me a less selective and more broad-ranged perceiver of the world and my own being; it shatters, or forces me to revise, concepts; and it insures my unceasing personal growth. If I chronically conceptualize the world, I "freeze" it in only one of its infinite possibilities. It presents only one face to me and conceals all of its others. I can navigate in such a stabilized world, to be sure. Indeed, I must freeze it anew for each project I undertake.

[*] This chapter was first published as a chapter in S. M. Jourard, ed., *To Be or Not To Be: Existential-Psychological Perspectives on the Self*, University of Florida Press, Gainesville, Florida, 1967.

But I must also be ready to let the structure collapse, so that new possibilities can present themselves to me when the projects are consummated. It is useless to continue experiencing the world as a businessman might, when one has no business to transact. One does not look for opportunities to make a profit when one is on a battlefield, when the task in hand is to slay the enemy and stay alive oneself, not to see what can be bought cheap and sold for a profit.* The transparent mode is available as a free choice. Operationally, it is attained by adopting the set, "What is the being of the world *beyond* my present concepts of it?" Or, it is acquired by developing the habit of asking, ". . . and what else? . . .", after one has conceptualized oneself, another person, a tree—to remind ourselves that everything *is more than* our present description and concept of it.

The other, overtly *behavioral* pole of transparency is disclosure of oneself. This entails the resolve to let another person know one's being-for-oneself, so that *his* present concept of one's being will be duly shattered or revised. To disclose one's being before others, in good faith, is to insure that one aspect of *his* world—namely, yourself—will not be falsely constant and congealed in his concepts.

I disclose myself in many ways—in words, by my actions, gestures, and facial expressions, by my omissions—all these acts reveal my aims, my feelings and attitudes, my beliefs, my memories of the past. My aim, in disclosing myself is to be known, *to be perceived by the other as the one I know myself to be.* This is a project in its own right, and we can properly ask, "When will we seek to be thus known?"

My hypothesis is that we seek to have a true being in the experience of others under two conditions: when we experience it as *safe* thus to be known; and when we believe that vital values will be gained if we are known in our authentic being, or lost if we are not.

If we resolve to be known, incidentally, we simultaneously choose to experience the *other* as a *person* rather than as a concept and a manipulandum. If he is a person-for-us, and we are persons-for-him, there is no effort to predict or control action on either part. If we choose instead to misrepresent or conceal our being to him, then we are indeed reducing him in ontological status from person to a manipulable being— we are striving to manipulate his perception of us to some expedient range, and we are concealing our true being from him. Thus, to disclose oneself to another is the expression of one's granting to him and willing for him the status of a person with freedom, rather than the status of an object with an essence, with predictable and controllable behavior.

* Unless, of course, one is Milo Minderbinder, the enterprising officer in Joseph Heller's (1961) novel, *Catch 22.*

The decision to be transparent is free. The activity of self-disclosure, once undertaken, follows the principles of operant behavior, in that its structure is shaped by the reinforcers that are yielded as feedback. Thus, the form and content of my disclosure, once I have chosen to disclose myself, is affected by my experience of partial reinforcers that guide me, like signposts, to the goal I seek in commencing to disclose, namely evidence provided by the other that he is receiving and understanding my disclosure, and changing his concept of me accordingly.

It is my hypothesis that both modes of transparency are correlated in a person. A man who can let the world be what it is, letting it disclose its being to him as freely as it can, will prove thereby that he has attained the courage and security and self-esteem to cope with and to disclose himself into that world. We typically receive only as much of the world's disclosure as is relevant to our projects, and as much as we can contend with. Let more "world" in, and it is catastrophic, as for Kurt Goldstein's brain-injured patients, provincial people who encounter novelty, or LSD "acid heads" who suffer a bad trip. A man in the mode of transparency will let his own embodied being disclose itself to him, as in moments of meditative introspection, when he discovers that he is not right now the person he hitherto believed himself to be. Transparency, thus, is a multifaceted mode of being—it calls for a courage and a willingness to let the world be what it is, to let the other be who he is, and to let oneself be whom one is. It calls as well for a commitment to truth, as it changeably presents itself. It calls for a readiness to suspend concepts and beliefs about self, others, and world, and to perceive what is. It calls for a readiness to suspend imagination, wish, and fantasy, a readiness to inform and revise concepts with fresh inputs of perception. That it calls for courage to disclose oneself *to* the world is self-evident, since untrammeled self-disclosure is rare. It must seem a very dangerous and hostile world in which we live, since so few of us experience it as a place where we can be and disclose the truth of our being, and where we dare not let the other freely disclose his being to us.

We might wonder why people largely experience *semblance* as safer than disclosure. We live in social systems that are organized in particular ways in order to produce and distribute goods, and to preserve a certain class and power structure. The social, economic, and political facts of life require that we learn roles and restrict our public performances to the limits that the roles impose. Agencies of social control insure that we confine our revealed being to the range that is deemed sane, legal, and good. Indeed, we are socialized to believe that if we even think, feel, and wish beyond the role-defined ways, then we will experience ourselves as mad, criminal, and evil. We may be imprisoned, hospitalized, or ostracized if others learn that there is more to our experience than they presently see. Psychiatrists and psychologists most often collude with this view, and define as mentally ill those whose experience departs from the socially sanctioned patterns. But the separation of one's authentic being from one's public semblance can and does lead to drastic surprises, when the authentic being can no longer be repressed. It is my thesis that America is populated with millions of people who seek always *to seem* in a certain expedient way, and who experience all of their being that departs from the image as dreadful. As they conceal their truth from others, they succeed in concealing it from themselves. The toll of physical breakdown from stress and dispiritation, and the frequency of the so-called nervous breakdown is to me evidence that such an "all-American" way is unlivable, or is not worth the price. Indeed, the strictly role-defined way of being-with-others is related to our economic and productive base. As we become increasingly automated, the relevance of the upwardly mobile, role-conforming way will cease; socialization will have to aim toward a new image of man— one who can relate to his fellows, not on the basis of controlling their perceptions and concepts of him so as to grease his upward path to promotion, but rather on the basis of dialogue, with its attendant risks, delights, and unpredictability.*

I have been speaking about transparency as a way for man to be in his everyday life, and I have noted some of the consequences that can follow from it, in his everyday life in contrast to the way of semblance. But we psychologists are men, and though we study life, there is no necessary gulf between the study and the living of life. What will our psychology be like *if psychologists become transparent?*

We psychologists live significant portions of our lives in the laboratory, the field-observation and interviewing setting, and in the consulting room. It is in these settings that we make the observations of our fellows that culminate in our articles and books, which laymen read to get an informed image of man. Our psychology is a psychology that is profoundly affected by the social system in which we live, by the sources of funds for our research and salaries, and by the way we present ourselves to our subjects and patients. Here is a hypothesis that is too shattering in its impact, if it is true, to be overlooked: *Our way of doing psychology and being psychologists serves to maintain a socio-*

---

* See, in this connection, Thomas Hanna's (1970) new book, *Bodies in Revolt: A Primer in Somatic Thinking;* and James C. Brown's (1970) utopian novel, *The Troika Incident.* Both authors give readers a prophetic view of the 21st century.

economic and political status quo. It encourages an elite few to seek ever-new ways to manipulate and mystify the many; and it produces an image of the being of man that is false, or at best, only partially true, and unlikely to be corrected unless there is a change in psychology's orientation and psychologists' way of being.

The research psychologist, seeking properly to be objective, presents himself impersonally, as an unknown entity, to his subject. Rosenthal (1967) has shown with vigor and ingenuity that an experimenter does not simply let a subject be and disclose himself; rather, the experimenter appears to influence his subject such that he experiences a pressure to comply with the experimenter's expectations as he "behaves" in the laboratory. But consider also the fact that *a subject's behavior is a mode of self-disclosure, a way of encoding his experience and showing it to another person.* From our studies, it is clear that the role, personality, and way of being of the other person are the most powerful influences upon anyone's disclosure. Indeed, the most effective way to invite authentic disclosure from another is to take the risky lead and offer it oneself, first. Now consider the possibility that the thousands of subjects who have been the source of our psychology do not know, like, or trust the researcher, and do not feel safe enough to disclose themselves authentically in his presence. Nor do they feel that their values would be served or defended by such transparency. And consider the possibility that the subject's very experience of themselves—that which they do disclose—is powerfully affected by the way in which the experimenter appears in their world as the high-status stranger. And consider, finally, the possibility that increasing numbers of subjects may distrust the experimenter, seeing him as a kind of spy for big business and government—agencies which aim to regulate and control his conduct, and profit from his predictability. Would it be incredible, if many subjects simply lied, or misrepresented their experience through their behavior in the research setting?

We have described a series of studies (in Part II) showing that there is a difference in the outcome of a research when the experimenter makes himself more transparent, or less a predictable role-player than has been customary. It is possible that further research conducted in this way will yield an experimental psychology of authenticity, and a more authentic psychology.

The Next Chapter

Next chapter is the last. There I look back over Part II and reflect upon some of the implications I see in that research for further research and for theory.

25. Summary, Conclusions, and Implications

In the first part of this book I reported a series of exploratory studies employing self-disclosure questionnaires. The data obtained in this manner are no more valid than the willingness and ability of the subjects to be authentic in their efforts to comply with the instructions for completing the questionnaires. I believe that we obtained useful information from our subjects about typical patterns of self-disclosing behavior in everyday life.

But nearly every psychologist is discontented with self-report data. He itches to see the behavior in which he is interested at first hand, *in statu nascendi* in the laboratory. The assumption is that by having control over the conditions which he sets up, he will be in a better position to understand and explain the behavior in question. I share this view, which is why we brought self-disclosure into the laboratory— actually, into rather grubby rooms available to us as "research space," that were equipped with chairs, a table, and a tape recorder. But that is laboratory enough.

We were able to show (I think convincingly) that self-disclosure from one person is the most powerful stimulus to self-disclosure from the other. Actually, I prefer the word "invitation" to the term "stimulus," because we are not talking about animals but about people.

I am quite intrigued by the fact that the subjects in psychological research disclose more (*cf.* Drag, Jaffe, Friedman), and behave differently when they are involved with an experimenter who has first let himself be known in various respects. It seems to me that experimenters are part of the situation or world within which an experimental subject is invited to appear, and it makes perfect sense that he will experience his situation differently (and hence behave differently) in the presence of a transparent investigator. Miss Graham's demonstration that attitude toward one's death affects one's readiness to be fully present and self-disclosing to an experimenter opens up paths for explorations in a more "existential" psychology. And the fact that students learn more readily (Frey), perceive the experimenter differently (Rubin), and are responsive to his risk-taking efforts to reduce distance are findings that psychologists cannot ignore. Mrs. Jaffe's and Friedman's studies have direct implications for those who are engaged in psychotherapy, that art of inviting people to make themselves known in order to be helped toward more effective lives. Mrs. Resnick's study shows that people tend to "move" from a "low" to a more highly disclosing mode of relating when given an opportunity to do so. Finally, Kormann's and Heifitz's tantalizing demonstrations that people responding to psychological tests vary their responses as a function of how well they have gotten to know the investigator is a lead that should be followed by more psychometricians, especially since important decisions are often grounded on people's responses to psychological tests.

Epilogue

This book is neither text nor monograph. I see it more as a report to students and colleagues of what I have done with an idea from the time it occurred to me up to the present. Interestingly enough, none of the research was done with outside financial support. I failed "grantmanship." I reckon that somewhere around a half-million dollars worth of support that I asked for, from various granting agencies, was denied me. Perhaps this is as it should be, because there is no immediate practical payoff for the research we have done. Moreover, I was spared, once I gave up trying to justify my way of working to funding-agency referees, the agonies of periodic progress reports, reviewing sessions, and the like. In short, I was free to follow my whims and inclinations. There is no order, rhyme, or reason to the sequence in which the research was done. One finding triggered lines of thinking that generated another study and so on—what Wilse B. Webb (1969) calls, with appalling punmanship but essential truth, "a *couple* of experiments."

If I did not think self-disclosure was the most important thing in the world to study, I would not have carried on with the work as far as we carried it. Of course, every investigator believes that what he is devoting himself to is the most important topic under the sun. That too is as it should be. The real value of this work is not the findings which I have reported; they raise more questions than they answer. The work is best likened, I think, to that of a prospector who looks here and there for signs of pay dirt, so that more exhaustive and systematic mining operations can be undertaken. The growing bibliography attests that this view is not inappropriate.

It is no easy task to be a human being. Non-humans simply live out their more or less programmed existences. Man must invent himself and his world, ever anew, daily. He usually reinvents, from day to day, the same self and the same world that he did the day before. Discovery and actualization of new selves in new worlds is a slow and sometimes

187

painful, sometimes joyous and exciting business. Authentic self-disclosure is a way of letting others know of one's self and world, to see if they approve or disapprove—and to see if one likes or dislikes this self and world oneself. I hope this book encourages readers to study, and to engage in, the magnificent act of self-disclosure, that embodiment of the "courage to be."

In the way of transparency, psychologists have exciting new vistas of relevance for their know-how and commitment. As we more nearly enter the age of automation, our task as psychologists will be, not to make man more like an automaton for those who would control him; but rather to explore *our own* possibilities, as men, and to explore ways to help *all* men discover their own potentialities and to enlarge their freedom from the determiners that limit freedom, that scientific psychology already has discovered. I look to the time when psychologists will not be detached spectators and manipulators of other men's action and experience, but will instead seek to identify and to transcend barriers to fullest self-fulfillment. Their task as scientists and as men will be to disclose, in words and by living example, how to live freely, responsibly, and creatively in social systems that tend to prevent authentic existence.

Appendix 1†

Topics of the Sixty-Item Self-Disclosure Questionnaire*

Attitudes and opinions

1. What I think and feel about religion; my personal religious views.
2. My personal opinions and feelings about other religious groups than my own, e.g., Protestants, Catholics, Jews, atheists.
3. My views on communism.
4. My views on the present government—the president, government policies, etc.
5. My views on the question of racial integration in schools, transportation, etc.
6. My personal views on drinking.
7. My personal views on sexual morality—how I feel that I and others ought to behave in sexual matters.
8. My personal standards of beauty and attractiveness in women—what I consider to be attractive in a woman.
9. The things that I regard as desirable for a man to be—what I look for in a man.
10. My feelings about how parents ought to deal with children.

Tastes and interests

1. My favorite foods, the ways I like food prepared, and my food dislikes.
2. My favorite beverages, and the ones I don't like.
3. My likes and dislikes in music.
4. My favorite reading matter.
5. The kinds of movies that I like to see best; the TV shows that are my favorites.
6. My tastes in clothing.
7. The style of house, and the kinds of furnishings that I like best.
8. The kind of party, or social gathering that I like best, and the kind that would bore me, or that I wouldn't enjoy.
9. My favorite ways of spending spare time, e.g., hunting, reading, cards, sports events, parties, dancing, etc.
10. What I would appreciate most for a present.

---

† *Note.* The questionnaires shown in the appendices were developed for the studies reported in this book. They may be used or modified by researchers without written permission.

* See Chapter 1 for instructions to subjects.

Work (or studies)

1. What I find to be the worst pressures and strains in my work.
2. What I find to be the most boring and unenjoyable aspects of my work.
3. What I enjoy most, and get the most satisfaction from in my present work.
4. What I feel are *my* shortcomings and handicaps that prevent me from working as I'd like to, or that prevent me from getting further ahead in my work.
5. What I feel are my special strong points and qualifications for my work.
6. How I feel that my work is appreciated by others (e.g., boss, fellow-workers, teacher, husband, etc.)
7. My ambitions and goals in my work.
8. My feelings about the salary or rewards that I get for my work.
9. How I feel about the choice of career that I have made—whether or not I'm satisfied with it.
10. How I really feel about the people that I work for, or work with.

Money

1. How much money I make at my work, or get as an allowance.
2. Whether or not I owe money; if so, *how much.*
3. Whom I owe money to at present; or whom I have borrowed from in the past.
4. Whether or not I have savings, and the amount.
5. Whether or not others owe me money; the amount, and who owes it to me.
6. Whether or not I gamble; if so, the way I gamble, and the extent of it.
7. All of my present sources or income—wages, fees, allowance, dividends, etc.
8. My total financial worth, including property, savings, bonds, insurance, etc.
9. My most pressing need for money right now, e.g., outstanding bills, some major purchase that is desired or needed.
10. How I budget my money—the proportion that goes to necessities, luxuries, etc.

Personality

1. The aspects of my personality that I dislike, worry about, that I regard as a handicap to me.
2. What feelings, if any, that I have trouble expressing or controlling.
3. The facts of my present sex life—including knowledge of how I get sexual gratification; any problems that I might have, with whom I have relations, if anybody.
4. Whether or not I feel that I am attractive to the opposite sex; my problems, if any, about getting favorable attention from the opposite sex.
5. Things in the past or present that I feel ashamed and guilty about.
6. The kinds of things that just make me furious.
7. What it takes to get me feeling real depressed and blue.
8. What it takes to get me real worried, anxious, and afraid.
9. What it takes to hurt my feelings deeply.
10. The kinds of things that make me especially proud of myself, elated, full of self-esteem or self-respect.

Body

1. My feelings about the appearance of my face—things I don't like, and things that I might like about my face and head—nose, eyes, hair, teeth, etc.
2. How I wish I looked: my ideals for overall appearance.
3. My feelings about different parts of my body—legs, hips, waist, weight, chest, or bust, etc.
4. Any problems and worries that I had with my appearance in the past.
5. Whether or not I now have any health problems—e.g., trouble with sleep, digestion, female complaints, heart condition, allergies, headaches, piles, etc.
6. Whether or not I have any long-range worries or concerns about my health, e.g., cancer, ulcers, heart trouble.
7. My past record of illness and treatment.
8. Whether or not I now make special efforts to keep fit, healthy, and attractive, e.g., calisthenics, diet.
9. My present physical measurements, e.g., height, weight, waist, etc.
10. My feelings about my adequacy in sexual behavior—whether or not I feel able to perform adequately in sex-relationships.

Appendix 2

The Parent-Cathexis Questionnaire

Below are listed a number of things characteristic of your mother and your father. Consider each item listed and encircle the number after each item which best represents your feelings toward that trait of your parent according to the following scale:

1: Have Strong Positive Feelings.
   Encircle a 1 for those aspects of the parent about which you feel proud or happy or which give you a pleasant feeling when you think about them. For example, if you feel happy about your mother's intelligence level, encircle the 1 after that item.
2: Have Moderate Positive Feelings.
   Encircle a 2 for those aspects of the parent about which you have some positive feeling but not as strong as that in category 1.
3: Have No Feeling One Way or the Other.
   Encircle a 3 for those aspects of the parent about which you have no feeling at all. For example, if you have no feeling at all about your mother's artistic talents (or lack of them) encircle the 3 after that item.
4: Have Moderate Negative Feelings.
   Encircle a 4 for those aspects of the parent about which you have some negative feeling but not as strong as that in category 5 (see below).
5: Have Strong Negative Feelings.
   Encircle a 5 for those aspects of the parent which you dislike very much or which cause you to feel unhappy when you think about them. For example, if you think that your mother is intolerant and this disturbs you when you think about it, or if you feel unhappy about this trait in your mother, encircle the 5 after that item.

Attitudes toward Mother (Father)
[check which parent you are rating]

1: Have strong positive feelings
2: Have moderate positive feelings
3: Have no feeling one way or the other
4: Have moderate negative feelings
5: Have strong negative feelings

Sense of humor 1 2 3 4 5
Degree of independence 1 2 3 4 5
Temper 1 2 3 4 5
Ability to express self 1 2 3 4 5
Self-understanding 1 2 3 4 5
Artistic talents 1 2 3 4 5
Tolerance of other's
  shortcomings 1 2 3 4 5
Moods 1 2 3 4 5
Extent of general knowledge 1 2 3 4 5
Imagination 1 2 3 4 5
Degree of popularity 1 2 3 4 5
Self-confidence 1 2 3 4 5
Ability to accept criticism 1 2 3 4 5
Memory 1 2 3 4 5
Thriftiness 1 2 3 4 5
Overall personality 1 2 3 4 5
Ability to concentrate 1 2 3 4 5
Procrastination 1 2 3 4 5
Degree of self-assertiveness 1 2 3 4 5
Ability to express sympathy 1 2 3 4 5
Sensitivity to others' feelings 1 2 3 4 5

Ability to lead 1 2 3 4 5
Ability to control impulses 1 2 3 4 5
Intelligence level 1 2 3 4 5
Athletic skills 1 2 3 4 5
Present degree of happiness 1 2 3 4 5
Creativeness 1 2 3 4 5
Love life at present 1 2 3 4 5
Sex appeal 1 2 3 4 5
Skill with hands 1 2 3 4 5
Gracefulness 1 2 3 4 5
Amount that he (she)
  worries 1 2 3 4 5
Capacity for work 1 2 3 4 5
Ability to discipline self 1 2 3 4 5
Vocabulary 1 2 3 4 5
Ability to discipline self 1 2 3 4 5
Degree of suggestibility 1 2 3 4 5
Present strength of will
  power 1 2 3 4 5
Ability to make decisions 1 2 3 4 5
Degree of self-consciousness 1 2 3 4 5

Appendix 3

Fifteen Disclosure Topics Used in Study of Nursing Faculty and Graduate Students in Psychology

1. When you were an undergraduate, did you participate in any extracurricular activities, e.g., clubs, dramatics, sports, etc.?
2. In what town were you born?
3. Have you ever gone steady or been engaged? If so, what was her (their) name(s)? OR In what year were you married?
4. Do you have any brothers or sisters? How many of each?
5. Do you have a main hobby or interest(s) outside of school? What?
6. What physical malady(ies) bother you at present, recurrently (if any)?
7. What characteristics of yourself bother you most?
8. Do you go to any church in town?
9. What aspect(s) of your physical appearance do you regard as your chief problem, that you dislike most, that you wish you could change or improve?
10. What is the name of the teacher whom you count as outstanding and most influential during your training?
11. Are there any sports you engage in at present or when there is an opportunity?
12. Is there any food or dish that you especially dislike?
13. With which faculty member do you find it most difficult to get along?
14. What is your usual monthly income (within $25)?
15. What is or was your father's chief occupation?

Appendix 4

The Forty-Item Self-Disclosure Questionnaire

Who Knows You?

Introduction

People differ in the extent to which they let other people know them. We are seeking to investigate what people tell others about themselves.

Naturally, the things that are true about your personality, your feelings, your problems, hopes and actions will change as you get on with living. Therefore, the idea that other people have about you will be out of date from time to time. What was true about you last week or last year may no longer be true. When you see people after a lapse of time, and you want them to know you as you now are, you tell them about yourself so that they will have a more up-to-date picture of you. If you don't want them to know, you don't tell them, even if they ask you personal questions.

Some of the things about yourself you will regard as more personal and private than others; people differ widely in what they consider appropriate to let others know, and what they consider is nobody's business but their own.

Instructions

Below there is a list of topics that pertain to you. You have also been given a special answer sheet. We want you to indicate on the answer sheet the degree to which you have let each of several people in your life know this information about you.

You have a reasonably good idea of how much about yourself you have let each of the people know about you in the past, and how current and up-to-date their knowledge about you is at the present.

Therefore, will you indicate on the answer sheet the extent to which each of the other persons *now* knows the pertinent facts about you. In other words, how complete, up-to-date, and accurate is their picture of you as you are now. Use the following scale to indicate your answers:

O: The other person *doesn't know me* in this respect right now, because I haven't told him, or let him know in any other ways.

1: The other person *has a general idea* of how I am now, of what is true in this respect, but his idea of me is not complete, or up-to-date.

2: The other person *fully knows me* as I now am in this respect, because I have talked about this topic to him fully in the recent past, and things have not changed. I have kept him fully informed about this aspect of me.

X: Write in an X instead of an O for those items which you *would not confide to the person* even if that person asked you to reveal the information.

1. What you dislike about your overall appearance.
2. The things about your appearance that you like most, or are proudest of.
3. Your chief health concern, worry, or problem, at the present time.
4. Your favorite spare-time hobbies or interests.
5. Your food dislikes at present.
6. Your religious activity at present—whether or not you go to church; which one; how often.
7. Your personal religious views.
8. Your favorite reading materials—kinds of magazines, books, or papers you usually read.
9. What particularly annoys you most about your closest friend of the opposite sex or (if married) your spouse.
10. Whether or not you have sex problems, and the nature of these problems, if any.
11. An accurate knowledge of your sex life up to the present—e.g., the names of your sex partners in the past and present, if any; your ways of getting sexual gratification.
12. Things about your own personality that worry you or annoy you.
13. The chief pressures and strains in your daily work.
14. Things about the future that you worry about at present.
15. What you are most sensitive about.
16. What you feel the guiltiest about, or most ashamed of in your past.
17. Your views about what is acceptable sex morality for people to follow.
18. The kinds of music you enjoy listening to the most.
19. The subjects you did not, or do not like at school.
20. Whether or not you do anything special to maintain or improve your appearance, e.g., diet, exercise, etc.
21. The kind of behavior in others that most annoys you, or makes you furious.
22. The characteristics of your father that you do not like, or did not like.
23. Characteristics of your mother that you do not like, or did not like.
24. Your most frequent daydream—what you daydream about most.
25. The feelings you have the most trouble controlling, e.g., worry, depression, anger, jealousy, etc.
26. The biggest disappointment that you have had in your life.
27. How you feel about your choice of life work.
28. What you regard as your chief handicaps to doing a better job in your work or studies.
29. Your views on the segregation of whites and Negroes.
30. Your thoughts and feelings about other religious groups than your own.
31. Your strongest ambition at the present time.
32. Whether or not you have planned some major decision in the near future, e.g., a new job, break engagement, get married, divorce, buy something big.
33. Your favorite jokes—the kind of jokes you like to hear.

34. Whether or not you have savings; if so, the amount.
35. The possessions you are proudest of, and take greatest care of, e.g., your car, or musical instrument, or furniture, etc.
36. How you usually sleep, e.g., well, or poorly, or with help of drugs.
37. Your favorite television programs.
38. Your favorite comics.
39. The groups or clubs or organizations you belong to, e.g., fraternity, lodge, bridge club, YMCA, professional organizations, etc.
40. The beverages you do not like to drink, e.g., coffee, tea, coke, beer, liquor, etc., and your *preferred* beverages.

Answer Sheet

Male or Female:_____

Birthdate: _____ Age:_____
　　　　Month　Day　Year

Marital Status　S　M　D　W

Home Town_____

Father's Occupation:_____

Father's Education:_____

Father's Income (Approx.)_____

Mother's Occupation:_____

Mother's Education: _____

Your Major Course: _____

Your Year in College: _____

	Mother	Father	Male Friend	Female Friend	Spouse		Mother	Father	Male Friend	Female Friend	Spouse
1.						21.					
2.						22.					
3.						23.					
4.						24.					
5.						25.					
6.						26.					
7.						27.					
8.						28.					
9.						29.					
10.						30.					
11.						31.					
12.						32.					
13.						33.					
14.						34.					
15.						35.					
16.						36.					
17.						37.					
18.						38.					
19.						39.					
20.						40.					

Appendix 5

The Twenty-Five-Item Self-Disclosure Questionnaire

Instructions

On the following page there is listed a number of items of information about oneself.

You are asked to indicate on the special answer sheet the extent to which certain other people know this information about you through your telling it or confiding it to them.

If you are certain that the other person knows this information fully—so that he or she could tell someone else about this aspect of you—write the number *1* in the appropriate space. If the other person does not know this information fully—if he or she has only a vague idea, or has an incomplete knowledge of this particular item, write in a zero.

Remember, do not write in a *1* unless you are sure that you have given this information to the other person in full enough detail, that they could describe you accurately in this respect to another person.

Information about Oneself*

1. What you like to do most in your spare time at home, e.g., read, sports, go out, etc.
2. The kind of party or social gathering that you enjoy most.
3. Your usual and favorite spare-time reading material, e.g., novels, non-fiction, science fiction, poetry, etc.
4. The kinds of music that you enjoy listening to most, e.g., popular, classical, folk-music, opera.
5. The sports you engage in most, if any, e.g., golf, swimming, tennis, baseball, etc.
6. Whether or not you know and play any card games, e.g., bridge, poker, gin rummy, etc.
7. Whether or not you will drink alcoholic beverages; if so, your favorite drinks—beer, wine, gin, brandy, whiskey, etc.

8. The foods you like best, and the ways you like food prepared; e.g., rare steak, etc.
9. Whether or not you belong to any church; if so, which one, and the usual frequency of attending.
10. Whether or not you belong to any clubs, fraternity, civic organizations; if so, the names of these organizations.
11. Any skills you have mastered, e.g., arts and crafts, painting, sculpture, wood-working, auto repair, knitting, weaving, etc.
12. Whether or not you have any favorite spectator sports; if so, what these are, e.g., boxing, wrestling, football, basketball, etc.
13. The places that you have travelled to, or lived in during your life—other countries, cities, states.
14. What your political sentiments are at present—your views on state and federal government policies of interest to you.
15. Whether or not you have been seriously in love during your life before this year; if so, with whom, what the details were, and the outcome.
16. The names of the people in your life whose care and happiness you feel in some way directly responsible for.
17. The personal deficiencies that you would most like to improve, or that you are struggling to do something about at present, e.g., appearance, lack of knowl-edge, loneliness, temper, etc.
18. Whether or not you presently owe money; if so, how much, and to whom?
19. The kind of future you are aiming toward, working for, planning for—both personally and vocationally, e.g., marriage and family, professional status, etc.
20. Whether or not you are now involved in any projects that you would not want to interrupt at present—either socially, personally, or in your work; what these projects are.
21. The details of your sex life up to the present time, including whether or not you have had, or are now having sexual relations, whether or not you masturbate, etc.
22. Your problems and worries about your personality, that is, what you dislike most about yourself, any guilts, inferiority feelings, etc.
23. How you feel about the appearance of your body—your looks, figure, weight— what you dislike and what you accept in your appearance, and how you wish you might change your looks to improve them.
24. Your thoughts about your health, including any problems, worries, or concerns that you might have at present.
25. An exact idea of your regular income. (If a student, of your usual combined allowance and earnings, if any.)

---

* Odd-even reliability coefficient, over all items and 4 target persons = .93 with N = 50 male, 50 female college students.

Appendix 6

Self-Disclosure Topics for Children Aged
6 to 12

1. Spare time—What kinds of things do you like to do in your spare time when you are by yourself? Have you told your best friend about this? Has he told you what he likes to do in his spare time when he is by himself?
2. Church—Do you go to church? Do you like to go to church? Have you told your best friend about this? Has he told you if he goes to church?
3. Reading—What do you like to read most? What kinds of books do you read? Have you told your best friend about this? Has he told you what he likes to read?
4. Opposite-sex friend—Do you have a girlfriend (boyfriend)? Have you told your best friend about her (him)? Has your best friend told you if he has a girlfriend?
5. Self—What do you not like about yourself? Have you told your best friend this? Has he told you what he doesn't like about himself?
6. Happy times—What are the happiest times you have had? Have you told your best friend about this? Has he told you about his happiest times?
7. Unhappy times—What are the unhappiest times you have had? Have you told your best friend about this? Has he told you about his unhappy times?
8. Favorite sports—What are your favorite sports? Have you told your best friend? Has he told you what his favorite sports are?
9. Parents—What do you like about your parents? Have you told your best friend? Has he told you what he likes about his parents?
10. Television—What are your favorite television shows? Have you told your best friend? Has he told you what his favorite television shows are?
11. Money—Where do you get your money? Have you told your best friend about this? Has he told you where he gets his money?
12. Chores—What do you have to do around the house? Have you told your best friend? Has he told you what he has to do around the house?
13. Bedtime—What time do you go to bed at night? Have you told your best friend? Has he told you what time he goes to bed?
14. Ambition—What do you want to be when you grow up? Have you told your best friend about this? Has he told you what he wants to be when he grows up?
15. Punishment: Why—What do your parents punish you for? Have you told your best friend? Has he told you what his parents punish him for?

16. Punishment: How—How do your parents punish you? Have you told your best friend about this? Has he told you how his parents punish him?
17. Fright—What are you most afraid of? Have you told your best friend about this? Has he told you what he is most afraid of?
18. Appearance: Like—What do you like about the way you look? Have you told your best friend? Has he told you what he likes about the way he looks?
19. Appearance: Dislike—What do you not like about the way you look? Have you told your best friend this? Has he told you what he doesn't like about the way he looks?
20. Subjects: Best—What subjects at school are you best at? Have you told your best friend this? Has he told you what his best subjects are?
21. Subjects: Worst—What subjects at school are you worse at? Have you told your best friend this? Has he told you what his worst subjects are?
22. Abilities: Best—What things outside of school are you best at? Have you told your best friend this? Has he told you what things he is best at?
23. Abilities: Worst—What things outside of school are you bad at? Have you told your best friend this? Has he told you what things he is bad at?
24. Food—What food do you not like? Have you told your best friend this? Has he told you what food he dislikes?
25. Teacher—What teacher do you like best? Have you told your best friend this? Has he told you what teacher he likes best?

Appendix 7

Protestant Religious Behavior Scale*†

Below is a seven-point rating scale dealing with amount of religious behavior, and frequency of participation in religious activities. Please describe yourself as you see yourself and respond to the items as if you were describing yourself to yourself. Read each statement carefully; then mark one of the responses underneath it. Remember, you are not trying to describe yourself as others see you, but only as you see yourself. All information will be strictly confidential. Do not sign your name.

1. I have discussed my religion, or matters pertaining to my religion, such as morality or the existence of God with my friends or relatives.

   yearly   monthly   several   weekly   several   daily   several
       or   times   times   times
      less   monthly   weekly   daily

2. I now participate, or have participated in the past, in church activities, such as social organizations or religious education groups.

   always   usually   very often   often   occasionally   seldom   never

3. When listening to a sermon, either at Church or over the radio, I pay attention to the speaker's words.

   never   seldom   occasionally   often   very often   usually   always

4. I now attend Church services.

   several   weekly   several   monthly   several   yearly   never
   times   times   times
   weekly   monthly   yearly

   Please be as honest and as objective as possible.

5. I recognize the tune of, or know most of the words to, approximately this many religious hymns sung at my church.

   0–5   5–10   10–15   15–20   20–25   25–30   30–35

6. I am familiar with the words and music, and try to participate in the singing of religious music sung in my church.

   always   usually   very often   often   occasionally   seldom   never

7. Whenever I do attend Church, I either carry my own hymnbooks, Bible, or prayerbooks with me, or else I use the ones provided.

   never   seldom   occasionally   often   very often   usually   always

8. I meditate, or think, for a period of time about specific religious topics.

   yearly   monthly   several   weekly   several   daily   several
   or   times   times   times
   less   monthly   weekly   daily

   Please be as honest and as accurate as possible.

9. I pray to thank God for favors received, or to ask Him for help approximately this often.

   several   daily   several   weekly   several   monthly   yearly
   times   times   times   or
   daily   weekly   monthly   less

10. I use the Ten Commandments, or my Church's standards of conduct in guiding my important ethical decisions.

    always   usually   very often   often   occasionally   seldom   never

11. I read the Bible, or other religious works by Christian leaders approximately this often.

    yearly   monthly   several   weekly   several   daily   several
    or   times   times   times
    less   monthly   weekly   daily

12. I own or possess, either here or at home, approximately this many books dealing with religion. This includes hymnbooks, prayerbooks, and Bibles, as well as books written by religious leaders.

    6 or more   5   4   3   2   1   0

13. I read religious magazines, newspapers, and church bulletins.

    never   yearly   several   monthly   several   weekly   several
            or   times   times   times
            less   yearly   monthly   weekly

14. I contribute approximately this amount of money to the usual Sunday collection.

    .00–.10   .10–.25   25–.50   .50–.75   .75–1.00   1.00–2.00   2.00–5.00

---

* Developed by Dr. Terence E. Cooke in 1961.
† Odd-even reliability coefficient = .90. Each item correlates with total score as follows, from item 1 to 14, respectively: .49, .75, .58, .80, .72, .74, .62, .70, .65, .69, .70, .63, .72, .41, with $N = 100$.

Appendix 8

A Forty-Item Self-Disclosure
Questionnaire with Topics Rated for
Intimacy Value

A Study of Confiding

Instructions[*]

You have been given a list of 40 questions asking for personal information about yourself. On the answer sheet, you will see two rule columns, A and B. A has the heading "I have revealed information about this item to someone in my past." B column has the heading "Willing to disclose information about this item to a same-sex stranger on a first encounter." *You are requested to indicate how much information about each question you have told someone in your past and how much you would be willing to disclose to a stranger of the same sex that you have just met.*

Write in a 0 in column A on each question if you know you have never talked about that item to another person.

Write in a 0 in column B on each question if you would be unwilling to talk about that item to a same-sex stranger.

Write in a 1 in column A on each question if you have talked in general terms about that item, but not in full detail. Another person has been given only a general idea about that particular side of you.

Write in a 1 in column B if you would be willing to talk in general terms about a given question to a stranger of the same sex.

Write in a 2 in column A only if you know that you have talked fully to another person about that particular question. Use a 2 only for those topics where you know that another person has full and accurate information about you because you have taken the trouble to confide fully.

Write in a 2 in column B only on those questions which you would be willing to confide completely to a stranger.

[*] Instructions used for selection of subjects in Phase One.

For example: If you have never told anyone how you feel about your overall appearance, you would write in a *0* in Column A. If you have told someone that you are more or less satisfied or dissatisfied with your looks, but have never confided more, you would write in a *1* in Column A. You would only write in a *2* if you had talked about your appearance to someone in full detail, something like this: "I like my face, but I'm not satisfied with the way my teeth look. I think I'm about 10 pounds overweight. My feet are too big." The same procedure would hold for column B depending upon how deeply you would be willing to confide this same information to a stranger.

Questionnaire

1. If someone sent you a bouquet of flowers, what kind would you like? (L)*
2. What do you dislike the most about having a complete physical examination? (H)
3. How do you feel about engaging in sex activities prior to, or outside of marriage? (H)
4. With whom have you discussed your sexual experiences? (H)
5. What are your favorite spare-time hobbies or interests? (L)
6. What do you feel the guiltiest about, or most ashamed of in your past? (H)
7. How many brothers and sisters do you have? (L)
8. What movies have you seen lately? (L)
9. What are your favorite subjects in school? (L)
10. What questions in the area of sex are you most curious to know about? (H)
11. What are your favorite colors? (L)
12. With how many boys have you "petted" in the last year? (H)
13. How can you tell when you are getting sexually aroused? (H)
14. On what parts of your body have you been kissed? (H)
15. What age do you think a President of the United States should be? (L)
16. What type of foods do you enjoy the most? (L)
17. What thoughts have you had that repulse you? (H)
18. What techniques of sex play do you know of? (H)
19. What type of reading material do you enjoy the most? (L)
20. What are your feelings about masturbation? (H)
21. What foods do you feel are best for your health? (L)
22. In what ways do you think various members of your family may be "maladjusted"? (H)
23. Where would you like to go on a trip? (L)
24. What kind of furniture would you like to have after you are married? (L)
25. How many colds do you usually have per year? (L)
26. What are your favorite sports? (L)
27. How do you feel about your love life? (H)
28. Would you like to travel and see what part of the country? (L)
29. What kinds of group activities do you usually enjoy? (L)
30. How tall do you like men to be? (L)

* Note: Items designated (H) are of high-rated intimacy, while those marked (L) are of low intimacy

31. How frequently do you like to engage in sexual activities? (H)
32. What schools have you attended? (L)
33. What are the persons like with whom you have had some type of sexual experience? (H)
34. How important do you feel education is to a person? (L)
35. How do you feel if someone sees you naked? (H)
36. How do you feel about having members of the opposite sex touch you? (H)
37. How do you feel about having members of the same sex touch you? (H)
38. Which movie or TV entertainers do you like the most? (L)
39. Which (if either or both) of your parents do you think might have had pre-marital sexual relations? (H)
40. What do you think makes a book a best-seller? (L)

Answer Sheet

Name_____Age_____Today's Date_____

Marital Status: S M D W   Your Year in College_____Major_____

	A	B		A	B
	I have revealed information to someone in my past	Willing to disclose to a same-sex stranger on a first encounter		I have revealed information to someone in my past	Willing to disclose to a same-sex stranger on a first encounter
1.			21.		
2.			22.		
3.			23.		
4.			24.		
5.			25.		
6.			26.		
7.			27.		
8.			28.		
9.			29.		
10.			30.		
11.			31.		
12.			32.		
13.			33.		
14.			34.		
15.			35.		
16.			36.		
17.			37.		
18.			38.		
19.			39.		
20.			40.		

Appendix 9

The Game of "Invitations"

You are already familiar with the rules for playing "Invitations"—it is a game of questions through which you identify yourself to other people, who in turn may or may not identify themselves to you.

Whenever you want to claim something at the post office, or cash a check, or open a charge account, you are "invited" to produce a driver's license, a passport, or a birth certificate, which usually gives certain information about yourself, e.g., name, address, date of birth, and other physical characteristics. When you do this you have entered into the spirit of "Invitations" with another person who has asked the question, "Who are you?" When the game is played at this level, however, you do not have to answer questions about who you are as a person.

At other levels, the game may be played with a perfect stranger on a plane, or in a bus, with a close friend or an acquaintance, with a husband or a member of your immediate family. And the set of rules by which it is played probably varies with each relationship.

Basically, the game of "Invitations" as you have probably guessed, involves the process of making ourselves known to other people and in turn getting to know who they are; the rules we use are generally based on our readiness to confide personal information to others.

By now, you have probably formulated some opinions about the person who will be your partner in playing the game. Based on what information you have about the other, you should be able to formulate certain rules for playing the game, which is as follows:

Directions

Both you and your partner have received a list of 40 questions varying in their degree of personal intimacy. When the game begins, both you and your partner will have selected 5 questions to ask of each other from this list. *The only firm rule in playing the game is that you may not ask your partner a question which you, yourself, are not willing to answer.* Otherwise, you are on your own and may explore the question at any level of intimacy you choose, until one of the players declines an "invitation" to disclose further information. At this point you should move on to another question.

Your score sheet for the game should be partially filled our *before* you begin to play. For each question indicate how much information you, yourself, would be willing to tell your partner. Mark each question on your score sheet as follows:

Mark a *O* for each question you would be unwilling to talk about with your partner.

Mark a *1* if you would be willing to talk about that question in general terms with your partner, but would not be willing to reveal any extremely personal information about yourself.

Mark a *2* only on those questions which you would be willing to confide completely and very personally to your partner.

Notice on the right-hand side of your score sheet a section marked (1) Questions I intend to ask my partner. As you initially go through the questions to score them as to your willingness to confide in your partner, *select 5 questions to ask your partner. Remember in selecting these 5 questions, that you are only to select those which you, yourself, are willing to talk about.* For your own reference, write the *numbers* of the 5 questions you intend to ask your partner in the space provided.

Notice on the right-hand side of your score sheet there is also a section marked (2) My Invitation was Refused by the other Person. When the Game actually begins, mark those questions on which your "invitation" to disclose was refused by your partner.

If your partner is willing to accept your invitation, after she has answered your question, you will also answer that question.

When to Accept or Decline an "Invitation"

In playing the game, you should try and feel as you might when attending a dance. Just as you feel no need to explain why you prefer not to dance with certain people, e.g., you do not like them, you do not want to be that close to them, you perhaps do not know the particular steps, etc., there is likewise no need to explain why you refuse an invitation to talk about yourself on a given question. The reasons why people decline invitations are many, e.g., they believe the question to be of too intimate a nature to discuss with a given individual; they believe the question is in poor taste; the question does not hold any interest for them, etc. Therefore, you should not feel embarrassed or in any way uncomfortable, if you do not wish to answer a question your partner may ask. Simply say, "I decline," and you both will move on to another question.

Final word . . .

> *Remember you are to select 5 questions to ask your partner which you, yourself, are willing to answer.*

Score Sheet

Name_____   Partner's Name_____

My Willingness To Disclose
_____

1. _____	21. _____
2. _____	22. _____
3. _____	23. _____
4. _____	24. _____
5. _____	25. _____
6. _____	26. _____
7. _____	27. _____
8. _____	28. _____
9. _____	29. _____
10. _____	30. _____
11. _____	31. _____
12. _____	32. _____
13. _____	33. _____
14. _____	34. _____
15. _____	35. _____
16. _____	36. _____
17. _____	37. _____
18. _____	38. _____
19. _____	39. _____
20. _____	40. _____

(1)	(2)
Questions I Intend To Ask My Partner	My Invitation Was Refused By The Other Person
1. _____	_____
2. _____	_____
3. _____	_____
4. _____	_____
5. _____	_____

Appendix 10

Measure of Subjects' Trust of Experimenter

Interview Rating Scale

Experiment: _____   Date: _____

Name: _____   Partner's Name: _____

Put a circle around each of the phrases (1 through 15) that best describes your experience with the person you have just met.

1. felt at ease   felt tense, anxious

2. felt that I made myself known to the   did not feel that I made myself known to
   other person   the other person

3. bored by other person   interested by other person

4. held back a lot, and was careful of   talked fully and freely
   what I revealed

5. liked the other person   disliked the other person

6. felt the other person was interested   felt the other person was not very inter-
   in me   ested in me

7. the other person was good at inter-   felt the other person was not very good at
   viewing and drawing me out   interviewing and drawing me out

8. wouldn't want to interact with the   would want to interact with the other
   other person again   person again

9. didn't mind the tape recorder   was bothered by the tape recorder

10. felt the other person could describe   did not feel the other person could de-
    me effectively to a third party   scribe me effectively to a third party

11. felt the other person was a good listener

did not feel the other person was a good listener

12. felt the other person made herself known to me

did not feel the other person made herself known to me

13. did not feel the other person could be trusted

felt like the other person could be trusted

14. would like to have the other person as a close friend

would not like to have the other person as a close friend

15. felt like the other person was judging me

did not feel like the other person was judging me

Appendix 11

Twenty Self-Disclosure Topics Rated for Intimacy Value*

1. The types of play and recreation I enjoy. — 1.01 (L)
2. Characteristics of my parents that I dislike. — 3.43 (H)
3. The things in my past or present life about which I am most ashamed. — 4.01 (H)
4. The type of literature that interests me the most. — 1.02 (L)
5. The aspects of my body that I am most satisfied or dissatisfied with. — 3.50 (H)
6. The amount and kind of primping I do. — 1.97 (L)
7. The extent of traveling I have done and hope to do. — 1.06 (L)
8. Radio and TV programs that interest me. — 1.01 (L)
9. Disappointments I have experienced with the opposite sex. — 3.40 (H)
10. How I react to other's criticism and praise of me. What are the things they criticize and praise in me? — 3.20 (H)
11. How often I have sexual experiences and the nature of these experiences. — 4.31 (H)
12. The kind of person with whom I would like to have sexual experiences. — 3.73 (H)
13. Places where I would like to work and live. — 1.07 (L)
14. My general reaction to a charming, flirtatious male. — 2.00 (L)
15. My opinion on foreign aid to pro-Communist countries. — 1.21 (L)
16. The most crucial decisions I have had to make.
17. The aspects of my personality that I dislike, worry about, or regard as a handicap to me. — 3.34 (H)
18. Feelings about my sexual adequacy. — 3.70 (H)
19. My opinion on marrying for money. — 1.57 (L)
20. The subjects I enjoy studying the most. — 1.03 (L)

---

* Numbers signify mean intimacy value, and letters (H, L) high and low intimacy value. These ratings were done by 80 female college students. The median (2.60) was used as the dividing point between high and low intimacy ratings.

Appendix 12

Twenty-One Self-Disclosure Questions Rated for Intimacy Value*

(1.)† What are your views on the way a husband and wife should live their marriage? 4.30 (L)

2. What are your usual ways of dealing with depression, anxiety and anger? 3.74 (M)

(3.) What are the actions you have most regretted doing in your life and why? 3.10 (H)

(4.) What are your personal religious views and the nature of your religious participation if any? 4.41 (L)

5. What are the ways in which you feel you are most maladjusted or immature? 3.30 (M)

(6.) What are your guiltiest secrets? 2.38 (H)

7. What are your personal views on politics, the presidency, foreign and domestic policy? 4.64 (L)

8. What are the habits and reactions of yours which bother you at present? 3.77 (M)

9. What are the sources of strain and dissatisfaction in your marriage (or your relationship with the opposite sex)? 3.16 (H)

(10.) What are your favorite forms of erotic play and sexual lovemaking? 2.56 (H)

(11.) What are your hobbies, how do you best like to spend your spare time? 4.98 (L)

12. What were the occasions in your life in which you were the happiest? 3.93 (M)

13. What are the aspects of your daily work that satisfy and bother you? 4.53 (L)

14. What characteristics of yourself give you cause for pride and satisfaction? 3.56 (M)

15. Who are the persons in your life whom you most resent; why? 3.16 (H)

16. Who are the people with whom you have been sexually intimate. What were the circumstances of your relationship with each? 2.21 (H)

17. What are the unhappiest moments in your life; why? 3.38 (M)

(18.) What are your preferences and dislikes in music? 4.92 (L)

19. What are your personal goals for the next 10 years or so? 4.39 (L)

20. What are the circumstances under which you become depressed and when your feelings are hurt? 3.51 (M)

(21.) What are your most common sexual fantasies and reveries? 2.56 (H)

---

* Numbers signify mean intimacy value, letters (H, M, L) signify high, medium and low intimacy value. Ratings conducted by 30 male and 30 female college students.

† The circled items are the 8 topics employed in Friedman's second experiment (Chapter 19).

Appendix 13

Haymes* (1969) Technique for Measuring Self-Disclosure from Tape-Recorded Interviews

Code and Scoring Manual for Self-Disclosure

Self-disclosure will include four major categories of response:

1. Expressions of emotion and emotional processes.
2. Expressions of needs.
3. Expressions of fantasies, strivings, dreams, hopes.
4. Expressions of self-awareness.

Self-disclosure will specifically exclude opinions about objects other than self unless the person obviously intends the opinion to be saying something about himself. Since this experiment deals with the acquaintance process, it is only rarely that one comes across such inferential statements without their being followed up by a clarifying remark which is scorable under one of the categories below.

Although much self-disclosure of the types described below is stated in the first person singular, it is possible to make self-disclosing statements in the third person. Examples of both types are included below.

Scoring Procedure

A score of 2 points will be given to disclosures of the defined types when they are first person references.

A score of 1 point will be given to the disclosures of the same types when they are reflexive third person references. These statements in the third person in which the word "you" is an obvious substitution for saying "I."

* From Haymes, M., *Self-Disclosure and the Acquaintance Process.* Unpublished article, in press, 1970.

Non-reflexive third person references, such as "people always . . . ," in which the person is not really revealing any information about himself will not be scored.

For this experiment, ratings will be given for each 30 seconds of interaction. In any *30-second segment*, only the score for the maximally disclosing statement will be used. In other words, if a person makes 1, 2, or 10 2-point disclosures in any 30-second segment his score is 2 *points* for that segment. This avoids inaccurately scoring for speech pattern repetitions. Similarly, if a person makes a 1-point statement, and a 2-point statement in the same 30-second segment, his score is 2 points for that segment.

Examples

1. Expressions of emotions and emotional processes:

Irritation—"It really bugs me . . ." "You get peeved at . . ." "It makes me sick when . . ." "It drives me crazy . . ." Also references to being agitated, irritated, testy, etc.

Anger, rage, hostility, hate, bitterness, resentment—"It gets me very angry when . . ." "You (I) just naturally hate people like her."

Excitement, involvement, concern, etc.—"I get all caught up in . . ." "It gets to me . . ." "It gets me goin' " "I'm really close to my father." "I'm excited by . . ." Also the opposite of invlovement. "I can't seem to get into the material." "Boredom is one of my big problems."

Sad, blue, apathetic, cheerless, depressed, grief, mournful, pensive, gloomy, etc.— "It depresses me when . . ." "I get blue frequently."

Happy, contented, delighted, feeling great, secure, feeling well (strong, confident, etc.), assured, pleased, jovial, elated, euphoric, merry—"I feel great when she . . ." "You really feel good when . . ." (Also the opposite of feeling well and strong, i.e., discussion of health problems, physical complaints, expression of general lack of the feeling of well being.) expressions which have been leached of their emotional content are not scored.

2. Expressions of needs, demands made upon others in contact with self: "I demand a great deal of attention." "I don't feel too motivated to do much of anything." "All I want is . . ." These will frequently be expressed in statement of self-awareness (see below).

3. Expressions of self-awareness, internal forces, processes, capabilities, and/or the lack of them. "You (I) tell yourself that . . ." "I rationalize that by . . ." "That's one of my handicaps." "I don't panic easily." "I get mad at myself . . ." "I have the worst time with writing." "It's not a natural thing for me . . ." "It's easy for me to . . ." "It's really bad for me when I . . ." "I'm torn between . . ." "I'm not mature." "I'm not too hot at . . ." "I can't possibly integrate all that stuff." "You (I) adjust to things . . ." "I can think logically but math is impossible." "I identify with people who . . ." "I get very sentimental when . . ." "I'm a night-time person."

4. Expressions of fantasies, hopes, strivings, long-range plans, etc. "I've wanted to be a doctor since I was five years old." "I frequently dream that I'm . . ." "I dream of the day when . . . ."

Surprise, shock, astonishment, amazement. "She really shocked me terrifically with her openess." "I love being surprised."

Sorry, repentent, ashamed, guilty, etc. "I feel very guilty about . . ." "I always feel sorry when . . . ."

Pride, self-esteem, feelings of fulfillment, self-confidence. "I felt good about what I did for her." "I've been feeling great lately."

Confused, perplexed, puzzled, cloudy, incoherent, disoriented. uncertain, etc. To be scored the statement must indicate some emotional disorientation or confusion. (i.e., "My math homework confuses me" is not scored.) "Situations like that puzzle the hell out of me." "I just don't know how I feel about it."

Anxious, tense, afraid, on-edge, overrought, upset, distressed, worried, etc. "I get really tense in situations like this." "It worries me when . . ." "She scares me." "You (I) get frightened when . . . ."

Love, tenderness, affection, warmth, caring-for another, passion, arousal (sexual), withdraw at times like that."

Love, tenderness, affection, warmth, caring-for another, passion, arousal (sexual), etc. "I loved her before she . . ." "I was so hung up on her that I couldn't even . . ." (Colloquial).

Appendix 14

Paired-Associate Word Lists

List A		List B		List C	
arm	—money	arm	—river	arm	—rain
car	—body	car	—bird	car	—ball
book	—river	book	—garden	book	—ice
chair	—bird	chair	—money	chair	—body
bed	—garden	bed	—tree	bed	—horse
bridge	—food	bridge	—hair	bridge	—dog
clothes	—tree	clothes	—food	clothes	—army
ship	—mouth	ship	—paper	ship	—garden
smoke	—head	smoke	—body	smoke	—hair
hole	—paper	hole	—dog	hole	—river
island	—skin	island	—horse	island	—face
egg	—horse	egg	—face	egg	—money
feet	—dog	feet	—ice	feet	—paper
doctor	—ice	doctor	—bag	doctor	—food
box	—face	box	—rain	box	—mouth
queen	—bag	queen	—ball	queen	—head
eye	—hair	eye	—army	eye	—skin
window	—army	window	—mouth	window	—bag
ear	—ball	ear	—skin	ear	—bird
mother	—rain	mother	—head	mother	—tree

Each list appeared on the memory drum in three different orders.

Appendix 15

Impression Scale

Below are 30 items, each of which contains two adjectives at opposite extremes. In each of these items, you are to indicate your impression of the other participant. For example, on item 1, if the person strikes you as being incompetent, then place a check mark in one of the spaces to the right of center. The more incompetent you believe him to to be, then the farther to the right you would want to check.

The same thing applies if you regard him as competent—only you then check to the left of center. If you feel you have absolutely no idea one way or the other concerning his ability, then you would mark the center of the line. The same rules apply to the other items. Try to be as frank and sensitive as you can be in your ratings and *be certain that every item is checked.*

1.	competent individual	: : : : : : :	incompetent individual
2.	inactive	: : : : : : :	energetic
3.	considerate of others	: : : : : : :	inconsiderate of others
4.	stubborn	: : : : : : :	pliable
5.	self-respecting	: : : : : : :	self-debasing
6.	slow-thinking	: : : : : : :	quick-witted
7.	competitive individual	: : : : : : :	noncompetitive individual
8.	warm person	: : : : : : :	cold person
9.	obstinate	: : : : : : :	flexible
10.	vengeful	: : : : : : :	forgiving
11.	intelligent	: : : : : : :	unintelligent
12.	easy-going	: : : : : : :	hard-driving
13.	not very likeable	: : : : : : :	likeable
14.	firm	: : : : : : :	wishy-washy
15.	irritating	: : : : : : :	pleasant
16.	well-organized	: : : : : : :	disorganized
17.	does his or her best	: : : : : : :	doesn't do his or her best
18.	hostile		friendly
19.	easy to influence	: : : : : : :	difficult to influence
20.	attractive	: : : : : : :	unattractive
21.	undependable	: : : : : : :	dependable

220

22.	happy	: : : : : : : :	sad
23.	active	: : : : : : : :	passive
24.	weak	: : : : : : : :	strong
25.	bad	: : : : : : : :	good
26.	slow	: : : : : : : :	fast
27.	deep	: : : : : : : :	shallow
28.	worthless	: : : : : : : :	valuable
29.	sharp	: : : : : : : :	dull
30.	large	: : : : : : : :	small
I am not at all confident about these ratings		: : : : : : : :	I am very confident about these ratings

Appendix 16
Ten Disclosure Topics

Discussion Topics

___ 1. Your hobbies; how you like best to spend you spare time.
___ 2. Your preferences and dislikes in music.
___ 3. Aspects of your daily work that satisfy and that bother you.
___ 4. What your personal goals are for the next ten years or so.
___ 5. The occasions in your life when you were happiest: in detail.
___ 6. The educational and family background of your parents.
___ 7. How you see and evaluate your parents' relationship with one another.
___ 8. Your personal religious views, nature of religious participation, if any.
___ 9. The main unfulfilled wishes and dreams, and failures in your life.
___10. The unhappiest moments in your life: in detail.

Appendix 17

The Experience of Being a "Subject"*

The following statements were derived in the hope of better understanding how you felt in the experimental situation. Your frankness will be appreciated because it will help make your feelings clear to me.

Instructions

Put a circle around the phrase in each pair that comes closest to describing how you felt in the experimental situation you have just been in.

1. I felt unsafe.
2. I felt the experimenter got to know me as a person.
3. I felt at ease and relaxed.
4. I don't think the experimenter liked me because he kept staring at me.
5. I feel that I showed the experimenter that I liked him.
6. I didn't feel that the experimenter co-experienced what things meant to me.
7. I don't feel I learned more about myself through serving in this study.
8. I felt comfortable because the experimenter was looking at me and showing interest.
9. I felt the experimenter didn't know or understand my feelings.
10. If I had any misgivings or worries about the experiment, I was soon relieved by the way the experimenter acted or what he did.
11. I don't feel the experimenter got to know me because he was staring at me as if I were an object.
12. I don't like the experimenter because I am annoyed by the way he stared at me.

1. I felt safe.
2. I felt that the experimenter didn't get to know me.
3. I felt tense, anxious or uneasy.
4. I felt that the experimenter liked me because he was looking at me with interest.
5. I don't feel that I showed the experimenter I liked him.
6. I felt the experimenter knew and understood my feelings.
7. I feel I learned more about myself from serving in the study.
8. I felt uncomfortable because the experimenter was staring at me.
9. I felt the experimenter knew and understood my feelings.
10. My misgivings or worries were not reduced or they were intensified.
11. I felt the experimenter understood me because he was looking at me and appeared attentive.
12. I like the experimenter because he looked at me and appeared interested in me.
13. I did not feel close to the experimenter.

13. I felt close to the experimenter.

14. I felt some satisfaction in my relationship with the experimenter.

15. I was on guard, reserved, I was very careful of what I showed or did.

16. I am not sure if my responses have any scientific value.

17. I think the experimenter felt close to me in the situation.

18. I don't think the experimenter wanted to get to know me very much.

19. I was indifferent to the experimenter or disliked him; wouldn't particularly like to have anything more to do with him.

20. During the course of my relationship with the experimenter I perceived signs of understanding from him.

21. I felt the experimenter liked me.

22. I would not want to serve in another study conducted by this experimenter.

23. I feel I got to know the experimenter pretty well.

24. I feel the experimenter was interested in me as a person, an individual.

25. I didn't see or feel anything that might have indicated that the experimenter liked me.

26. I feel the experimenter was comfortable with me.

14. I was dissatisfied with my relationship with the experimenter.

15. I was open, expressive and made my experience known to the experimenter.

16. I feel my responses in the experiment were valuable data for science.

17. I don't think the experimenter felt close to me.

18. I think the experimenter showed an interest in wanting to get to know me.

19. I liked the experimenter and would like to get to know him better as a person.

20. I didn't see or feel anything that might have indicated that the experimenter understood my feelings.

21. I felt that the experimenter was indifferent to me or didn't like me.

22. I would be willing to serve in other research conducted by the experimenter.

23. I don't think I got to know the experimenter very well.

24. I feel that the experimenter regarded me, not as a person, but as a source of data.

25. During the course of the experiment I perceived signs that the experimenter liked me.

26. I feel the experimenter was uncomfortable with me.

---

* This was the form used for Group III. Wording of items changed slightly for Groups I and II.

Appendix 18

Instructions to Subjects for Reporting Past Disclosure, and Willingness to Disclose the Twenty-One Topics in Appendix 12

Instructions

You have been given a list of 21 questions asking for personal information about yourself. On the answer sheet on the next page you will see two ruled columns, A and B. A has the heading "I have revealed information about this item to someone in my past." B column has the heading "Willing to disclose information about this item to a male experimenter." You are requested to give a number indicating how much information about each question you have told someone in your past and how much you would be willing to disclose to a male experimenter. Rate each question for both columns A and B using the following scale as a guideline.

Write a 0 in column A for the question if you know you have never talked about that item to another person.

Write a 0 in column B for the question if you would not be willing to reveal anything about that question to a male experimenter.

Write a 1 in column A if you have disclosed almost nothing about this question. No one whom you know or have known knows very much about you with respect to this question.

Write a 1 in column B if you would tell almost nothing about this question to a male experimenter.

Write a 2 in column A if you have talked about this topic in general terms with someone but you have left out most of the specific details.

Write a 2 in column B if you would be willing to talk about this topic in general terms, leaving out most of the specific details to a male experimenter.

Write a 3 in column A if you have talked about some of the specific details in relation to this question, that is, if you have disclosed about an average amount about this question to someone.

Write a 3 in column B if you would be willing to talk about some of the specific details, that is, would be willing to disclose about an average amount to a male experimenter.

Write a *4* in column A if you have talked about most of the important details in regard to this question. Someone knows a great deal about you in relation to this question.

Write a *4* in column B if you would be willing to disclose most of the important details in regard to this question to a male experimenter.

Write a *5* in column A if you have brought someone completely up to date on this question. Someone knows all there is to know about you in relation to this question.

Write a *5* in column B if you would be willing to disclose everything about this question to a male experimenter.

Appendix 19

Self-Disclosure Questionnaire Used to Select High- and Low-Disclosing Subjects

---

A Pilot Study in Self-Disclosure

Your name _____ Student No._____

Classification_____ Age_____ Race _____

Telephone No. where you may be reached_____

Instructions

People differ in the extent to which they let other people know them. We are seeking to investigate what people tell others about themselves.

1. Below there is a list of 40 topics that pertain to you. Read the topics carefully and check those topics that you have disclosed fully to *somebody* in your life. If there is nobody to whom you have *fully* revealed that aspect of your life, leave that space blank.

2. After you have completed the above procedure, turn the page in the booklet. The same 40 topics are listed. Check the topics you would be willing to discuss fully with a partner, who would be an unknown female of your own age and peer group. If you would be reluctant for any reason to discuss a topic fully, leave that space blank.

Topics (listed on each of 2 separate pages)

In the space provided at the left, check those topics on which you have disclosed yourself *fully* to *somebody* [or would be willing to with a strange partner].

1. The different kinds of play and recreation I enjoy.
2. My smoking habits.
3. The best friendship I ever had.
4. The religious denomination to which I belong.

5. The number of children I want to have after I am married.
6. Bad habits my mother or father have.
7. Times I have felt lonely.
8. The things in my past or present life about which I am most ashamed.
9. What I am most afraid of.
10. What annoys me most in people.
11. Times I have been in the hospital.
12. How satisfied I am with different parts of my body—legs, waist, weight, chest, etc.
13. How often I usually go on dates.
14. The description of a person with whom I have been or am in love.
15. How I would feel about marrying a person of a different religion.
16. Whether or not I want to travel and see the country.
17. Radio and television programs that interest me.
18. What I dislike about making new friends.
19. My feelings about people who try to impress me with their knowledge.
20. What I daydream about.
21. Good times I had in school.
22. My school grades.
23. How much I care about what others think of me.
24. How often I have had sexual relations in my life.
25. The kind of person with whom I would like to have sexual experiences.
26. Why some people dislike me.
27. Whether I like doing things alone or in a group.
28. My opinions about how capable and smart I am compared to others around me.
29. Places where I have worked.
30. How I budget my money—the proportion that goes for necessities, luxuries, etc.
31. What would bother me, if anything, about making a speech or giving a talk.
32. How important I think sex will be in making my marriage a good one.
33. Things I liked about my home life.
34. Where my parents and grandparents came from.
35. Feelings about my adequacy in sexual behavior—my ability to perform adequately in sexual relationships.
36. My opinion on marrying for money.
37. Whether or not I think the federal government should support persons who cannot find work.
38. How I feel about girls' new fashions styles.
39. Whom I most admire.
40. The aspects of my personality that I dislike, worry about, or regard as a handicap to me.

Appendix 20

Twenty Disclosure Topics Used as Guides for Mutual Interviewing by "High" Disclosers, "Low" Disclosers, and in Mixed, "High-Low" Dyads*

1. Your hobbies; how you best like to spend your spare time. (L)
2. Your favorite foods and beverages, and chief dislikes in food and drink. (L)
3. What your personal goals are for the next 10 years or so. (L)
4. The description of a person with whom you have been or are in love. (H)
5. Characteristics of yourself that give you cause for pride and satisfaction. (M)
6. The unhappiest moments of your life: in detail. (M)
7. What you regard as the mistakes and failures your parents made in raising you. (M)
8. The kind of person with whom you would like to have sexual experiences. (H)
9. Your educational background and your feelings about it. (L)
10. Your present financial position: income, debts, savings, sources of income. (M)
11. Your opinions about how capable and smart you are compared to others around you. (H)
12. Why some people dislike you. (H)
13. The things in your past or present life about which you are most ashamed. (H)
14. How satisfied you are with different parts of your body—legs, weight, chest, etc. (H)
15. The happiest moments of your life: in detail. (M)
16. Your personal religious views, nature of religious participation, if any. (L)
17. The people with whom you have been sexually intimate; the circumstances of your relationship with each. (H)
18. The aspects of your personality that you dislike, worry about, or regard as a handicap to yourself. (H)
19. How much you care about what others think of you. (H)
20. Feelings about your adequacy in sexual behavior—your abilities to perform adequately in sexual relationships. (H)

---

* *Note:* The (H) refers to items of high rated intimacy value, (M) refers to items of medium, and (L) refers to items of low rated intimacy value.

Appendix 21

Greene's (1964) Sentence Completion Blank for Measuring Self-Disclosure

Name_____ Age_____ Date_____
       (please print)

Class: freshman_____sophomore_____junior_____senior_____graduate school_____

Instructions

This sentence completion blank is designed to help gain an understanding of your basic feelings concerning yourself and your personal world. Please complete these sentences to express *your real feelings,* trying to be as frank as possible about matters which are personally important to you.

Try to do every sentence. Be sure to make a complete sentence

1. Sometimes I_____
2. I can't_____
3. Sexual thoughts_____
4. I often wish_____
5. There have been times when_____
6. My biggest problem is_____
7. I secretly_____
8. I feel_____
9. Loneliness_____
10. I feel guilty_____
11. I have an emotional need to_____
12. I regret_____
13. I hate_____
14. I am afraid_____
15. I_____
16. I am best when_____
17. I am worst when_____
18. I need_____
19. I punish myself_____
20. I am hurt when_____

Scoring Manual

Purpose and Scoring Procedure

The Self-Disclosure Sentence Blank is an attempt to standardize a method for scoring a subject's sentence completions for the degree to which he *willingly* reveals core aspects of his private and personal world.

The subject is asked to complete 20 sentence stems which have been designed to have "high pull" for self-disclosure. Although the subject's responses can be used for general interpretation in the same manner that a clinician trained in dynamic psychology uses any projective material, this particular scoring procedure is *not* designed to take into account information about the subject which he in fact does not purposely disclose. This is important for the scorer to keep in mind so that he does not "read in" meaning to responses as he is scoring them. For example, if a female should respond to the stem, "I hate . . . . ," with "umbrellas," this may yield rich information for anyone interested in Freudian dynamics, but in keeping with the purposes of this scale, it would be scored as grossly evasive and unrevealing (Level Five).

Another error to guard against is the incorrect scoring of a response as unrevealing because the scorer finds it difficult to believe that the subject was serious in his response. Such completions might be: "I feel . . . crazy," "I regret . . . my whole life," "I . . . fear this test too much," or, "I am worst when . . . I am sober." In all instances, the scorer is admonished to accept subject responses at face value, and to score each response, *as it is written*, for its closeness to what are likely to be core issues in a person's personal life. For example, both the completions, "I feel . . . with my hands," and "I feel . . . crazy," *might* not be meant seriously, but the scorer is to assume that they are, and to rate their revealingness accordingly. Thus, even if a subject is serious when saying that he feels "with his hand," he is still being grossly unrevealing of his personal life. But if a subject is taken seriously when he says that he "feels crazy," he is being quite open about an important aspect of his personal life. To repeat, all responses are to be judged by their verbal content, and not the inferred intentions of the subject.

The instructions for the Self-Disclosure Sentence Blank are intended to give the subject a clear understanding of what the examiner is interested in. These instructions are:

> This sentence completion blank is designed to help gain an understanding of your basic feelings concerning yourself and your personal world. Please complete these sentences to express *your real feelings*, trying to be as frank as possible about matters which are personally important to you.
>
> Try to do every sentence. Be sure to make a complete sentence.

These instructions are meant to say in effect, "I'd like to get to know you as well as possible in the short time we have together. Please tell me as frankly as you can what kind of person you really are deep down under the skin."

To score the subject's responses, the scorer assigns each response a scale value from 1 to 5, depending on its judged degree of revealingness. (Level One disclosures are very revealing; those at Level Five are evasive.) The responses can be scored in a relatively objective manner if the scorer (1) makes himself thoroughly familiar with the descriptions which provide the rationale for the five levels, and (2) compares each response with typical examples provided for each level in the scoring-by-matching section of this manual. The sum of the individual scale values for all stems provides the index of self-disclosure.

In order to minimize the tendency to score all responses in light of the overall impression made by the subject, each completion is to be scored independently of all others, except when there is a clear reference to a previous disclosure. When scoring a number of individuals, each stem should be scored for all subjects before proceeding on to the next stem, that is, all stems numbered 1 before going on to all stems numbered 2, etc. If, while scoring a particular stem, the scorer should find a response which, in and of itself, makes little sense, the immediately preceding completions should be re-read to see whether or not the subject is continuing a train of thought from a previous disclosure. For example, if a completion number 4 should read, "I often wish . . . and pray they didn't,) it would make little sense, as it stands alone. But if this subject's completion number 3 is found to read, "Sexual thoughts . . . possess me all the time and make me guilty," then completion number 4 gains meaning and revealingness when viewed as a continuation of this previous disclosure.

The scorer may find on occasion that despite his best efforts, he cannot decide at which of two levels a response best fits. In order to achieve some consistency in such cases, the response should be scored at the higher level of self-disclosure.

The Five Scoring Levels

The question to be kept in mind is this: How much does this disclosure, taken alone, and at face value, contribute to an understanding of this person's private and personal world? Or, to shift the emphasis slightly, how willing has this person been to allow the examiner to know him as he sees himself?

Level One

He reveals basic feelings and emotions of a personally relevant nature about a central aspect of his private and personal life. This material is likely to play a major role, or have a fundamental effect, on the shaping of a large part of the subject's personal as well as public experience. His point of reference is his own inner experience—his own subjective world. He speaks as an internal observer reporting on internal events, even when the comment also includes mention of the external world.

What is disclosed is likely to be the sort of thing which one would never know unless told, and which would ordinarily be told only to a close and trusted friend. There is no attempt to present himself in a socially desirable manner. Facades are absent, and as a result, core constructs by which he maintains his identity and existence, as well as areas of extreme conflict, are likely to be directly and frankly discussed. For instance, statements concerning his self-image, his approach to fundamental interpersonal relationships, sexual conflicts, severe family problems, and strong feelings of personal confusion are likely to be scored at this level.

This self-disclosure, taken alone, and at face value, contributes significantly to an understanding of the subject's personal world of experience.

Level Two

He expresses feelings and emotions of "secondary" importance and/or of a less personal nature than at Level One. He may hint at or speak in a qualified or more distant way about material which might otherwise fall within Level One. Distance from the core theme may be along a dimension of person, place, time, intensity, or frequency. Disclosures at this level, while personally important, often tend to be more content and situation specific than at Level One. That is, the content does not play as major a role over as wide an area of the subject's life.

The focus remains, however, on internal experience which seems of direct relevance to the person's personal life. What is revealed would not ordinarily be said to casual acquaintances. He does not necessarily present himself in socially favorable terms. He seems to be honestly trying to express himself about important aspects of his subjective world, but is unwilling or unable to reach the degree of openness expressed at Level One. He does, however, purposely reveal something important and fundamental about his basic personality.

Level Three

He reveals important facts and/or details of an "external" nature. Material revealed at this level probably plays a major role in the shaping of the subject's private life. The focus of attention is generally not on his subjective inner experience, but rather on people and events in the world outside of himself, things happening to him, and things which he does. When feelings or emotions are expressed, they do not seem deep-seated or closely tied to the core constructs by which he maintains his identity and existence.

Although what is revealed is probably important to the subject and his public life, it might be revealed to a casual acquaintance, and in general would not prove embarrassing if publicly known. Some guardedness may be apparent, and personal statements of a socially undesirable nature tend to be avoided. Although this material may help in coming to know the subject, he is (purposely) revealing little or nothing of significance about his private, experiential world.

Level Four

He discloses facts and/or details of "secondary" importance and of an "external" nature. This material probably plays a relatively minor role in a limited area of the subject's life, and would appear to have little or no lasting effect on his moment to moment personal experience. His point of reference is clearly the external world, and he may speak as a detached, nominally interested external observer.

Guardedness is often apparent, and socially undesirable statements are almost nonexistent. What is revealed might easily be said to a stranger or made public with embarrassment. Problems, when they are mentioned at all, are never deep-seated or in any manner incapacitating. If feelings or emotions are expressed, they are distant from the core constructs by which the subject's identity and existence are defined. Minor incidents, facts, wants, beliefs, etc., may be disclosed, but their sphere of influence is quite likely to be content and situation specific, and relatively trivial when compared with what might be said about central areas of a person's personal or public life.

Vague or highly qualified reference may be made to material which might otherwise fall within Level Three. The subject may reveal strong negative attitudes, but only in socially approved ways.

Level Four statements help give the examiner very little, if any, understanding of the subject's personal and private world.

Level Five

Essentially neutral, meaningless, or grossly evasive material is offered at this level. Omissions are scored at this level, as well as stereotype answers, cliches, catch phrases, etc. The subject represents himself as having no real problems. Statements at this level give the examiner no understanding of the subject's personal or public life.

Appendix 22

Disclosure Profiles Used in Lefkowitz's Study

Low Disclosure Profile

As your date I would be willing to disclose to you in none of the areas listed. It would be pertinent for me, however, to make many other particular kinds of disclosing statements. I would reveal my food preferences and my favorite athlete. It would also be important to disclose my likes and dislikes in clothing and who I consider to be my favorite professor. I would be concerned with relating what kind of car I drive. I would also disclose a recent escapade with my best friend.

I would reveal something about my previous girl friends. It would also be important to disclose my drinking habits and abilities—whatever they might be. I would divulge my favorite television show and my age. I would be concerned with disclosing how many people I know and who some of them are. I would indicate my usual class schedule during the week.

I would reveal what I did during the day before I picked you up for our date. I would disclose my favorite recording artist. It would also be important to disclose something about my high school days. I would be willing to reveal to you any material possessions that I may own. I would divulge my financial status. I would be concerned with disclosing certain political beliefs that I have.

I would reveal what I usually do for entertainment. I would disclose what I perceive the level of my social status to be. It would also be important to disclose my feelings about a recent movie that I have seen and to disclose my general feelings about pets. I would be concerned with disclosing my place of birth. I would also divulge what newspaper I usually read.

Low-Medium Disclosure Profile

As your date I would be willing to disclose to you in a few of the areas listed. I would reveal the extent to which I have traveled and the places I have visited. I would include my learning experiences from these travels and from the people whom I have met. It would also be important to disclose my general attitude toward Greek versus Independent living and to provide you with some "fraternity data"—whether I am in a house; if so, what house, and so on. I would be concerned with disclosing my general philosophy with regard to life and man. I would also divulge my feelings about individuality and conformity.

It would also be pertinent for me to make a number of other particular kinds of disclosing statements. I would reveal something about my previous girl friends. It would also be important to disclose my drinking habits and abilities—whatever they might be. I would divulge my favorite television show and my age. I would be concerned with disclosing how many people I know and who some of them are. I would indicate my usual class schedule during the week.

I would reveal what I did during the day before I picked you up for our date. I would disclose my favorite recording artist. It would also be important to disclose something about my high school days. I would be willing to reveal to you any material possessions that I may own. I would divulge my financial status. I would be concerned with disclosing certain political beliefs that I have.

I would reveal what I usually do for entertainment. I would disclose what I perceive the level of my social status to be. It would also be important to disclose my feelings about a recent movie that I have seen and to disclose my general feelings about pets. I would be concerned with disclosing my place of birth. I would also divulge what newspaper I usually read.

Medium Disclosure Profile

As your date I would be willing to disclose to you in some of the areas listed. I would reveal my hobbies or areas of interest and discuss my involvement in sports and my general athletic ability. It would also be important to disclose my general attitude—whether pro or con—toward drugs. I would be willing to reveal if I have been personally involved with drugs and, if so, my experiences with them. I would divulge my feelings about civil rights, racial unrest, minority groups, and equality. I would be concerned with disclosing my attitude toward certain political organizations on campus, for example, whether I am for or against protest groups.

I would reveal the extent to which I have traveled and the places I have visited. I would include my learning experiences from these travels and from the people whom I have met. It would also be important to disclose my general attitude toward Greek versus independent living and to provide you with some "fraternity data"—whether I am in a house; if so, what house, and so on. I would be concerned with disclosing my general philosophy with regard to life and man. I would also divulge my feelings about individuality and conformity.

It would also be pertinent for me to make some other particular kinds of disclosing statements. I would reveal what I did during the day before I picked you up for our date. I would disclose my favorite recording artist. It would also be important to disclose something about my high school days. I would be willing to reveal to you any material possessions that I may own. I would divulge my financial status. I would be concerned with disclosing certain political beliefs that I have.

I would reveal what I usually do for entertainment. I would disclose what I perceive the level of my social status to be. It would also be important to disclose my feelings about a recent movie that I have seen and to disclose my general feelings about pets. I would be concerned with disclosing my place of birth. I would also divulge what newspaper I usually read.

High-Medium Disclosure Profile

As your date I would be willing to disclose to you in most of the areas listed. I would reveal the kind of relationship I have with my parents and the rest of my family. It would also be important to disclose my feelings about what I think an ideal parent-child relationship should be like. I would divulge my general sexual philosophy and the sexual expectations I have in the first date situation. I would be concerned with disclosing my academic major and the reason for my choosing this area of study.

I would reveal my hobbies or areas of interest and discuss my involvement in sports and my general athletic ability. It would also be important to disclose my general attitude—whether pro or con—toward drugs. I would be willing to reveal if I have been personally involved with drugs and, if so, my experiences with them. I would divulge my feelings about civil rights, racial unrest, minority groups, and equality. I would be concerned with disclosing my attitude toward certain political organizations on campus, for example, whether I am for or against protest groups.

I would reveal the extent to which I have traveled and the places I have visited. I would include my learning experiences from these travels and from the people whom I have met. It would also be important to disclose my general attitude toward Greek versus independent living and to provide you with some "fraternity data"—whether I am in a house; if so, what house, and so on. I would be concerned with disclosing my general philosophy with regard to life and man. I would also divulge my feelings about individuality and conformity.

It would also be pertinent for me to make a few other particular kinds of disclosing statements. I would reveal what I usually do for entertainment. I would disclose what I perceive the level of my social status to be. It would also be important to disclose my feelings about a recent movie that I have seen and to disclose my general feelings about pets. I would be concerned with disclosing my place of birth. I would also divulge what newspaper I usually read.

High Disclosure Profile

As your date I would be willing to disclose to you in all of the areas listed. I would reveal my professional aspirations by indicating the field or area I am interested in and the reason for my choice. It would also be important to disclose my religious denomination and to engage in a discussion of my general religious beliefs. I would be concerned with relating whether I receive enjoyment from being with others, that is, whether I am an inner-dependent or outer-dependent person. I would also disclose my prejudices, if I had any.

I would reveal the kind of relationship I have with my parents and the rest of my family. It would also be important to disclose my feelings about what I think an ideal parent-child relationship should be like. I would divulge my general sexual philosophy and the sexual expectations I have in the first date situation. I would be concerned with disclosing my academic major and the reason for my choosing this area of study.

I would reveal my hobbies or areas of interest and discuss my involvement in sports and my general athletic ability. It would also be important to disclose my general attitude—whether pro or con—toward drugs. I would be willing to reveal if I have been personally involved with drugs and, if so, my experiences with them. I would divulge my feelings about civil rights, racial unrest, minority groups, and equality. I would be concerned with disclosing my attitude toward certain political organizations on campus, for example, whether I am for or against protest groups.

I would reveal the extent to which I have traveled and the places I have visited. I would include my learning experiences from these travels and from the people whom I have met. It would also be important to disclose my general attitude toward Greek versus independent living and to provide you with some "fraternity data"—whether I am in a house; if so, what house, and so on. I would be concerned with disclosing my general philosophy with regard to life and man. I would also divulge my feelings about individuality and conformity.

It would not be pertinent for me to make any other particular kinds of disclosing statements.

Bibliography

llport, G. W. *Pattern and growth in personality.* New York: Holt, 1961.

rdrey, R. *The territorial imperative.* New York: Atheneum, 1966.

rgyle, M. and Dean, J. Eye-contact, distance, and affiliation. *Sociometry,* 1965, **28,** 289–304.

ıkan, D. *The duality of human existence.* Chicago: Rand McNally, 1966.

ock, J. The assessment of communication. Role variations as a function of interactional context. *Journal of Personality,* 1952, **21,** 272–286.

ock, J., and Bennett, Lillian. The assessment of communication. Perception and transmission as a function of social situation. *Human Relations,* 1955, **8,** 317–325.

own, J. C. *The troika incident.* Garden City, N.Y.: Doubleday, 1970.

ıgental, J. F. T. *Challenges of humanistic psychology,* New York: McGraw-Hill, 1967.

hittick, E. V., and Himelstein, P. The manipulation of self-disclosure. *Journal of Psychology,* 1967, **65,** 117–121.

ooke, T. F. Interpersonal correlates of religious behavior. Unpublished doctoral dissertation, University of Florida, 1962.

ronbach, L. J. *Essentials of psychological testing.* New York: Harper, 1959.

aninos, P. *The secret of Major Thompson.* New York: Knopf, 1957.

rag, Lee R. Experimenter-subject interaction: a situational determinant of differential levels of self-disclosure, Unpublished master's thesis, University of Florida, 1968.

rag, Lee R. The bus-rider phenomenon and its generalizability: a study of self-disclosure in student-stranger versus college room-mate dyads. Uupublished doctoral dissertation, University of Florida, 1971.

rag, R. M. Self-disclosure as a function of group size and experimenter behavior. Unpublished doctoral dissertation, University of Folrdia, 1968.

utton, E. Some relationships between self-reports of emotional and social behavior and measures of academic achievement, interest, and talent. Paper read at 1963 annual meeting of the National Council on Measurement in Education.

ymond, Rosalind F. Personality and empathy. *Journal of Consulting Psychology,* 1950, **4,** 343–350.

iske, D. W. Some hypotheses concerning test adequacy. *Educational and Psychological Measurement,* 1966, **26,** 69–88.

ɔa, U. Empathy or behavioral transparency? *Journal of Abnormal and Social Psychology,* 1958, **56,** 62–66.

rank, L. K. Tactile communication. *ETC, Review of General Semantics,* 1958, **16,** 31–79.

rey, M. The effects of self-disclosure and social reinforcement on performance in paired-associate learning. Unpublished senior honors paper, University of Florida, 1967.

Friedman, R. Experimenter-subject distance and self-disclosure. Unpublished master's thesis, University of Florida, 1969.

Fromm, E. *Man for himself*. New York: Rinehart, 1947.

Fromm, E. *The sane society*. New York: Rinehart, 1955.

Gendlin, E. The concept of congruence reformulated in terms of experiencing. *Counseling Center Discussion Papers*, University of Chicago, 1959, **5**, (12).

Gibson, J. J. *The senses considered as perceptual systems*. Boston: Houghton Mifflin, 1966.

Glazer, Victoria. Body-cathexis and physical intimacy. Unpublished master's thesis, University of Florida, 1967.

Goldstein, K., and Scheerer, M. Abstract and concrete behavior. An experimental study with special tests. *Psychological Monographs*, 1941, **53**, No. 239.

Graham, Sharon. Level of self-disclosure as a variable of death attitudes. Unpublished master's thesis, University of Florida, 1970.

Green, R. A sentence-completion test for measuring self-disclosure. Unpublished master's thesis, Ohio State University, 1964.

Gunther, B. *Sense relaxation*. New York: Macmillan, 1967.

Guttman, L. A basis for scaling quantitative data. *American Sociological Review*, 1944, **9**, 139–150.

Hall, E. T. *The hidden dimension*. Garden City, N.Y.: Doubleday, 1966.

Hanna, T. *Bodies in revolt: A primer of somatic thinking*. New York: Holt, 1970.

Haymes, M. Self-disclosure and the acquaintance process. Unpublished paper, Cornell University, 1969.

Heidegger, M. *Being and time*. London: S. C. M. Press, 1962.

Heider, F. *The psychology of interpersonal relations*. New York: Wiley, 1958.

Heifitz, M. L. Experimenter effect upon the openness of response to the Rotter Incomplete Sentence Blank. Unpublished senior honors paper, University of Florida, 1967.

Heller, J. *Catch 22*. New York:, Simon & Shuster, 1961.

Himelstein, P., and Kimbrough, W. A study of self-disclosure in the classroom. *Journal of Psychology*, 1963, **55**, 437–440.

Himelstein, P., and Lubin, B. Relationship of the MMPI K scale and a measure of self-disclosure in a normal population. *Psychological Reports*, 1966, **19**, 166.

Hollingshead, A. Two-factor index of social position. Mimeographed manuscript privately circulated, 1959.

Hora, T. The process of existential psychotherapy. *Psychiatric Quarterly*, 1960, **34**, 495–504.

Horney, Karen. *Neurosis and human growth*. New York: Norton, 1950.

Hurley, J. R., and Hurley, S. J. Toward authenticity in measuring self-disclosure. *Journal of Counseling Psychology*, 1969, **16**, 271–274.

Inkeles, A. and Levinson, D. J. National character: the study of modal personality and sociocultural systems. In G. Lindzey (Ed.), *Handbook of social psychology*, Volume 2, Cambridge, Mass.: Addison-Wesley, 1954.

Jaffe, Peggy E. Self-disclosure: an example of imitative behavior. Unpublished master's thesis, University of Florida, 1969.

Jourard, S. M. Self-disclosure and other-cathexis. *Journal of Abnormal and Social Psychology*, 1959, **59**, 428–431.

———. Religious denomination and self-disclosure. *Psychological Reports*, 1961, **8**, 446 (a).

———. Rorschach productivity and self-disclosure. *Perceptual and Motor Skills*, 1961, **13**, 232 (b).

————. Self-disclosure in British and American college females. *Journal of Social Psychology*, 1961, **54**, 315–320 (c).

————. Self-disclosure scores and grades in nursing college. *Journal of Applied Psychology*, 1961, **45**, 244–247 (d).

————. Age trends in self-disclosure. *Merrill-Palmer Quarterly of Behavior and Development*, 1961, **7**, 191–197 (e).

————. *Personal adjustment. An approach through the study of healthy personality.* New York: Macmillan, 1963 (2nd edition, 1958, 1st edition).

————. *The transparent self. Self-disclosure and well-being.* Princeton, N.J.: Van Nostrand, 1964.

————. An exploratory study of body-accessibility. *British Journal of Social and Clinical Psychology*, 1966, **5**, 221–231.

————. Some psychological aspects of privacy. *Law and Contemporary Problems.* Durham, N.C.: Duke University School of Law, 1966.

————. Experimenter-subject dialogue: a paradigm for a humanistic science of psychology. In J. F. T. Bugental, *Challenges of humanistic psychology.* New York: McGraw-Hill, 1967, (a).

————. To be or not to be transparent. In S. M. Jourard, *To be or not to be: existential-psychological perspectives on the self.* Gainesville, Fla.: University of Florida Press, 1967 (b).

————. *Disclosing man to himself.* Princeton, N.J.: Van Nostrand, 1968.

————. The effects of experimenters' disclosure on subjects' behavior. In C. Spielberger (Ed.), *Current topics in clinical and community psychology.* New York: Academic Press, 1969.

Jourard, S. M., and Devin, Linda. Self-disclosure in Puerto Rico and the United States. Unpublished manuscript, University of Florida, 1962.

———— and Friedman, R. Experimenter-subject 'distance' and self-disclosure. *Journal of Personality and Social Psychology*, 1970, **8**, 278–282.

———— and Jaffe, Peggy E. Influence of an interviewer's behavior on the self-disclosing behavior of interviewees. *Journal of Counseling Psychology*, 1970, **17**, 252–257.

———— and Kormann, L. Getting to know the experimenter and its effect on psychological test performance. *Journal of Humanistic Psychology*, 1968, **8**, 155–160.

———— and Landsman, M. J. Cognition, cathexis, and the "dyadic effect" in men's self-disclosing behavior. *Merrill-Palmer Quarterly of Behavior and Development*, 1960, **6**, 178–186.

———— and Lasakow, P. Some factors in self-disclosure. *Journal of Abnormal and Social Psychology*, 1958, **56**, 91–98.

———— and Remy, R. M. Perceived parental attitudes, the self, and security. *Journal of Consulting Psychology*, 1955, **19**, 364–366.

———— and Resnick, Jaquelyn L. Some effects of self-disclosure among college women. *Journal of Humanistic Psychology*, 1970, **10**, 84–93.

———— and Richman, Patricia. Factors in the self-disclosure inputs of college students. *Merrill-Palmer Quarterly of Behavior and Development*, 1963, **9**, 141–148.

———— and Secord, P. F. Body size and body-cathexis. *Journal of Consulting Psychology*, 1954, **18**, 184.

———— and Secord, P. F. Body-cathexis and the ideal female figure. *Journal of Abnormal and Social Psychology*, 1955, **50**, 243–246.

———— and Secord, P. F. Body-cathexis and personality. *British Journal of Psychology*, 1955, **46**, 130–138.

Kormann, L. Getting to know the experimenter and its effect on psychological test scores. Unpublished master's thesis, University of Florida, 1967.

Laing, R. D. *The divided self.* London: Tavistock, 1960.

Leary, T. *Interpersonal diagnosis of personality.* New York: Ronald Press, 1957.

Lefkowitz, M. B. The role of self-disclosure and physical attractiveness in person-perception: a hypothetical first date situation. Unpublished master's thesis, University of Florida, 1970.

Lewin, K. Some social-psychological differences between the United States and Germany. In Gertrude Lewin (Ed.), *Resolving social conflicts: selected papers on group dynamics, 1935–1946.* New York: Harper, 1948.

Macmurray, J. *The self as agent.* London: Faber and Faber, 1957.

Maslow, A. H. *Toward a psychology of being.* Princeton, N.J.: Van Nostrand, 1962.

Matarazzo, J. D., Wiens, A., and Saslow, G. Studies of interview speech behavior. In L. Krasner and L. P. Ullman, *Research in behavior modification.* New York: Holt, 1965.

Melikian, W. C. Self-disclosure among university students in the Middle East. *Journal of Social Psychology,* 1962, **57,** 257–263.

Middleton, W. C. Some reactions toward death among college students. *Journal of Abnormal and Social Psychology,* 1958, **56,** 295–299.

Moloney, J. C. *The magic cloak. A contribution to the psychology of authoritarianism.* Wakefield, Mass.: Montrose Press, 1949.

Morris, C. W. *Varieties of human value.* Chicago: University of Chicago Press, 1956.

Mowrer, O. H. *The crisis in psychiatry and religion.* Princeton, N.J.: Van Nostrand, 1961.

Mullen, H., and Sanguiliano, Iris. The subjective phenomenon in existential psychotherapy. *Journal of Existential Psychiatry,* 1961, **2,** 17–34.

Osgood, C. E., Suci, G. J., and Tannenbaum, P. H. *The measurement of meaning.* Urbana, Ill.: University of Illinois Press, 1957.

Plog, S. C. The disclosure of self in the United States and Germany. *Journal of Social Psychology,* 1965, **65,** 193–203.

Powell, W. J., Jr. Differential effectiveness of interviewer interventions in an experimental interview. *Journal of Consulting and Clinical Psychology,* 1968, **32,** 210–215.

Rickers-Ovsiankina, Maria, and Kusmin, A. A. Individual differences in social accessibility. *Psychological Reports,* 1958, **4,** 391–406.

Riesman, D. *The lonely crowd.* New Haven, Conn.: Yale University Press, 1950.

Rivenbark, W. H. Self-disclosure patterns among adolescents. Unpublished doctoral dissertation, University of Florida, 1966.

Rogers, C. R. The characteristics of a helping relationship. *Personnel and Guidance Journal,* 1958, **37,** 6–16.

Rogers, C. R. A theory of psychotherapy with schizophrenics, and a proposal for its empirical investigation. In J. G. Dawson, H. K. Stone, and N. P. Dellis, *Psychotherapy with schizophrenics.* Baton Rouge, La.: University of Louisiana Press, 1961.

Rosenthal, R. *Experimenter effects in behavioral research.* New York: Appleton-Century-Crofts, 1967.

Rubin, Jane E. Impression change as a function of level of self-disclosure. Unpublished master's thesis, University of Florida, 1968.

Schutz, W. *Joy.* New York: Grove Press, 1967.

Schutz, W. *FIRO. A three-dimentional theory of interpersonal behavior.* New York: Rinehart, 1958.

Secord, P. F., and Jourard, S. M. The appraisal of body-cathexis: body-cathexis and the self. *Journal of Consulting Psychology*, 1953, 17, 342–347.

Shapiro, A., and Swensen, C. Patterns of self-disclosure among married couples. *Journal of Counseling Psychology*, 1969, 16, 179–180.

Simmel, G. Sociology of the senses: visual interaction. In R. E. Park and E. W. Burgess, *Introduction to the science of sociology*. Chicago: University of Chicago Press, 1921.

Shapiro, J. G. Variability in the communication of affect. *Journal of Social Psychology*, 1968, 76, 181–188.

Skinner, B. F. *Verbal behavior*. New York: Appleton-Century-Crofts, 1957.

Skypeck, Genevieve. Self-disclosure in children ages six through twelve. Uupublished master's thesis, University of Flordia, 1967.

Small, L. Personal values and self-disclosure. Unpublished master's thesis, University of Florida, 1970.

Smith, S. A. Self-disclosure behavior associated with two MMPI code types. Unpublished master's thesis, University of Alabama, 1958.

Sullivan, H. S. *The psychiatric interview*. New York: Norton, 1954.

Taylor, D. A. Some aspects of the development of interpersonal relationships: social penetration process. *Technical Report No. 1*, Center for Research on Social Behavior, University of Delaware, 1965.

Taylor, D. A., and Altman, I. Intimacy-scaled stimuli for use in studies of interpersonal relations. *Psychological Reports*, 1966, 19, 729–730.

Truax, C. A scale for the measurement of accurate empathy. *Psychiatric Institute Bulletin*, Wisconsin Psychiatric Institute, University of Wisconsin, 1961, 1, 12.

Truax, C. Personal communication, 1970.

Webb, W. B. A "couple" of experiments. *American Psychologist*, 1968, 23, 428–433.

Author Index

245

Subject Index